SUPERVISOR'S SURVIVAL KIT

YOUR FIRST STEP INTO MANAGEMENT

Ninth Edition

Elwood N. Chapman
Cliff Goodwin

NETEFFECT SERIES

Prentice Hall

Upper Saddle River, New Jersey 07458

Library of Congress Cataloging-in-Publication Data

Chapman, Elwood N.
 Supervisor's survival kit : your first step into management / Elwood N.
 Chapman and Cliff Goodwin.—9th ed.
  p. cm.
 ISBN 0-13-029031-9
  1. Supervision of employees.   2. Personnel management.   I. Goodwin,
 Cliff, 1948–   II. Title.
 HF5549.12.C44   2001
 658.3′02—dc21   2001021475

Publisher: *Steve Helba*
Executive Editor: *Elizabeth Sugg*
Director of Production and Manufacturing: *Bruce Johnson*
Managing Editor: *Mary Carnis*
Manufacturing Buyer: *Cathleen Petersen*
Production Liaison: *Brian Hyland*
Design Director: *Cheryl Asherman*
Senior Design Coordinator: *Miguel Ortiz*
Cover Illustration: *Alex Bloch/SIS*
Cover Design: *LaFortezza Design Group*
Full Service Production/Formatting: *BookMasters, Inc.*
Editorial Assistant: *Anita Rhodes*
Printing and Binding: *Banta Harrisonburg*

Pearson Education LTD.
Pearson Education Australia PTY, Limited
Pearson Education Singapore, Pte. Ltd
Pearson Education North Asia Ltd
Pearson Education Canada, Ltd.
Pearson Educación de Mexico, S.A. de C.V.
Pearson Education—Japan
Pearson Education Malaysia, Pte. Ltd
Pearson Education, Upper Saddle River, New Jersey

10 9 8 7 6 5
ISBN 0-13-029031-9

Contents

About this Book   v

From the Publisher   ix

Introduction   x

GETTING INTO SUPERVISION   1

1
Should You Be a Supervisor?   3
Case Study: Choice   11

2
Making the Transition   12
Mini-Game: Strategy   20

3
The New Star in the Management Hierarchy   22
Mini-Game: Downsizing   28

HUMAN RELATIONS AND COMMUNICATIONS: THE KEY TO SUCCESSFUL SUPERVISION   31

4   **Achieving Productivity Through People**   **33**
Case Study: Approach   44

5   **The Supervisor-Employee Relationship**   **45**
Mini-Game: Intervention   52

6   **Five Irreplaceable Foundations**   **54**
Case Study: Request   61

7   **Creating a Productive Working Climate**   **62**
Mini-Game: Climate   74

8   **The Shift to Total Quality Management**   **77**
Mini-Game: Philosophy   83

9   **The Effective Work Team**   **85**
Mini-Game: Pyramid vs. Circle   98

10   **Communicating Privately**   **99**
Case Study: Technique   109

11   **The Problem Employee**   **110**
Mini-Game: Confrontation   121

12   **Staffing**   **123**
Case Study: Staffing   136

13 **Delegation**   **137**
       Mini-Game: To Delegate or Not   144

14 **Use Your Knowledge Power**   **146**
       Case Study: Training   153

15 **The Formal Appraisal**   **154**
       Mini-Game: Option   169

MANAGING YOURSELF   **171**

16 **Learning to Concentrate**   **173**
       Case Study: Thinking   179

17 **Establishing Goals and Planning**   **180**
       Case Study: Planning   190

18 **Setting Priorities**   **191**
       Mini-Game: Priorities   198

19 **Managing Your Time**   **200**
       Case Study: Analysis   208

20 **Make Decisive Decisions**   **210**
       Mini-Game: Termination   219

WHERE DO I GO FROM HERE?   221

21 Common Mistakes You Don't Want to Make   223
Case Study: Intimidation   231

22 Converting Change into Opportunity   232
Mini-Game: Change   238

23 Having a Personal Plan B   239
Case Study: Decision   248

24 Leadership: What Every Manager Should Know   249
Mini-Game: Reward Trade-Offs   262

Suggested Answers to Case Problems   264

Role Profiles for Cases and Mini-Games   268

Index   275

About this Book

For the past several years, *Supervisor's Survival Kit* has enjoyed increasing success. A major reason for this popularity is that the book works effectively in a variety of situations. It is sufficiently comprehensive and substantive to be used as a text for a formal college course, yet brief enough to meet the needs of an industrial seminar. *Supervisor's Survival Kit* is also effective as a self-study publication. A powerful and intriguing feature of the book is Mini-Games or Cases at the end of each chapter. The authors have also developed the following support materials:

1. A Study Wizard for students that enhances self-study as it applies the concepts to the world of work

2. A Leader's Guide that provides teaching ideas on the most effective ways to use the material

Professor Chapman authored several books, including his all-time best seller *Your Attitude Is Showing: A Primer on Human Relations*. Another of his popular books is *Leadership: What Every Manager Needs to Know*.

Professor Cliff Goodwin, from the Purdue School of Engineering and Technology at Indianapolis, Indiana, has graciously offered to continue on with Professor Chapman's legacy, while adding contemporary insights into the many aspects of becoming an effective supervisor.

Professor Goodwin has been on the faculty of the Purdue School of Engineering and Technology for the past seventeen years. His primary teaching emphasis is in the area of supervisory skill development. He has conducted research, authored articles, and presented seminars on a wide variety of supervision and management-related topics. In addition to his university work, Professor Goodwin has acted as a consultant to numerous businesses throughout Indiana. Prior to his University appointment, he was in management in the automotive manufacturing industry.

Professor Goodwin holds degrees from Purdue University and Ball State University in management and industrial training areas. He completed his Doctorate of Education at Indiana University.

From the Publisher

Few books ever achieve the success of *Supervisor's Survival Kit*. Since its original publication in 1970, nearly a million readers have benefited from this brief, to-the-point, practical book. We know that people like *Supervisor's Survival Kit* because they regularly tell us so in many unsolicited letters. We also know that the book works, because the same customers continue to reorder it.

Perhaps the most amazing feature about *Supervisor's Survival Kit* is the variety of markets it serves. Prentice Hall has customers ranging from major universities and two-year community colleges to technical and private business schools; from small companies to those in the *Fortune* 500. All seem delighted with the way the book provides students and employees with their first step into management.

Although *Supervisor's Survival Kit* remains basically the same—with lively vignettes and Mini-Games—it has been updated. In this edition you will discover new information throughout the book. In particular, Chapter 7 addresses monitoring and controlling the personal use of computers during working hours as well as tips on how to create and maintain a motivating work environment. Chapter 9 on teams has been revised to include a thorough look at the role functions in a team and the normative conditions needed for effective work team behavior. Chapter 10 now presents some specific methods the supervisor can use to improve interpersonal communications with employees. More helpful hints on time management and goal setting were added to Chapter 19.

It is the hope of Prentice Hall that this unusually effective book will continue to win the support of those professionals who prepare men and women for demanding management roles.

Introduction

Someday, if it hasn't happened already, you may become a supervisor and be responsible for the productivity of others. Should it happen, your life will change.

Will you be ready for your new responsibilities? Will you earn the respect of those who work for you? Will those who promoted you be pleased with your work? The answers lie in how you go about motivating, appraising, and building relationships with those you supervise, the kind of working climate you create, the quality of the decisions you make, the skill you demonstrate in handling a wide variety of human problems, the way you manage your time, how you set your priorities, your ability to mold employees from different cultures into a team, and the amount of leadership you put into your supervisory style.

Common sense will help you somewhat in becoming a good supervisor, but to make a really successful transition you will need the kind of help this book provides. It is both a classroom text and an on-the-job guide for the "instant" supervisor who has not had the advantage of formal preparation. It can help make your move into management graceful, rewarding, and permanent and help you provide the foundation for moving into even more challenging management roles in the future.

At the end of each chapter in this book you will find either a case study or a mini-game designed to involve you in a realistic management problem. The case studies can be used for discussion, written assignments, or self-instruction. Suggested answers are provided in the back of the book. The mini-games are intended primarily for role or game playing in the classroom or seminar. A game can be played in fifty minutes or less; specific instructions are provided for each game. Mini-games can also be used as traditional case studies.

Cases and games are built around nine different roles that are profiled in detail in the back of the book beginning on page 264.

Please become acquainted with each character before reading any of the cases or playing any of the mini-games.

Getting into Supervision

"There is more credit and satisfaction in being a first-rate truck driver than a tenth-rate executive."

B. C. FORBES

Should You Be a Supervisor?

After you have finished reading this chapter, you should be able to (1) list a minimum of ten characteristics needed by a good supervisor and (2) identify which of these you can develop in yourself.

Patti drove home from her job with a financial institution feeling both elated and troubled. After less than two years with the firm, she had been offered a promotion to a supervisory role. *Should she accept it?* Manuel has been happy as a short-order chef for three years. Yesterday he was offered a position as night manager at a substantial increase in pay. *Should he accept the challenge?* Gerald was surprised when he was invited to apply for a management position with his electronics firm. *Should he leave his highly paid, satisfying, skilled position for the headaches of management?* Mrs. B reentered the labor market in the health care industry at the age of forty-three. After less than six months, she has been invited into management. *Should she make the move?* George has been encouraged to start thinking about a supervisory role with his national supermarket chain. *Should he leave the security of his union for the problems of management?*

Whether to make the transition into management is a difficult and serious decision. When your opportunity comes, you should weigh both the advantages and disadvantages. Would you be happier as an employee with fewer responsibilities? Which would mean more—the personal satisfaction of being a specialist

or the status that comes from being a leader? Some people wouldn't consider becoming supervisors, as you can see by the following comments:

> As a supervisor you are squeezed between a rock and a hard place. You have to please management and at the same time keep your employees happy. It's an impossible situation. No, thanks.

> I've seen too many burned-out supervisors to want the impossible headaches of a supervisor for a few more dollars each week. I'd rather be happy without the pressure and additional income, and my family agrees with me.

> I'm a skilled person who takes pride in and receives pleasure from doing my specialized job well. Why should I abandon a skill it took me years to develop? I consider myself to be an excellent technical person, but after taking a management seminar I could tell that being a supervisor would never be in my comfort zone.

MANAGEMENT DEFINED

What is management? Managing is getting things done within an organization through other people. It means guiding people's efforts toward organizational objectives; it means inspiring, communicating, planning, organizing, controlling, and evaluating; it means setting goals and moving employees toward them. Management is leadership.

Obviously management is not for everyone. Most employees in all classifications are wise to remain nonmanagers, especially when they do not have the temperament or personality for successful careers as supervisors. But how about you? Should you seriously consider a permanent career in management? Would it satisfy your personal needs and values? Would you achieve greater self-fulfillment? Would you be successful? To help you think it through, try answering the ten questions in the following checklist.

CHECKLIST FOR PROSPECTIVE SUPERVISORS	Yes	No
1. Do you consider yourself a highly ambitious person?	❏	❏
2. Do you sincerely like and have patience with people?	❏	❏
3. Do you like solving problems that don't have just one correct answer?	❏	❏
4. Is making more money important to you?	❏	❏
5. Would recognition from others be more important to you than taking pride in doing a detailed job well?	❏	❏
6. Would you enjoy learning about psychology and human behavior?	❏	❏
7. Would you be happier with more responsibility?	❏	❏
8. Would you rather work with problems involving human relationships than with mechanical, computational, creative, clerical, or similar problems?	❏	❏
9. Do you desire an opportunity to demonstrate your leadership ability?	❏	❏
10. Do you desire the freedom to do your own planning rather than being told what to do?	❏	❏

Total Number: _____ Yes _____ No

If your total number of yes answers exceeds your no answers, you probably make an excellent candidate for a supervisory position.

This checklist was intended to start you thinking, not to tell you definitely whether to become a supervisor.

If most of your answers are yes, it would appear that the role of supervisor might be attractive and comfortable for you. If, however, you gave more no than yes answers, it would appear (at least at this stage of your life) that you should proceed with caution. Such a checklist also helps by pointing out that many important factors are involved in such a decision. Here are four that should receive your special attention.

- *How deep is your need for recognition?* We may all dream about showing everybody how things should be run, but some people are more content with a nonmanagement job. The need for recognition can account for this difference in people. How strong is your drive to gain recognition from others? Would you be willing to work hard enough to parlay your first job in supervision into a middle or top management position? If you can become a superior beginning supervisor, more responsible management positions will be open to you. In fact, you will be able to go as far as your ambition and management skills will take you. If, however, your need for recognition is easily satisfied—perhaps by good fellowship with your co-workers—you may not be willing to pay the price that management requires. You might be happier as a nonsupervisor.

- *How important are people to you?* Most jobs require some contact with people, but the job of supervisor requires much more than most. You must be a personnel director, counselor, teacher, and practical psychologist at the same time. You must learn to work constructively with and accept people who irritate, frustrate, disappoint, and hurt you. You must develop your interpersonal or "people" skills. Active listening and use of correct grammar in written and spoken communication are examples of these skills. You must familiarize yourself with employment laws (e.g., Title VII of the Civil Rights Act of 1964). This law is important for all supervisors because it pertains to the civil rights of your employees. You must be receptive to assist new employees from diversified cultures. You must have a great deal of patience, perception, and compassion. In other words, you must like people—*all* kinds of people. You can't fake it. Yet, if people are truly important to you, building lasting relationships with those you supervise can be highly rewarding—sometimes more rewarding than the money you make.

- *Do you consider yourself a good planner? Are you an organizer?* Supervisors must prepare and implement plans. They must spend quiet periods reorganizing their departments. They must *think ahead.* If you prefer to leave planning to others, you may not be happy as a supervisor.

- *Do you have leadership potential?* A supervisor, department manager, or crew chief is, more than anything else, a leader. He or she must set the tempo, provide the inspiration, and sometimes nurse the employees along, while at other times exercise harsh discipline and hand out constructive feedback. It is a constant balancing act designed to keep the team spirit of the department alive. Although some people seem to have a natural leadership ability, most managers have had to develop their skills through training, experience, and reflection on their experiences. Don't worry about whether you have been able to demonstrate your leadership yet—it's the desire that counts. If you feel you have the potential, look ahead with confidence to your role as a supervisor. Opportunities to demonstrate your leadership will come later.

ADVANTAGES OF MANAGEMENT

If you have never been a leader, it may be difficult to predict how you will react or perform in a management role. If you have the slightest interest in finding out what your chances are, why not try? Start preparing now and accept the first opportunity that presents itself. Here are some advantages to consider.

1. *Opportunities abound.* One out of every nine employee positions is a supervisory or management one so there must be room for you. The police officer who is on a beat can prepare to become a sergeant. The registered nurse can plan to become a superintendent. The factory worker can aspire to become a supervisor. The young person at McDonald's can set the goal of becoming its CEO. The opportunity to move up is nearly always present in those who are willing to plan ahead and prepare. *The Upper Level Leadership Dearth Theory* states that the further up the management ladder you climb, the fewer qualified people exist for the most responsible roles. Translated, this theory means that the further you go, the more opportunity there will be. Also, top leaders are more apt to move to another organization, thus creating opportunity for advancement.

2. *Becoming a supervisor is often the best way to achieve a better-than-average income quickly if you don't have a technical skill or a professional speciality.* If you have a general educational background and do not have a trade, specialized skill, or professional or semiprofessional license or certificate, you should consider becoming a supervisor. The opportunities, especially in service organizations, are excellent.

3. *Supervisors can learn more because of the greater opportunity to participate in company training.* They can attend more classes, read more, and associate with experts. In fact, supervisors must continue to improve and grow with the company. Organizations experience many changes that require their employees to learn new skills. Along with technical training that supervisors or managers get, they are often given the opportunity to attend seminars on leadership, team dynamics, or in technical areas like inventory control, production planning, or quality assurance. Employees may be able to find a little niche where they can hide, but supervisors cannot. *The Bigger Pot Principle* applies here. For example, if you feel your personal growth is restricted as an employee, moving into supervision would be like transplanting a plant to a bigger pot where greater root growth is possible in many directions.

4. *Supervisors almost always know what is happening within the organization.* As part of the management team, they attend meetings, receive more written communications, and are often consulted by upper levels. They interact with other departments and deal with a wide variety of challenges.

5. *Supervisors are in an ideal position to contribute to the welfare of others.* As managers they can go to bat for the employees they supervise. The supervisor is the employee's link to policy makers in the organization. The process of meeting the special needs of employees often begins with the supervisor.

6. *Supervisors are more mobile than workers.* Front-line supervisors usually find it easier to locate a new job should their firm downsize, right size, or simply shut its doors and go out of business. There are two reasons for this: (1) having additional knowledge and experience and (2) having demonstrated leadership.

DISADVANTAGES OF MANAGEMENT

In addition to many other advantages in becoming a manager, a few of the disadvantages are listed here. Think about them before making a final commitment.

1. *Problem employees can be difficult.* As an employee, you have already noticed that some co-workers have unusual behavior patterns that cause problems for their supervisors. Handling confrontations, working with grievances, and doing corrective interviews can be traumatic for some people. Supervisors have sometimes found themselves in the middle of complex human problems that seem to have no possible solution.

2. *Expect to be more alone as a supervisor.* Successful supervisors—even team leaders—must isolate themselves to some extent from the employees they supervise. It can be difficult to be a supervisor and a close friend at times. You must frequently back away when you might rather be a part of the group. You may be asked to withhold confidential information from your employees until an official announcement is made. As a member of the management team, you may be perceived as being one of "them" and not one of "us" by your employees. You will feel this isolation most when you make an unpopular decision and the people you supervise let you know you are on opposite sides. It is an unreasonable expectation to think that you can please everyone all the time.

3. *You may not receive constant reinforcement from your supervisor.* Management people usually treat other managers differently from the way supervisors treat their employees. As a supervisor, you will be expected to support and protect your employees at all times. You must give them day-to-day security and constant personal attention. Do not, however, expect this same treatment from your supervisor. Because you are a manager, you are expected to be stronger, so your supervisor may not feel the same need to reinforce you. He or she will take it for granted that you will provide your own personal confidence and self-motivation and will deal more openly and directly with you.

4. *You may have to change your behavior more than you expect.* Becoming a supervisor for the first time may become one of the most important things to happen to you in your lifetime. It can be a bigger transition than people expect. In becoming a supervisor, you lay your career and reputation on the line; if you fail, your adjustment to a lower level can be brutally difficult and often impossible. The change requires realigning your thinking because your

whole approach to your career must be different. Your daily routine, your human relationships, and your self-concept may have to change. To underestimate the degree of change you might have to make could cause you to fail as a supervisor.

5. *A position as a supervisor could mean longer hours without overtime pay.* It may also mean taking extra work home with you. You may be asked to attend seminars on your own time. You will be expected to manage your time and the time of others. Many deadlines can only be met with appropriate planning and time management techniques. You may not be paid extra for the time this planning takes. Often, a supervisor's schedule is so tight during the regular working day that he or she might typically take work home. This extra home work can cut into family time. Such is the price for those who wish to lead.

6. *High productivity and high quality standards are more important today than they were during the last decade.* Your challenge will be to gain higher quality standards and greater production with fewer people. These demands will increase the pressure on supervisors to learn new technology and approaches in work flow and job design.

7. *Your skills as a supervisor may need to be developed.* Often, the best and most capable technician may be given a promotion to supervisor. Even though technical skills are important, other skills are needed too. As mentioned earlier, you will need interpersonal skills, such as people and leadership skills, as well as time management skills.

THE PRESSURES OF MANAGEMENT

The promises and the pitfalls of management are many. But is there any truth in the belief that becoming a manager is a sure way to get an ulcer? A first-class ticket to a heart attack? A one-way passage to a nervous breakdown? Not really.

This frequently expressed fear—that becoming a manager is injurious to one's physical and mental health because of excessive pressures—is a myth. Management people, in general, are as healthy as those not in management. The supervisor can learn to deal with organizational pressures just as the politician must deal with public pressures. Certainly the job may tax your nervous system a little more than some other kinds of work, and the emotional and mental strain may be greater in some careers than in others. Every job has its own special demands. The solution, of course, is to handle the job without letting it become too much of a strain. Special courses teach strategies for dealing with stress. Some individuals who are highly self-motivated apply pressure to themselves by setting difficult goals that force them to live up to their potential. Properly controlled, stress increases productivity.

Let's look at an example of one individual who wanted the challenge and involvement of a supervisory role. Hank recently accepted an opportunity to become a supervisor. He is approaching his new assignment with an excellent attitude, as is apparent in this conversation with his friend Pamela, who is already a supervisor.

"I admit that I have many fears about becoming a supervisor. I've never thought of myself as a natural leader and have never really had an opportunity to work under pressure. But I've got to cross over the line sometime or I'll never know whether I can make it. I might as well start now and find out what it's like. I realize the days ahead will be the most critical of my career, even though I will supervise only four people at first.

"I see the whole thing as a sort of laboratory experiment. I'll be able to try out all the principles and techniques of good supervision, and if they work well with four people now, they should work well with four hundred people later. It's my first chance to test my ability as a leader. I feel somewhat like a young senator on his first trip to the capitol. I've won the election, but now I must prove to myself that I can survive."

"Good way to look at it, Hank," replied Pamela. "I agree with you all the way. If you decide to go the management route, give it all you've got. Be a professional."

THE PRIOR-IMAGE PROBLEM

Should you decide to make the move into management in a firm where you started as a new employee, understanding the *Prior-Image Predominance Theory* will assist you. Wherever you are now as an employee, those above you may have an image of you built on first impressions. When you first joined the organization, you went through a period of adjustment. You were less confident and less capable than you are now. A prior image based on first impressions is no longer fair to you, and you may need to make special efforts—like new grooming, new confidence, more forthright communication—to change it. You may need to make these changes even before a supervisory appointment is made, but the process should continue after the announcement so that everyone will sense your new maturity and not treat you unfairly because of a less favorable image established in the past.

DISCUSSION QUESTIONS

1. For you, right now, is the price of becoming a supervisor too high to pay?

2. Should a college student who does not have specific clerical, mechanical, technical, or professional skills take courses in management? Defend your answer.

3. From your personal experience as a employee, what percentage of supervisors are truly professional?

4. Describe the job of your supervisor. As you do so, ask yourself whether the rewards justify the sacrifices.

Being in management at the supervisory level holds many unique and rewarding opportunities. A supervisor's job can be exciting, challenging, and growth producing. The ideas expressed throughout this book will provide you with sound principles and guidelines on which to build a rewarding management career. To those of you who are currently a supervisor and to those of you who plan to become one, I dedicate this edition.

Case Study

Please turn to page 268 and become acquainted with the roles of Mr. Big, Supervisor Joe, Mr. G, and Mrs. R before analyzing this case.

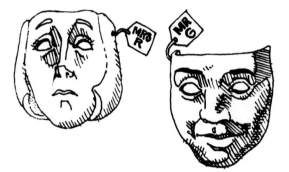

Choice[1]

Mr. Big asked Supervisor Joe to choose one of his employees for promotion. Joe must name a new supervisor for a department similar to his by next week. Joe has narrowed the choice to either Mrs. R or Mr. G but is ambivalent about the final selection. Joe knows that Mrs. R feels she is entitled to the promotion because she leads the department in personal productivity. She is the better choice on the basis of educational background and mental ability, but Joe is not sure that other employees will respond well to her assertive ways and high demands. Mrs. R's relationships with others are not as good as Mr. G's.

Joe also knows that Mr. G believes he is ready to make the move. Having seniority, Mr. G has paid his dues. His ability is sufficiently high, and he might be more sensitive to the needs of employees. Joe must consider one additional factor: Mrs. R seems to have more personal confidence than Mr. G.

No matter what happens, Joe knows he will have a human relations problem with the employee not selected. Even so, he wants credit from Mr. Big for providing the most successful candidate.

Supervisor Joe comes to you for your advice. Base your choice upon the preceding information and your interpretation of the roles of Mrs. R and Mr. G (as described on pages 272). How would you proceed? Upon what factors would you base your decision? What process would you follow? What information will you need to make your choice? You know you will be expected to justify your choice to Mr. Big and to the one not chosen.

Do you feel qualified to make such a decision? Is Mr. Big using this situation as an opportunity to test your skills in leadership? If so, can you identify your leadership skills?

[1]Turn to page 264 to compare your thoughts to those of the author.

Making the Transition

After you have finished reading this chapter, you should be able to write a specific step-by-step plan outlining your successful transition from the role of an employee to that of a supervisor in the same department.

Last year Marsha was a quiet, unassertive computer operator; today she is an efficient office manager. Last year Craig was a graduate student doing research; today he is supervising the work of a dozen employees. Marsha and Craig have successfully made one of the most difficult transitions of their lives. Last year they were followers—today they are leaders. Could this transition happen to you?

You will probably move into your first supervisory position from a nonsupervisory job within the same organization. You may move up within the same department or be transferred from another section. Either way, you will have a challenging experience ahead of you. To help you explore this transition, let's look at two examples.

Harry and Lin, who just completed such a transition, are the same age, with similar personal goals and track records. They became supervisors for the same organization at almost the same time. Their appointments, however, occurred under quite different circumstances.

Because Harry knew about his promotion three months in advance, he was able to prepare for his new responsibilities by taking a supervision course at a nearby college, doing some reading about management, and working closely as an understudy to the person he was to replace. This preparation was designed to guarantee a smooth transition for both Harry and the organization. Lin, on the

other hand, was a regular employee one day and a supervisor the next. Unlike Harry, who was groomed for his new role, Lin became an "instant supervisor," with almost no opportunity to prepare.

Why didn't Lin receive the same training and preparation time as Harry? The answer is simple: Management cannot always predict supervisory vacancies caused by resignations, transfers, and promotions. Sudden growth sometimes causes the demand for supervisors to be greater than the supply. As a result, management is often forced to fill slots quickly. Every day remarks like the following are being made somewhere:

> I realize, Palmer, that you have been with us for only three months and haven't had supervisory experience, but because of an emergency situation, we want you to take over the department tomorrow morning.

> It may come as a shock, Susan, because we haven't had a chance to groom you as a team leader, but we'd rather give you the opportunity than to bring in an outsider.

> Remember when you came to work, Sam, you said you wanted to be a supervisor within a year? Well, you have made it ahead of schedule. Drop by my office later, and we will talk about salary and other details.

Each month men and women of all ages take their first step up the management ladder without preparation. If it happens so often, why all the fuss? *To impress on you that the time to prepare is now.*

No matter what your age, education, or experience, you can't predict what opportunities will occur in the future. You can't anticipate when your supervisor will leave or when some other supervisory opening will occur. Even in periods of recession, when some firms cut back, an opportunity may surface.

YOUR FIRST STEP AS A SUPERVISOR

When you move into your first management role, you will want to keep your eyes open and, as quickly as possible, get the lay of the land. Every position of leadership responsibility entails certain unwritten agreements or ground rules of operation.

- Are you about to encounter some sensitive human relations situations you need to know about in advance?

- Will you be inheriting a problem employee?

- Do any special legal or safety precautions require your attention?

- Does your leadership style differ significantly from that of your predecessor?

- Should you be apprised of some informal reports or unusual protocol?

- Do you know how to handle an incident of employee theft or a problem of sexual harassment?

You hope answers to such questions will come automatically from your new superior either before or shortly after you make your transition. But do not depend on it. You may have to uncover the problems and dig up some answers on your own. Some new supervisors make a list of questions similar to those just given so that they can get answers in advance and avoid unnecessary initial mistakes.

Even if you do an outstanding job of learning which hurdles to jump and which to avoid, the position will likely hold other pitfalls for you to guard against. It is one thing to learn theory and prepare for management, but it's quite another to put that knowledge into practice. No matter how much formal preparation you receive in advance, your first few weeks are critical. If at all possible, you should begin on the right foot.

RECOGNIZING THAT BECOMING A GOOD SUPERVISOR IS NOT A PIECE OF CAKE

Making the move from a follower to a leader is a difficult passage involving behavioral changes on your part and adjustments on the part of those who will work for you. If you underestimate the challenge, you will not live up to your own expectations, let alone those of your superiors.

HOW TO SURVIVE YOUR FIRST FEW WEEKS AS A MANAGER

To help you survive during your first few weeks as a supervisor, try the suggestions presented in the following pages. They can help make the difference between a sound, easy transition and a needlessly difficult one that will cause you problems before you can show your real ability. They may get you through the crucial period when people's reactions to you may be the most critical.

Use Your New Power in a Sensitive Manner

You may think it can't happen to you, but sudden authority has a strange way of inflating your feelings of self-importance without your being aware that it is happening. Guard against this danger by neutralizing your new power with a strong dose of humility. Keep reminding yourself that you are basically the same person you were before you became a supervisor. You must now succeed through the efforts of others, but you do not want to abuse your new authority and create hostility in those who must now look to you for leadership.

Be Patient with Yourself

Your first days as a supervisor may be hectic. You will likely face paperwork and deadlines you didn't expect, meetings that will gobble up your time, and problems you didn't anticipate. At the same time, you may become impatient because you want to try new things right away. Relax. Back away. Try taking the long view. You may wish to confide in a fellow supervisor or with your supervisor. Support from others you trust can help you deal effectively with change.

Decide to Be a Professional

The only way you will be happy as a supervisor is to satisfy your belief that you are effective. Personal pride will come only *after* you feel comfortable with your new role—not before. Recognition from both your employees and superiors will signal your arrival.

Stay in Close Contact with All Employees

The temptation to please management by increasing productivity may cause you to be less sensitive to the people in your department and their problems. This insensitivity would be a serious mistake. Despite all your pressing new responsibilities, it is important that you take time to make personal, positive contacts with each employee in the department during your first few weeks as their supervisor, regardless of whether you were promoted from within the department or were brought in from outside. These contacts can be accomplished through brief stand-up conversations, by coffee-break talks, or by invitations to talk things over, depending on the number of employees, the time available, and other circumstances. The purpose of each contact is to let each person know that you appreciate her or him as an individual. It is your responsibility to initiate the contact and build the relationship.

Make Changes Gradually

Sudden change scares many people. Unless management demands immediate changes, it is best to get used to the way the department operates before introducing major innovations. When you are ready to make changes, explain them to the people who will be affected by them. And remember, people are more motivated to make changes when they have been involved in the planning of the change.

Watch the Up Side—Protect the Down Side

Naturally you will want to satisfy your superiors during your first few weeks because you must earn their support. In doing so, however, be sure to protect those who work in your department. Don't pass on to your people the sudden pressures you feel from above. You must act as a buffer and keep your frustrations and disappointments to yourself if you are to keep a smoothly operating, productive department. Your job is to make the work of those in your department easier, not harder.

Save Some Planning Time

The hustle and bustle of being a new supervisor may cause you to spin your wheels and try to operate without a plan. You may spend too much time moving in one direction and not enough in another. You might solve one problem only to discover that a problem having a much higher priority has been neglected. Take the time to think and plan. Evaluate yourself and your performance on a day-to-day basis. If you cannot find any time for planning while you are on the job, do it at home.

Redefine Your Workplace Friendships

It is possible that some of your close on-the-job friends may try to capitalize on a previous personal relationship now that you are a supervisor. In other words, they may seek preferential treatment. *Do not permit this manipulation.* Your first responsibility as a supervisor is to keep all relationships with your people fair and equal. If you violate this principle at the beginning, you may jeopardize the respect and confidence you receive from others.

NEW STANDARDS OF INTEGRITY

Previous co-workers with whom you have mature friendships will recognize your new responsibilities and will not expect favoritism. These friendships can continue to be close, although both parties may need to redefine their agreements and expend additional energy to keep them in balance. As you adjust to these situations, new standards of integrity on your part may be necessary. Such matters as confidentiality (keeping management matters to yourself), self-control, and personal adherence to company rules come into play.

Let Your Employees Help You

Some of your employees may know more about your department than you do. How can you handle this situation? By all means, go to them with questions. Ask their advice and accept it. Involve them in as many decisions as possible, especially those decisions that will affect them personally. You need their help, especially at the beginning.

Adopt a Learning Attitude

Once you become a supervisor, do not become so preoccupied with pleasing everyone that you neglect your education. Do not hesitate to ask necessary questions of your superiors, fellow supervisors, and knowledgeable employees; continue to read and study this book (it is most helpful *after* you become a supervisor); and enroll in any available outside courses that can offer important direction to your success. For example, if you discover that your new role is putting extra demands upon you in a specific area such as data processing, then study these skills on the outside while you are performing inside. It is widely accepted among educators that when you can apply what you learn immediately, you are motivated to learn faster, cover more material, and understand it better. Once you are a supervisor, your learning should accelerate, not decline. To be an effective supervisor, one must first be an effective human being. Lifelong learning is necessary in our modern world. Take the opportunity to learn new skills when you can. Do not become obsolete.

INITIAL GOALS AS A SUPERVISOR

More than ever, it is a time to read and listen. The new supervisor should attempt to accomplish the following during the first few weeks:

1. *Maintain productivity.* Try to keep the productivity and efficiency of the department at previous levels, with some improvement if possible.

2. *Build relationships with employees.* Redefine and start building a new, strong relationship with each employee. Get to know your people. Introduce yourself. Let them get to know you. Self-disclosure can help employees see you as a person, not just as a supervisor.

3. *Build relationships with peers.* Keep in mind that fellow supervisors can often assist you in making your transition.

4. *Think like management.* Make some progress in the direction of becoming a solid member of the management team. Start the process by thinking like a manager, not like an employee. Do not fall into the trap of criticizing management openly to your employees. Work as a member of management to correct problems, and do so with a spirit of unity and teamwork.

5. *Stay positive.* No matter how you feel on the inside, stay positive and appear confident on the outside.

Later, you can attempt to accomplish more dramatic results. If the first steps have been successful, your future goals are attainable. The willingness of your followers to follow you rests on your track record. Success begets success. The way you pace yourself during the first few weeks will determine to a large degree your long-range success or failure. Let's look at an example of what to avoid.

After two years of waiting, Ron finally became a supervisor with the Acme Discount Stores. He was given a clothing department with seven full-time employees. He began with great enthusiasm, stirring up the employees, making changes on the run, and generally applying the new-broom technique. Predictably the immediate results were gratifying. Sales jumped and management was pleased. Ron was the new hero around the store. In a few weeks, however, some problems slowly became evident. First came some rumbles from the employees. Next came the resignation of one long-time employee, followed soon after by another. Finally, sales dropped drastically, and management's enthusiasm for Ron changed to discouragement. They soon realized he had committed the cardinal management sin: He had sacrificed the relationships between himself and the people in his department in order to make a big show with immediate results. He had taken the short view instead of the long one, and the price both Ron and the company paid was high.

BALANCING HOME AND CAREER

New supervisors have two important reasons for learning more about how to balance home and career. One is to improve immediately their own "balancing act" so that they can survive as supervisors; the other is so that they will be in a position to teach and counsel their employees to do the same later on. With more single parents in the workplace, the need for such training has increased dramatically. Here are four tips to assist you in getting started:

1. Apply the same management techniques you learn in this book to do a better job of leading your family. Remember that home can be a good, safe place to practice newly acquired techniques of leadership.

2. Demonstrate to your employees and superiors that you know how to balance home and career by not jeopardizing one for the other. Stresses at work can cause stress at home, and vice versa. It can be difficult sometimes to keep one from spilling over into the other.

3. Use your weekends to catch up on home responsibilities and enjoy a few leisure activities so that you arrive in the office on Monday morning fresh and organized.

4. Arrive ahead of your staff so that you have some quiet time to plan your daily activities.

When you first become a supervisor, be careful not to create more problems than you solve. Move in with confidence and enthusiasm, but keep your eyes open and don't destroy previous relationships instead of building new ones. Create a climate of excitement, but don't sacrifice your long-range goals for immediate gains. Remember that it is easier to win popularity than to achieve respect. The management ladder has many rungs; if you don't make a smooth transition to the first one, you may never climb the others.

DISCUSSION QUESTIONS

1. In moving from the position of a worker to that of a supervisor, what basic behavioral changes should you anticipate?

2. In making the transition to supervisor in the same department, how would you go about building a supervisor-employee relationship with an employee you were close friends with before the switch?

3. If you were the director of human resources, how would you communicate with and try to change the attitude of a new supervisor who had become overly impressed with the power of his or her new position?

4. How will you balance home life and work life so that one does not jeopardize the other?

Players

Mini-Game

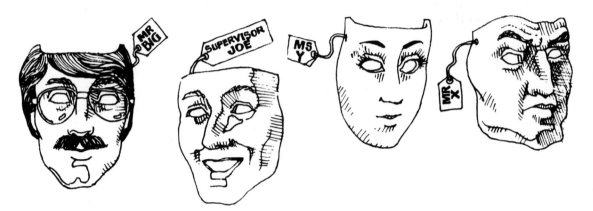

Strategy

Objective

To evaluate alternatives and choose the best approach to use in taking over a new department.

Problem

Mrs. R has been promoted and will take over a new department tomorrow. She wants your advice on one of these basic strategies:

1. Move in openly and freely in a warm and friendly manner. Get acquainted with each employee quickly. *Eliminate any hint of a threatening climate.* After one week, slowly withdraw and let the employees know you are the boss by establishing a friendly but firm discipline line.

2. Move in quietly and maintain a discreet distance from each employee. Make little effort to build personal relationships. Give them time to watch your leadership style. *Let them discover who is the boss the easy way.* After using this approach for a week, relax a little and slowly attempt to establish the warm, friendly relationships and discipline discussed in strategy 1.

Remember, the problem deals only with which approach Mrs. R should take. Support the strategy that will put her in the best position by the end of her second week.

Players

(If the Mini-Game is used in the classroom.)

Use only the four management roles (Mr. Big, Supervisor Joe, Mr. X, and Ms. Y). Students may draw roles as they enter the classroom; then form a panel in front of the class.

Procedure

Have a lively twenty-five-minute discussion of the problem after all players have become involved in their roles. Each player must strongly defend and support one strategy or the other during this period. Every player should have an equal opportunity to defend her or his choice. At the end of the discussion all four players vote by secret ballot for either strategy 1 or 2, but they need not vote for the one they defended. Votes are then collected and tallied. Nonplayers as well as players win if they select the strategy that receives the most votes.

Postgame Discussion

Discuss a possible blend of the two strategies to fit the leadership style of the supervisor involved (in this case, Mrs. R).

The New Star in the Management Hierarchy

After you have finished reading this chapter, you should be able to provide compelling reasons why the front-line supervisor is increasingly vital to the management team.

For years the role of the working or front-line supervisor has been considered by many organizations to be little more than a stepping stone into management. Business and management schools have devoted their attention primarily to principles and theories applicable to upper management. Many professors figured their graduates would hold down beginning supervisory roles for a short period and then move into something more challenging. How things have changed!

Due to the downsizing and restructuring of corporations, the role of the front-line supervisor has been upgraded dramatically. Instead of being a bit player at the bottom rung of the management ladder, the supervisor has become a key position. The obvious reason is because many middle-management positions have been eliminated as illustrated on next page.

MORE RESPONSIBILITY—LESS SUPPORT

The final result is that more responsibility has fallen upon the shoulders of the supervisor who is next to the workers. She or he must play a larger part in the

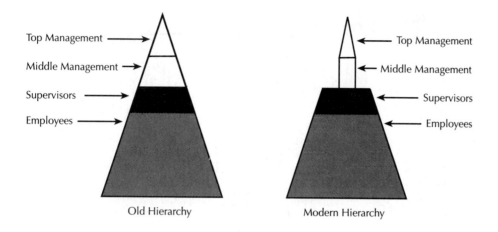

Old Hierarchy   Modern Hierarchy

firm, even though she may receive less support from above. On top of that, supervisors must deal with a wide assortment of new factors that have recently entered the picture.

- A more culturally diverse work team.

- Flex-scheduling, which may mean molding a productive team out of a mix of full-time, part-time, "temps," and home workers.

- Dealing with employees on issues of sexual harassment, child care, and absenteeism.

EX-MIDDLE MANAGERS SPEAK OUT

If you wish the full story of how these changes impacted many middle-management people, listen to a few who dropped back into supervisory roles.

> "I now have a new appreciation for what it means to be a working supervisor in today's lean and mean organization. The pace is hectic. The number of decisions I must make each day astounds me. In stepping down from middle management to supervisor, I should have received an increase in pay."

> "Returning to a supervisory role is a big reversal. Instead of pondering decisions, I have to make them fast; instead of assigning paperwork to others, I often must do it myself; instead of attending middle-management meetings, I must create training sessions that will give my 'team' a boost. No question about it, I should have had more respect for the job of the supervisor when I was supervising them. Talk about learning things the hard way. That's me!"

> "As a working supervisor instead of a middle manager, I find myself more energized and each day goes faster. I have daily contact with real problems instead of trying to manipulate policies. Best of all, I can see the results of my 'team' immediately without waiting until the end of the month to get a written report. When I get back up into a higher management position I will know how to work with supervisors to make their roles easier instead of harder."

What does it all mean?

MINOR CHANGES

It means many minor changes and three major changes. Some of the smaller things include the following:

- More decisions will be made at the production level.
- College professors will devote less time to theory and more time to "supervising techniques" in preparing those who aspire to management roles.
- Effective supervisors will be easier to spot and will receive "first call" on promotional possibilities.
- Women who excel as front-line supervisors will discover that the so-called "glass ceiling" is less apt to exist in their organizations.

MAJOR CHANGES

The three major changes are highlighted here.

1. *Empowerment of the line supervisor will occur.* Some of the "power" previously held by those whose jobs have been eliminated will be delegated to the supervisors they used to supervise. This shift means that the line supervisor or "team

leader" of the past can take a more positive stance. She or he can submit new suggestions with more freedom and more influence. In short, the line supervisor will play a bigger role in the total management team. Upper management (those left) will have to listen more and react to what they hear.

2. *Supervisors will have more autonomy.* With fewer directives to follow, fewer inspections from those above, and fewer people to please, supervisors will feel free to run their departments or "teams" more like the owner of a small business might do. Supervisors will be encouraged to operate with more authority while expecting to be held accountable.

3. *Supervisors will receive more advance training.* As upper management shifts additional responsibilities to their front-line supervisors, they will provide more training to help them succeed. In addition, more supervisors will appoint assistants and prepare them for temporary "takeover" roles when they are absent. In other words, front-line supervisors will move closer to those upper management leaders who remain with the firm and whose roles, in turn, will be expanded.

All these changes mean that employees or team members who aspire to become supervisors will be expected to demonstrate their acceptability with more force and enthusiasm. Not only will their personal performance and contribution to the higher performance of others be evaluated, but management will evaluate how well prepared they are academically to assume the STAR role of the supervisor. Obviously, being accepted as a new supervisor will be more of an achievement in the future than it has been in the past.

If, at this point, your long-term career goal is to get into upper management and you wish to qualify as a supervisor as soon as possible to speed things up, what steps might you consider? Here are three necessary steps.

WALK BEFORE YOU RUN

Step 1: *Put practical experience first.* The job of the supervisor in most organizations is 90 percent application. It is getting the job done. Theory is great, but it is even greater when practical techniques are learned and practiced first. The focus on experience does not mean that strategy theories are to be ignored. The more theoretical background one has the better. But in starting a career your first goal should be to survive as a supervisor, your second goal should be to become a superior supervisor, and your third goal should be to make the move into upper management.

Marty desires to eventually graduate from a four-year university, but being a realist, she knows she must earn her own way step by step. Her first step is to earn an Associates or two-year degree from a local community college. Her next step is to become a supervisor to obtain some practical experience in management. After gaining experience she expects to graduate from an accredited university with a Bachelors of Arts or Bachelors of Science degree. Marty figures that the theory and advanced courses in statistics, data processing, etc., will have more meaning to her after she has had some supervisory experience. It will speed up her transition and put her in a position to occupy a higher management role.

Step 2: *Learn the techniques of supervision by becoming an assistant supervisor for at least sixty days.* You can learn a lot about being a supervisor from working as an employee. You can learn even more by completing a course in supervision. The best option is a combination of both. You will not find, however, a substitute for being an understudy to an outstanding supervisor for a period of time. In most situations it is better to learn to walk before you run. Many colleges have internships or cooperative education opportunities in which you can gain experience and earn college credits at the same time.

> Drake recently graduated from a university as a business management major. He anticipates it may take him the better part of a year, perhaps more, to become eligible for a job as a supervisor. He is more than willing to build his experience, but he wants to qualify as a supervisor by first being an assistant. Drake wants the experience of working closely with a model supervisor who can give him the kind of help he can never get from a textbook. He feels he must become a star supervisor if he is to move into upper management within a two- or three-year period. The right mentor could be the ticket he is seeking.

LEARN TO MANAGE YOURSELF FIRST

Step 3: *Place emphasis on managing your personal life better now so that you can manage a department or team better at a later date.* At first this step may not seem appropriate. What does the way you manage your personal life—going to college, working part-time, working out regularly, and so on—have to do with becoming a superior supervisor? The answer is *plenty*. Take these typical subjects covered in most books on management and you will see the connection.

- Learning to concentrate
- Establishing goals
- Setting priorities
- Managing your time
- Making good decisions

All these skills will assist you in reaching the lifestyle you desire. The same basic skills will help you become an effective supervisor and manager.

Changes in the business environment during the last few years have, without question, focused more attention on the line-supervisor—the man or woman who is willing to assume the growing responsibility of leading a department or team to greater productivity. It may have been easier to become a supervisor and survive in the past because the rules were less complicated and the job had fewer responsibilities. It was more like playing ball in the minor leagues. Today, being a supervisor is a major-league job. The challenge is greater but so are the rewards. The supervisory role is a key player in the management hierarchy.

DISCUSSION QUESTIONS

1. Do fewer middle-management people and the same number of supervisors in most firms mean that the competition for upper management roles among supervisors will be greater in the future? Explain.

2. Have the majority of existing supervisors welcomed and taken advantage of their new powers, autonomy, and opportunities today? Defend your position from practical experience as a worker.

3. Do you agree with the author that the changes described in this chapter put women in a stronger position to occupy upper management roles in the future?

Mini-Game

Players

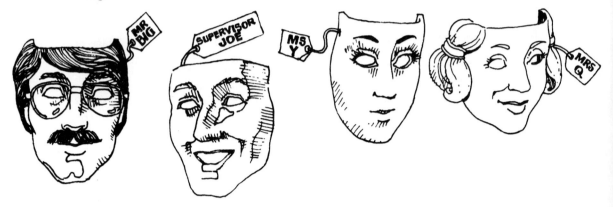

Downsizing

Objective

To measure and understand the impact on employees when downsizing takes place in an organization.

Problem

Mr. Big's job may be eliminated. If this happens, another manager in a job similar to Mr. Big's will look after Joe and Joe's department along with departments the manager already supervises. Mr. Big, however, will be offered Joe's job at his same salary if he wants it. Supervisor Joe, in turn, will be offered Ms. Y's job, and Ms. Y will replace Ms. Q. Ms. Q will be given notice of termination on the basis that her job has been eliminated and all other employees in the department have seniority over her.

Players

All roles may be assigned.

Procedure

Have everyone take five minutes to study *all* the roles. The instructor then picks a student for each role and provides another five minutes to study the assigned roles. At this point the instructor invites each role player to respond to the following two questions *as that person* might:

Question 1:   What do you think your reaction might be if Mr. Big refuses to accept Joe's job and resigns, leaving Supervisor Joe with a new boss who can spend less time with him, which means Joe will have more power with less guidance?

Question 2: What would your reaction be (playing your designated role) if Mr. Big accepted Joe's job?

Postgame Discussion

How does one prepare for the possibility of having her or his job eliminated or downgraded? Will this shifting of personnel continue? Does anyone have intimate knowledge of an individual whose job has been eliminated and how this person made the adjustment?

Human Relations and Communications: The Key to Successful Supervision

"The only things that evolve by themselves in an organization are disorder, friction, and malperformance."

PETER DRUCKER

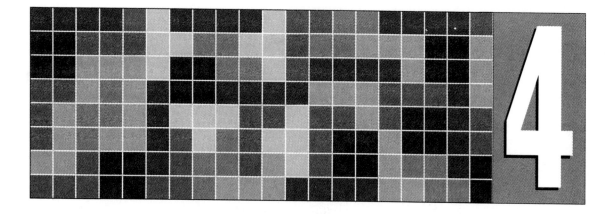

Achieving Productivity Through People

After you have finished reading this chapter, you should be able to list three fundamental reasons why a supervisor must work through people to gain hoped-for productivity and thereby survive.

As you move successfully from the role of worker to that of supervisor, an amazing transformation will take place in the way you look at things. You will suddenly find yourself more interested in John than in the machine he operates; more concerned with Helen than with the records she keeps; more involved with Hank as an individual than with the work he turns out.

Your attention will shift from things to people, from the job itself to the person who performs the job. In short, you will need to become people oriented.

Terms such as *human relations, human behavior, motivation, attitude, sensitivity,* and *leadership style* will take on new meaning. Human understanding will earn the same priority in your scheme of things as job know-how. Helping Roberta increase her productivity will be as important as getting one of your reports out on time. Improving Dick's attitude will command your attention along with production figures, deadlines, and work schedules. You must make the shift from a job-centered employee to a people-centered supervisor.

Why is this transition necessary? Why must the new supervisor become so people oriented? Why must she or he learn to focus attention more on people

than on the job itself? The answer lies in a simple, basic truth: *A supervisor achieves productivity through people.* Your success will be determined by the outputs of those you supervise.

YOU CAN NO LONGER DO IT YOURSELF

The moment you become a supervisor, the production work you do yourself becomes secondary to the relationships you build with the people who do most of the actual work. Even though you may be able to do the job better or faster than those who work for you, and even though you would enjoy doing it yourself, you must turn it over to your employees. You must achieve productivity by learning how to direct, train, create, and maintain a motivating environment. You can seldom afford the luxury of doing it yourself. In other words, in terms of production work in the department, you will contribute more by doing less. Here is how the process works.

1. If you remain an employee, you are primarily responsible for your own job performance and productivity. Your productivity is measured and compared with that of others, and is the focus of your concern. As a supervisor, you are responsible for the productivity of *everyone* in your department. Conse-

quently, management will be interested in measuring departmental productivity and not what you produce yourself.

2. Obviously you cannot increase productivity substantially through your own production. You cannot supervise effectively and produce at a high level at the same time—you are only one person, not two or three. Even if you arrive at work two hours early and leave two hours late every day to do production work, the increase in total productivity would not be substantial, and, of course, you could not continue at such a pace for long.

3. Therefore, as a supervisor, you can maintain or increase productivity substantially only through others. You cannot do it by yourself. If you do not accept this fact, you will never be happy as a manager.

When you become a supervisor, you must learn to let the personal satisfaction of working with people replace the satisfaction you previously enjoyed in working with things. Your future is in the hands of those you supervise, so you must take pride in creating the kinds of relationships that will motivate people to achieve the productivity you desire. First, create the relationships; then work through them to achieve your productivity goals.

Create and maintain an atmosphere of respect and trust. By listening and following through on your employees' suggestions, going to bat for them with your superiors, recognizing their individuality, and, above all, demonstrating two-way communication, you will build trusting relationships.

KINDS OF PRODUCTIVITY

Because your future as a supervisor is so dependent on a clear understanding of this principle, the next few pages will be devoted to the facts and theory involved. First, a sound understanding of productivity is important. *Productivity* is a word dear to the hearts of all managers. And well it should be. Productivity in its broadest meaning is the major purpose of all American business and government organizations and forms the foundation of our profit system. It permits us to compete favorably with other countries and is responsible for all the materials and services we enjoy. Only through the productivity of individuals (and machines operated by individuals) do we achieve our gross national product (GNP), the sum total of all tangible goods and services produced in this country during a given period of time. As a supervisor, however, you are concerned with only two kinds of productivity: *individual productivity* and *departmental productivity*.

Individual Productivity

As the term implies, *individual productivity* is the performance or contribution of one person over a specified period of time. It may mean the amount of materials produced, the ideas contributed, the sales achieved, or the quantity or quality of clerical services rendered. Every job has its own special kind of productivity or contribution. Most jobs, however, will fit into one of the following classifications.

- *Tangible productivity.* The factory worker who operates a machine on an assembly line contributes to the manufacture of the item in a form that can be seen and measured by management, so standards or norms can easily be established. For example, if the average employee produces sixty units per hour, and employee A produces seventy units, then it is easy to measure how far above the standard A's productivity is. In addition to factory work, tangible productivity applies to repairing or altering tangible products.

- *Sales productivity.* A salesperson in a retail store knows how her or his performance compares with that of others because management keeps a record of each person's dollar sales per hour. An individual's productivity can also be compared with a norm. For example, if sales amounting to $90 per hour is the standard for salespeople of a given classification, and one salesperson's sales amount to $100 per hour, her position above the norm is easily measured. However, retail salespeople should not be measured entirely on the basis of dollar sales. Because they must also contribute stock work, housekeeping, and other departmental nonselling functions, their productivity base is larger than selling alone.

- *Service productivity.* Many employees who do not produce tangible goods or generate dollar sales perform vital services that contribute a different form of productivity. Most of these services come under the classification of customer relations. For example, telephone operators do not produce anything you can see, nor do they normally sell to customers, yet the services they perform are basic to the company they represent. The same is true of the services provided by police officers, bank tellers, nurses, supermarket checkers, waiters and waitresses, postal employees, and many others. Although these intangible forms of productivity are sometimes difficult to measure and compare scientifically with norms, they are important to supervisors and the organizations they represent.

The productivity of all individuals is measured to some extent. If an objective measurement is impossible, a subjective measurement is attempted, perhaps comparing one individual with another. The measurement of individuals is vital to good personnel administration and management and must be accepted as part of employment (see Chapter 15). The important thing, of course, is to measure the productivity and not the personality of the individual.

Departmental Productivity

Departmental productivity is the sum total of all productivity (by machines and people) that comes from a department or section within an organization. Like individual productivity it can also be tangible, sales, service, or a combination of these and other forms. Just as one individual is compared with another, so are departments. It is easier, however, to measure the productivity of a department scientifically because it can usually be reduced to figures and accounting data from which management can make its analysis. The important thing to realize is that department productivity becomes your responsibility the moment you become a supervisor. You must live with the figures, reports, and comparisons on a day-to-day basis. If productivity goes up, you are rewarded; if it goes down, you must come up with some explanations. Your reputation in the company will be tied to the productivity record of your department regardless of how much you contribute individually.

Management is defined as planning, organizing, directing, coordinating, and controlling activities to achieve productivity goals. From a human relations point of view, this process boils down to specific things you do to get work done through and with other people. No manager or supervisor can do it all alone, and frequently the more tasks he or she does personally, the lower the total departmental productivity. Working supervisors, those who are expected to produce pieces or render services, often have lower departmental productivity than non-working supervisors.

Shipping department example. Despite the fact that Woody felt he already had more than he could handle, he was given new duties in addition to running the shipping department at the paint factory where he had been a supervisor for five years. How could he pitch in during high-activity periods to maintain shipping schedules if he had to supervise workers in another section? He decided to lay the cards on the table with his six-person shipping department staff. His basic comment was, "I've been able in the past to help out during peak periods, but I can no longer do it. In the future it will be up to you to maintain schedules without my personal productivity unless there is an emergency. How you do this is up to you. If you can come up with some time-saving procedures, I will go along with them."

Six weeks later, after the crew had made a number of helpful suggestions, shipping schedules were achieved without personal help from Woody, and when one member of the staff resigned, a replacement was not necessary. Woody learned that his crew had not been working up to their potential because they could rely on him to step in and produce during busy periods.

Banking example. Alice, operations officer for a savings and loan facility, devoted so much time to training a few people to operate computers that other employees felt neglected. She finally turned computer training over to another. Result? Because she was able to improve relationships, efficiency increased to the point where the facility was able to maintain a high level of service with one less employee.

Health care example. Frieda, a registered nurse in a long-term health care operation, decided to delegate a series of duties to her three ward nurses so that she could devote more time to building relationships with the twenty nurses aides under her supervision. Result? The quality of care increased and costs went down.

Please study the chart below for a moment. Notice that each employee has an individual productivity gap. This gap represents the difference between what each employee is currently producing and what *could* be produced under ideal conditions. Notice, also, a departmental productivity gap between what the department is currently producing and what *could* be produced.

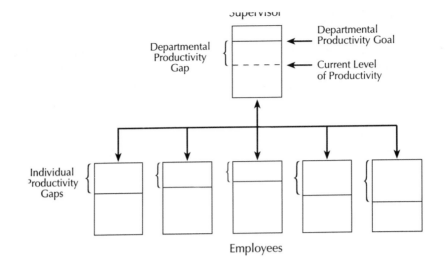

The goal of the supervisor is to close the departmental productivity gap. Because supervisors have a limited supply of time and energy, their time and energy should be spent helping employees close individual productivity gaps. This goal is accomplished primarily by building better human relationships with employees and creating an environment where they will be motivated to reach their own potentials. The remainder of this book will be devoted to helping you learn how to accomplish this goal.

The new supervisor soon learns that almost always a difference exists between an employee's daily performance and his or her capacity to perform. Whether large or small, a productivity gap of some size is natural and should be expected in all employees. Such gaps are, of course, difficult to measure accurately for two reasons: (1) the true potential capacity of an individual cannot really be determined because it is made up of elusive factors such as mental ability, inner drive, perception, attitude, physical stamina, and emotional stability; and (2) job productivity is difficult to measure. The actual performance of a worker is fluid, moving up and down on an hourly, daily, and weekly basis. At one time an employee can have a wide gap (anybody can have an off day), while at other times it can be narrow. In other words, productivity levels quickly move up and down, depending upon many internal and environmental factors. The supervisor can control some, but not all, of these factors.

It is only natural that supervisors should be sensitive to changes in productivity levels in their employees. When an employee shows progress in closing the gap between the current level of productivity and the potential capacity, the supervisor is happy. When the opposite happens, she or he becomes disturbed. The smaller the gap, the greater the total productivity, and nothing is more important to the supervisor's personal success. Small wonder the supervisor wants to know every technique that will help to close such gaps.

Okay, you may be saying, I get the picture. I see why I must step in and help my people perform in line with their capabilities. But how do I learn to motivate my people to work more closely to their capacities? How can I increase productivity in my department without more equipment or more employees?

MOTIVATION TECHNIQUES

Many things can happen, either on or off the job, to cause an excellent employee to drop suddenly in personal productivity. In dramatic situations of this nature (when the cause might be highly personal), the supervisor may wish to give the employee a few days to bounce back without interference. But if too much time passes with no improvement, the supervisor should try to discover the cause and take immediate steps to bring productivity back to the previous level. Hoping that time will take care of the problem can be wishful thinking. Take the case of Bernie, for example.

> For the past week, Bernie had been producing far beneath his potential as a home-appliance repairman. Most of his co-workers averaged thirty-two house calls the previous week (average labor billings $2,400), while Bernie was averaging only twenty-one calls (average billings $1,600). Why? Were Bernie's calls more difficult and time-consuming? Is he less capable, so that it takes him longer? Are some unknown personal reasons behind the gap between what he is doing and what he could do?
>
> Bernie's supervisor took time to look at his previous record and discovered that Bernie had been above average in productivity until the previous Friday, when his productivity gap dropped suddenly to about 50 percent of his normal level. Bernie's supervisor tried to remember any specific event that day that might have been the cause. Then it hit him. That was the day the new truck arrived and was assigned to Frank. Was Bernie upset about it? Through a quick counseling session with Bernie, the supervisor verified his hunch. Bernie, thinking he had seniority over Frank, had expected to be assigned the new truck and was understandably upset when he didn't get it—so upset, in fact, that he seriously thought about resigning. In a long heart-to-heart talk, the supervisor was able to convince Bernie that his assumption had been all wrong and that Frank was entitled to the new truck. The next day Bernie's productivity started going back up. The supervisor had done a successful emergency repair job. Rather than wait around, he moved in and corrected the situation before Bernie's productivity drop seriously hurt the department or before Bernie resigned.

Communication failures, misunderstandings, and damaged egos can occur in any department, so the supervisor must constantly be on the alert for sudden drops in individual productivity. You cannot always afford to wait to discover whether the problem is job-related.

Not all drops in productivity are sudden and dramatic. Sometimes a slow deterioration does not show up for weeks or months. In such instances the supervisor may not be able to find a tangible cause for the widening gap, making corrective action much more difficult. For example, what about the person who has become disenchanted with the job and the company? What do you do when an employee has temporarily lost sight of a previous goal or has a change in attitude that defies understanding? To illustrate the problem, let's look at the case of Gilbert.

> In less than two years with the organization, Gilbert had reached a position of high responsibility in his department. During the past three months, however, he had shown a noticeable productivity gap. Gilbert's slow loss of drive was reflected in reduced efficiency and generally weaker performance. Gilbert's

supervisor decided to try some motivational counseling. She called Gilbert into her office and began as follows.

"Good morning, Gilbert. Thanks for accepting my invitation to drop by. It's been a few months since you and I had a good chat. Tell me, how are things going for you?"

"Well, pretty good, I guess. I still like the job and the company. I haven't heard any complaints."

"Yes, I still feel you have excellent long-range potential with us. By the way, have you ever thought about where you might like to be in our organization in five years? Do you have a personal goal? Are you, for example, preparing for a job similar to mine?"

"Well, at first when I was really gung-ho, I decided to become a supervisor within three years, but I guess my goals are less crystallized now. Reality is quite different from optimistic first plans, I guess."

The conversation that followed between Gilbert and his supervisor lasted forty minutes. During that time, they had a free exchange of ideas on many subjects, but most of the talk centered on Gilbert's future. At the end, Gilbert admitted that he had lost his focus on a goal, and it had been affecting his work. He expressed his pleasure in getting the problem out in the open. It was forty minutes well spent because Gilbert's productivity started going back up within the next few days. In fact, soon it was higher than it had been previously. Before the year was out, Gilbert was promoted to supervisor of another department. Talking things over had apparently restored Gilbert's goal and renewed his personal confidence in his ability to achieve it.

In addition to counseling, many other steps can help you to help your employees keep their motivation. First and foremost, keep practicing the five irreplaceable foundations:

Five Foundations:

1. Give clear and complete instructions.

2. Communicate: Let your people know how they are doing.

3. Give credit when due.

4. Involve people in decisions.

5. Maintain an open door.

These foundations are thoroughly covered in Chapter 6. You can sometimes improve motivation by giving employees special assignments, rotating jobs when feasible, or providing special learning opportunities. Everything you do as a supervisor will have an impact upon the motivation of those who work for you. In turn, the degree of their motivation will determine the productivity level of your department.

MOTIVATION THEORIES

Management books are full of motivational theories. Some, properly interpreted, can be useful to the beginning supervisor. Here are two examples.

From 1927 to 1932 the Western Electric Company conducted what are now known as the *Hawthorne experiments*. These experiments showed that no matter what improvements were made (rest periods, free hot lunches, and so forth), the productivity of the group increased. Why? The employees were made to feel important; making any improvement gave them more status and respect. Until these experiments were made, management had accepted as self-evident that the way to improve the rate of production was to improve machinery, provide better lighting, and make similar physical changes. The Hawthorne experiments proved that the emotional climate of the worker is just as important.

Many psychologists claim that employees' inner needs must be satisfied before they can reach their personal potentials. They divide needs into primary and secondary. A primary need is physiological, such as hunger; a secondary need is one that satisfies the mind, ego, or spirit.

Maslow's Hierarchy of Needs

One of the best-known "need priority" lists was established by A. H. Maslow.[1] He ranked needs as follows:

The bottom need is physiological—food and good health. The next is safety and security. The third from the bottom is social needs: to be accepted and to enjoy the company of others. Next are ego needs—recognition from others. Finally, at the pinnacle, is one's need for self-fulfillment or self-realization.

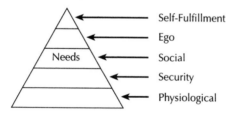

The crux of this theory is that the bottom needs must be fulfilled before the others come into play. In other words, you must satisfy your need for food and security before social needs become motivating. You must satisfy social and ego needs before self-fulfillment is possible.

Suggestions. Because the first three levels of your employees' needs are probably already satisfied, concentrate on their ego and self-fulfillment needs. As you implement the basic idea of this chapter—achieving greater productivity by closing individual productivity gaps—keep these four important principles in mind.

SUPERVISOR-EMPLOYEE RELATIONSHIPS AND PRODUCTIVITY

1. Once you become a supervisor, building good relations with employees is more important than being able to do the job skillfully yourself.

---

[1]A. H. Maslow, "A Theory of Human Motivation," *Psychological Review* 50(1943), pp. 370–96.

The technical skills you have are important because you must know how to do something before you can teach and supervise others; however, your emphasis as a supervisor will be on transmitting your skills through sound relationships rather than on doing all the tasks yourself.

2. Spending time to restore or improve your relationship with an employee whose productivity has slipped is the most important thing you can do with your time.

As a supervisor, you will have multiple responsibilities. In all likelihood, you will have more things to do than time to do them, so it will be necessary to sift out and assign suitable priorities to your responsibilities. Top priority should always go to keeping the productivity of others as high as possible. When the productivity of one employee slips, you must be aware of it immediately and begin trying to do something about it within a reasonable period of time.

3. Management expects you to achieve high productivity from new employees in a hurry.

Today a faster payoff is expected from new employees than was true in the past for several reasons: (a) Employees have a shorter span of employment today, moving from one job to another more quickly. So, if the mobile employee is going to make a productivity contribution, he or she should do so without wasting any time. (b) The pace in most organizations is faster today. Orientation periods have been speeded up, and training time (both on the job and in formal classrooms) is more limited. (c) Training today is more expensive.

What do these factors mean to you as a supervisor? It means you must build relations with new employees as early as possible and train them quickly so that they reach a good productivity level in a shorter span of time.

4. Your future promotions will be based on the productivity of the people who work for you now.

Many factors are considered when management promotes a first-line supervisor to a more responsible middle-management position, but nothing influences a favorable decision more than a supervisor's having the human relations skill to motivate sustained productivity from people. To ignore, underestimate, or downgrade this principle in any way will surely damage your career.

5. When you think of higher productivity, you must think of quality. A term circulating today that you must understand thoroughly is TQM, which stands for *Total Quality Management*.[2] Corporations have discovered that higher productivity and higher quality are necessary to compete domestically and internationally. Stockholders and executives know they are dependent upon front-line supervisors to achieve these goals.

Supervisors occupy a unique and sometimes contradictory role. Although they must possess the knowledge and skills to do specific jobs they ask their em-

---

[2]See Chapter 8 for a close look at TQM.

ployees to do, they must refrain from doing these jobs so that they can manage. They must be content to teach others how to reach their potential. They must reach their own goals through the efforts of others. It takes a special perspective and sensitivity to achieve success in this role.

DISCUSSION QUESTIONS

1. Why might it be extremely difficult—perhaps impossible—for a worker who has been in a highly skilled job for ten years to become a successful supervisor?

2. When, if ever, would a supervisor be justified in saying, "It's easier to do it myself"?

3. Does it take as much patience and understanding to be a good supervisor as it does to be a good teacher, coach, or minister?

4. What things might supervisors do in order to create an atmosphere in which their workers can meet their social, ego, and self-fulfillment needs?

Case Study

Approach[3]

Yesterday Mr. G was promoted to the role of supervisor in a department where customer relations has top priority. In fact, Mr. Big told him he received the promotion because of his outstanding skills with people and his contagiously positive attitude.

Mr. G is pleased with the opportunity and hopes that it will be the first step on a path that will bring him additional promotions. He decides on the following approach.

First, he thinks he can eliminate all training in how to handle customers by being an ideal model. He feels strongly that to work well with people an individual must be natural, and he does not want to impose his own customer relations techniques on the personalities of others. He feels that if he sets the pace and becomes a good example, employees will accept the challenge and develop their own style. They will not need specific suggestions from him. He intends to come to work early and stay late to do supervisory paperwork so that he can spend more time out front with customers.

Second, because satisfied employees are the key to success, he wants to be a "good guy" instead of a disciplinarian. He feels a permissive, relaxed working environment is essential if employees are to be natural and effective with customers. He feels that if he is more accessible to his employees, they will come to him with their problems, and he can develop stronger personal relationships.

Do you see any pitfalls in Mr. G's approach? What suggestions might you make?

---

[3]Turn to page 264 to compare your thoughts with those of the author.

The Supervisor-
Employee Relationship

After you have finished reading this chapter, you should be able to (1) identify the psychological ingredients or factors in a typical supervisor-employee relationship, and (2) write a specific plan that would enable you (as a supervisor) to achieve a better-than-average relationship with an employee.

"Sorry to put this additional responsibility on you at this time, but you know how it is. . . ."

"Here's a new report we have to get back to headquarters by Friday, even if it means letting something else slide."

"J. B. has called another special meeting for tomorrow afternoon. . . ."

The supervisor soon learns that a constant stream of additional and unexpected time-consuming duties filters down from above. Most supervisors occasionally feel that they need more arms and legs and a twenty-four-hour work day to give full attention to their growing list of responsibilities. But no matter how many or how urgent your multiple responsibilities may be, one must take priority over all others: your responsibility to *build and maintain a productive relationship with each employee under your immediate supervision.* No other single responsibility demands the same degree of attention.

Why? As we discovered in the last chapter, building a good relationship with an employee is the best way to close the employee's productivity gap. In addition, only through good relationships combined with strong, sensitive leadership can a cohesive department be built. The *quality* of relationships constitutes the fabric of the department. If relationships fall apart, the whole operation is weakened. If you do not learn to build and maintain these relationships skillfully, your days as a supervisor will be full of turmoil, and you will not reach your potential as a manager. As we shall see in Chapter 9, building interpersonal relationships is the key to success as a team leader.

What is the all-important relationship that exists between the supervisor and each employee? What is its function? How can a productive relationship be built?

THE RELATIONSHIP CHANNEL

Perhaps a supervisor-employee relationship is best perceived and understood as a line that exists between the two, a kind of psychological channel through which all communications, reactions, and feelings must flow back and forth.[1]

---

[1]E. N. Chapman, *Your Attitude Is Showing,* 8th ed. (Upper Saddle River, NJ: Prentice-Hall, Inc., 1996), Chapter 8.

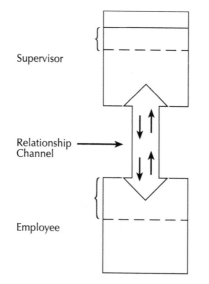

Through this relationship channel each party views, interprets, and reacts to the other. The openness—the amount of freedom or naturalness—of this line contributes to the quality or tone of the relationship, which, in turn, is the essence of the working arrangement. Here are three characteristics found in all relationships; these apply to the relationship itself and do not describe the individual at the other end.

1. *Two-way communication is the lifeblood of the relationship line.* You keep a relationship alive and healthy through an input of words and nonverbal signals from both ends. Just as all parts of the human body must receive a constant supply of fresh blood to survive, a relationship is kept alive with an exchange of ideas, given strength by words, and kept in good repair through talking. Parties at both ends of the line must contribute. An open dialogue keeps the relationship healthy.

2. *Mutual reward theory (MRT).* The MRT states that the relationship between supervisor and employee is enhanced when a good reward exchange occurs between them. For example, the supervisor may provide the employee with the freedom to work with minimum supervision, personal recognition, and involvement in decision making (all are ways to help the employee meet self-fulfillment needs according to Maslow). In return, the employee may provide high personal productivity, dependability, and cooperation with co-workers. When such an exchange takes place, both parties benefit. The employee is happy with his or her job; the supervisor is creating a good image with superiors. Without a reasonably good reward exchange, a healthy, productive long-term relationship is difficult to achieve.

3. *The relationship line can become emotionally charged.* Extreme emotional feelings of either the employee or the supervisor can sometimes enter the line and make it difficult to handle. Therefore, you must often take special care in dealing with a highly charged situation. You must go about the work in a quiet,

sensitive way. Sparks generated by uncontrolled emotionalism are dangerous to the supervisor-employee relationship. Although both parties share in this responsibility, it is the supervisor who must keep the line under control.

You, as the supervisor, are primarily responsible for the condition of any given employee relationship. You must take the initiative to keep it healthy. If it fails, you cannot blame the employee. You need the cooperation of the employee and must assume the responsibility for getting it.

What happens if you fail to build a workable relationship? You may have a problem employee. When faced with this situation, you have at least three possible solutions: (1) Involve the employee by asking for suggestions on how to improve the relationship. If nothing comes of this approach, you may have to (2) initiate action to transfer the individual to another supervisor who has a different leadership style and personality, which might be more successful than yours. This action should be taken in all cases where the employee has made a sincere effort to be productive. (3) Consider terminating the employee. This option may be the most difficult thing you are called upon to do as a supervisor, but sometimes it is inevitable. More often than not, such action is best for both the employee and the organization. If you choose to take this action, be sure that all company procedures and policies are honored. In most cases it means checking with the human resource department to make sure that the rights of the employee have been protected and that no laws have been violated.

A variety of supervisory jobs are available. Some supervisors direct large numbers of employees, others only a few. Some work with highly technical equipment, others with customer services. But no matter what the supervisor's scope or the complexity of the job, a supervisor faces no greater challenge than building and maintaining healthy relationships with those who look to her or him for leadership. To accept the challenge fully means to plunge deeply into human relations. It means taking a deep, clear look at your own behavior, for one thing is certain: *You get back the kind of behavior you send out.*

BUILDING SOUND RELATIONSHIPS

Now that you see why you must build and maintain good employee relationships, how will you do it? Listed here are some suggestions.

See the relationship first and the employee second. The previous pages have invited you to view the employee through a relationship channel in order to become more objective and professional in dealing with employees. By concentrating more on the relationship, you will become less involved in the personality of the individual and will probably be less motivated by any unconscious prejudices that you may have. You will also be more scientific in your approach to problems, more aware of your own responsibilities, and more successful in achieving the productivity you seek. This approach also provides insulation against unwise personal investments.

When Sylvia first took over the department, she dealt only in personalities, attempting to understand and deal with the individual traits of her staff. Resentment developed because her employees thought she was prying into their private lives. Later, Sylvia backed away and started to view each worker through the *relationship channel* for which she had primary responsibility to keep open and healthy. Not only did this more professional approach result in more respect from her staff, but Sylvia felt better about herself because she knew she was more objective and fair.

Don't play games with relationships. A relationship is not a toy or game that the supervisor is free to experiment with lightly. Relationships should be honored and treated with deep respect and sensitive consideration. If you hurt the relationship between you and your employee, you may lower productivity. The employee may at times seem too far away to be hurt by your actions, but she or he will certainly be aware of your attitude.

Keep all relationships on a business basis. In most cases, it is best to keep your business and personal lives balanced. You may find it hard to have both a working and a personal relationship with the same person (regardless of sex) without losing your objectivity and hurting both your careers. For some people in some situations, a working and a social relationship can be combined. However, if either you or those you supervise cannot handle this kind of closeness without a distortion of the on-the-job relationship, do not try to blend the two.

Don't build one relationship at the expense of another. The goal of the supervisor should be to build and keep relationships with all employees equally. Like the parent of several children, the supervisor should show no favoritism, despite the fact that one employee may need more help than another. In building one relationship, it is easy to neglect others, resulting in increasingly negative reactions from the other employees. It is similar to the problem faced by the stagecoach driver who attempts to get each of six horses to pull an equal share of the weight at the fastest possible speed over the long haul. It is difficult to hold the reins with just the right touch. To avoid imbalances, the supervisor must occasionally review the state of relationships with all employees in the department. If one relationship has been built at the expense of another, immediate repair work should be the first priority.

The following checklist can assist you in equalizing communications and rotating assignments.

SUPERVISOR'S CHECKLIST

❑ Talk to employees with the same frequency.

❑ Pay as much attention to employees whose interests are different from yours as those with whom you have more in common.

❑ Find *something* to appreciate about each employee.

❑ Rotate less desirable tasks.

❑ When assigning new tasks, follow criteria clearly defined and known to your employees.

❑ When assigning new tasks, keep in mind opportunities for cross training and skill building.

❑ Communicate your expectations of what is a fair workload for all employees.

Build your relationship with a new employee quickly and carefully. When a new employee comes into your department, you have a good opportunity to build a healthy, lasting relationship from scratch. Take time for this task. Do what is necessary to make new employees feel at home, give them the confidence needed to be productive, and help them build sound working relations with the other employees. Orient new employees to their new surroundings, taking time to introduce them to their co-workers. If you move in quickly and build the right kind of relationship with new employees, especially those from different cultures, they will respond with quick productivity, and the relationship itself will last through the many demands made on it later.

Relationships require daily maintenance. Just like certain pieces of complex machinery, relationships need daily maintenance. They need to be constantly lubricated with recognition, oiled with attention, and polished with kindness. A good relationship must be protected, nurtured, and closely observed lest it fail because of neglect. Experience shows that the productivity payoff is more than worth the attention.

Repair damage quickly. No matter how skillful you become in building relationships, a break now and then is likely to occur. When such disturbances surface, you should quickly make whatever repairs are necessary. Sometimes it means readjusting workloads, schedules, or procedures, or perhaps it requires an apology from you. Whatever it takes, you must move quickly. If the break is beyond repair or requires an outsider, take the problem to your supervisor or human resource director.

In addition to building and maintaining good relationships with employees, you must not neglect relationships with fellow supervisors.

DEALING WITH A DEMANDING SUPERIOR

Your most difficult challenge as a new supervisor may be dealing effectively with your own boss. It is one thing to deal with a superior as a regular employee; it is another ballgame when one management person (you) must build and maintain a strong, open relationship with another. Upper management people can often be more demanding (with vastly different behavioral patterns) than those at the beginning supervisory level. This distinction does not mean you should be intimidated by a powerful person. Three suggestions might assist you in this respect.

- Your new supervisor is more of an equal because you are both members of the management team.

- You can initiate communications more easily because the traditional employee-boss barrier has been eliminated.

- You can often be more assertive (express greater leadership) because you represent the welfare and productivity of your own team.

Your responsibility to your employees in no way means that you have less of a responsibility to build a stronger relationship with your supervisor. Just the opposite! In building these relationships, the following tips may be helpful:

1. Keep in mind that the more you act like a manager, the more you will be treated like one by other managers.

2. Be concerned with the relationship between you and your boss, and not with her or his personality. If you concentrate on the relationship, you can (with experience) get along with almost any personality your supervisor may possess, including those with unusual quirks, mannerisms, and styles of leadership.

3. Demonstrate productivity and quality performance first and good human relations second. You want your department to excel, but you do not want disruptive employees to go over your head by jumping the chain of command.

4. As a supervisor, you do not want problem employees in your department; by the same token, your superior does not want problem supervisors. He or she may be less apt to intervene and counsel you on your behavior than you would one of your own employees because it is expected that you have outgrown the need.

5. The more effectively you handle your own departmental problems, the more you will be appreciated.

Hopefully, your new superior will become a mentor and show you the "ropes" of upper management. Your challenge is to give her or him a reason to help you learn and succeed.

Supervisors can employ many relationship-building techniques, depending upon their styles and environments. Near the top of any list is becoming a good listener. Only when supervisors listen can they discover the special rewards their employees seek that will make the Mutual Reward Theory (MRT) effective; only through listening can problems be identified and solutions sought before they grow into major conflicts that destroy productivity.

Supervisors should remain flexible enough to accommodate harmless personal requests (like leaving early to take care of important personal business) when productivity is maintained and problems with other employees can be avoided. Consistency in style is also significant. Employees do not respond well to supervisors who are unpredictable in their behavior or in their expectations of others.

Becoming a good one-on-one counselor (Chapter 10) is another skill all supervisors need to master. The list goes on and on, but nothing—absolutely nothing—is more important than application of the five foundations outlined in the next chapter. They can literally make or break you as a supervisor.

DISCUSSION QUESTIONS

1. How important is MRT in maintaining good relationships between supervisors and employees? Use your personal experiences to support your answer.

2. What are the advantages of successfully separating the relationship between two people from the personalities involved?

3. How much time should the new supervisor devote to building relationships with their supervisors and peers? What, if any, precautions should be taken?

Mini-Game

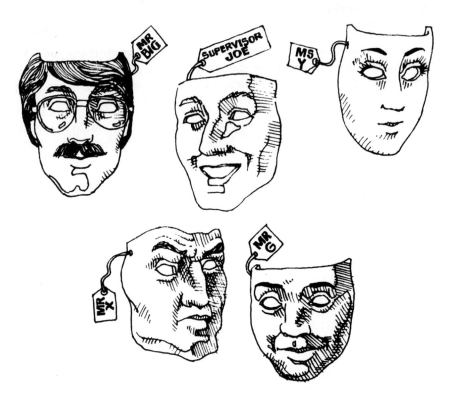

Intervention

Objective

To discover the dangers of intervening when an employee's attitude becomes highly negative.

Problem

Mr. G showed up this morning with a dramatic change in his attitude. Normally positive and pleasant, he is sullen and uncooperative today. Already indications are that his attitude may hurt the productivity of others. Supervisor Joe has always been proud of the quality of his relationship with Mr. G. He is certain that this problem is personal and not connected with the job. Joe feels he has three possible alternatives for dealing with the situation, and he would like your advice. Which should he choose?

1. Immediate intervention through a private talk. Nip the problem in the bud by moving in before group productivity suffers.

2. Give Mr. G two or three days to solve his problem before intervening. Even if productivity suffers, he has a right to solve his own problems. He has been an excellent employee. Why take the risk of offending and possibly losing him?

3. No intervention. Mr. G will eventually solve his own problem, and Supervisor Joe should do nothing in the meantime. Supervisors have no right to invade the privacy of employees, no matter what happens to productivity.

Players (For Classroom Role-Playing Situations)

Use all four management roles, plus Mr. G. All five participants form a panel in front of the class. The role of Mr. G should be assigned in advance to a perceptive student.

Procedure

The panel will discuss the three choices for a minimum of twenty minutes. Mr. G plays the key role. He should sit with the panel but remain silent until all players have discussed and voted for one of the three choices. Then Mr. G announces the alternative he feels is best. He should assume that the problem he faces is personal and not connected with his job. If you make the same choice as Mr. G, you win.

Postgame Discussion

Discussion should center on the way Supervisor Joe might intervene without offending Mr. G. The key should come from the individual who plays the role of Mr. G. What were his feelings as the problem was discussed? What kind of intervention would he have accepted? When would he be most receptive to intervention?

Five Irreplaceable Foundations

After you have finished reading this chapter, you should be able to (1) list the five foundations for good human relations, and (2) describe how you as a supervisor would put them into practice.

If someone offered you a free formula that would measurably enhance your appearance with little effort on your part, you would be skeptical. It would sound too easy. The same is true of the five foundations presented in this chapter. They sound too good to be true. Yet, these simple, somewhat obvious **fundamentals** really work and are recognized as irreplaceable by many management experts. They are easy to understand, are psychologically healthy, and, although they have been around for a long time, nobody has come up with a more modern or sophisticated substitute that works as well.

WHAT ARE THE FIVE FOUNDATIONS?

You will make a serious mistake if you take the five foundations lightly. On the other hand, if you weave them deeply into your leadership style, your success as a supervisor is almost guaranteed. Best of all, you can start practicing them immediately.

1.   Give Clear and Complete Instructions

As a supervisor, you have a certain amount of "knowledge power." You know more about how to perform certain tasks than most of your employees. How effectively you transmit this knowledge to them is the key to the relationship created.

When such instructions are given clearly and completely, the employee knows exactly what to do and feels good about it; however, when the instructions are hazy and incomplete, the employee loses confidence in the supervisor, and the relationship between them deteriorates. To feel secure, the employee must know what is expected and possess the skills to do his or her job. This kind of help comes mainly from the supervisor.

As a supervisor, take time in giving instructions. When possible, use visual illustrations. Follow the basic teaching techniques of keeping things simple and logical and providing examples. Of equal importance, make sure that instructions have been clear and complete by asking for feedback from the employees at the time the instructions are given, and then follow up by checking the following day to see whether the instructions were put into practice correctly.

With many important problems facing him, Supervisor Jake nevertheless took time to demonstrate patiently to Mary, an insecure new employee, how to operate a complicated, dangerous machine. Jake gave Mary more than two hours of his time, including two follow-ups, so that all errors were eliminated. On her second day at work, Mary felt completely competent and her productivity was almost up to average. This training happened more than a year ago, and Mary has yet to have an accident. Furthermore, Jake has had a strong, sound relationship with Mary from the very start.

2. Communicate: Let People Know How They Are Doing

To keep supervisor-employee relationships in good repair, take time to let employees know how they are getting along. Tell them whether they are doing well. *But tell them.* Most employees (especially new ones) want to know how to do their jobs better and will welcome help if it is provided in the right way. They also want to know when things are going well and when you are pleased with their performance. Don't let them feel that they are working in a vacuum and that you do not care.

Employees respond quickly to any stimuli created by you and can also sense the reaction of fellow employees. But the thing that hurts them most is neglect. They want to feel that they are an important part of the department, and they know that their future depends upon your training and support. An excellent way to keep the relationship in good working order is to provide both training and support. Being open to the needs of your employees will help create effective two-way communication.

Mrs. Browne is a highly capable night supervisor of nurses in an Atlanta hospital. She does not, however, believe in letting people know how they are doing. She almost never tells a nurse when she or he does well, but she comes down heavily when a violation occurs. As a result, she has more personnel problems than any supervisor on the staff. Nurses are constantly asking to be transferred to other wards. Mrs. Browne has been passed over for a promotion for three years in succession.

3. Give Credit When Due

Employees need positive reinforcement now and then if they are to keep their personal productivity at a high level. They need the compliment you intend to give before you get too busy with something else; they need recognition. Look for extraordinary quality performance from those who work for you. Sometimes it is best to give credit in front of the entire department. More often, however, it is best given privately. Praise should be given freely, sincerely, and most important, when it is due. To achieve this goal, you must constantly have your "radar" turned on to observe behavior that is deserving of credit. Supervisors who fail to give credit when it is due often have standards that are far above levels the employee is capable of reaching and are afraid that giving credit would be misinterpreted as undeserved flattery. This attitude leaves the employee feeling small and insignificant and usually results in lower productivity. It is necessary to be sincere in giving credit, and it is wise to be generous with giving it.

Karen handles certificates of deposit for her bank, which means she frequently deals with senior citizens who have accumulated enough money to purchase them in amounts of $10,000 or more. Many of these people become extremely nervous when making decisions. A few are overtalkative and difficult to send on their way. Others have hearing impediments. Last week at a staff meeting, Karen's supervisor complimented the entire staff on the improvements they had made in dealing with these customers and singled out Karen for special mention. The following day Karen told her supervisor that she had been thinking of leaving because she did not feel appreciated. She thanked the supervisor.

4.   Involve People in Decisions

Certain problems may arise that only the supervisor can solve. The wise supervisor knows, however, that many problems can be solved with employee participation. In such cases, the supervisor must give people the opportunity.

When you involve employees in departmental problems that concern them, you accomplish at least three goals:

1. You give them a chance to learn about the operations of the department, thus preparing them for future promotions.

2. You build their confidence by providing decision-making opportunities, and as a result, their productivity increases.

3. You improve the departmental climate by bringing people closer together, thereby reducing friction and misunderstandings.

Often the secondary benefits of letting employees come up with solutions to problems are more helpful than the solutions themselves. When employees help make decisions, they grow and you gain. Involvement makes people feel important, challenged, and stimulated. It can release talent and increase productivity as nothing else can.

Make it a practice to turn over appropriate problems to the people who work for you. Let them struggle with solutions even though you could easily find the answer alone. Once they have an answer, accept it gracefully, giving their solution your full support. Employees often give greater support to their decisions than to those handed down by the supervisor. Do not, however, come up with your own answer and just wait for someone to match it, intending to do what you planned all along. Tricking employees into thinking that they are helping you find a solution to a problem that you have already picked is manipulative and easily spotted. Employees find out quickly that you cannot be trusted.

> Marty, the owner of a successful boutique in an enclosed shopping center, had been paying a freelance window trimmer to change the front display twice each month. Her three full-time salespeople were so critical of the displays that she asked them to decide whether to keep the professional or to rotate the job among themselves. They said they would like to do it themselves. After two months, Marty had to agree that not only were the displays better, but all three salespeople were better motivated.

5.   Maintain an Open Door

The supervisor who is easy to approach builds better relationships than the aloof supervisor who is hard to see and difficult to talk with. Encourage your employees to come to you freely with suggestions, with complaints, or for counsel. To allow this communication to happen, you must avoid building physical or psychological barriers between yourself and each employee. Rather, try to establish and practice an open-door policy through which free, open, healthy communication practices can be built. Fear or distrust can prevent good communication and hurt relationships. Merely keeping the door to your office open and telling employees to drop by is not enough. You must work to create a nonthreatening atmosphere of welcome that will cause employees to come to you. Seeking them out by walking around and visiting them is an effective strategy for opening doors.

Ms. Trent was the supervisor of an office staff of twelve. Unfortunately, her office was enclosed in glass and visible to all employees. They could not hear Ms. Trent's conferences, but they could observe them. As a result, despite her best efforts, no one wanted to be made conspicuous while talking over problems in the supervisor's office. Her solution was to schedule and conduct short discussions once a month with each employee at a special location in the employee cafeteria. These meetings took time she could ill afford, but it greatly strengthened relationships and productivity increased.

USING THE FIVE FOUNDATIONS

These five irreplaceable foundations, then, serve the supervisor in building and keeping healthy, productive relationships with employees.

- Give clear and complete instructions.

- Communicate: Let people know how they are doing.

- Give credit when due.

- Involve people in decisions.

- Maintain an open door.

Obviously, it doesn't take a mental giant to understand them, nor does it take a supervisor with twenty years of experience to put them into practice. Why, *then, are they so frequently taken for granted and so seldom used?* Here are three possible reasons:

1. Some ambitious supervisors spend their time seeking more sophisticated replacements instead of realizing that these five foundations will serve them well.

2. Some supervisors give these foundations lip service by claiming to use them when in fact they do not. They say one thing and do another; only the people they supervise know the truth.

3. Some supervisors accept the foundations at face value and honestly try to use them but fail because they do not use them consistently day after day.

How can you sense the need for the five foundations and use them naturally in your daily contact with employees? First, you must make a personal commitment to the five foundations, convincing yourself of their value. You must believe they are sound human relations principles. Second, you must incorporate them into your way of working with your employees, integrating them into your daily routine. You must practice what you believe. The more you practice these five foundations, the better you become at using them.

MASTERING THE FIVE FOUNDATIONS

Here is a three-step formula to accomplish this goal.

Step One

Write the five foundations on a wallet-sized card. Cut a piece of paper or cardboard to a size that will fit into your wallet without being folded. When you have the card in front of you, write the five foundations in your own words. Turn back to the first part of the chapter if you need to do so. When you have finished writing all five foundations to your satisfaction, you are ready to continue.

Step Two

Memorize the five foundations. Holding the card in front of you, take the next five or ten minutes to memorize the five foundations, using any system you wish. (Some people use the "silly word" technique: They devise a five-letter meaningless word and build the five foundations around each letter in the word.) You need not memorize the foundations word for word or learn them in sequence, but you should be able to repeat them to yourself without looking at the card.

Without looking at your card, write them in the following spaces.

Foundation (1)_____
Foundation (2)_____
Foundation (3)_____
Foundation (4)_____
Foundation (5)_____

Now that you have committed these foundations to memory, repeat them over and over to yourself for the rest of the day in order to fix them in your mind for easy recall later. You are now ready for the final step.

Step Three

Apply the five foundations. If you are currently a supervisor, **explain how you plan to apply them during the next two or three weeks with the people you supervise.** If you are not a supervisor, try to apply the five foundations hypothetically. You might assume that you are Supervisor Joe and explain how you would apply them to the five employees under your supervision.

For this exercise, make any assumptions you wish. Try to be specific. The idea is for you to think through each foundation and then practice using it.

Putting the foundations into practice is similar to learning to type without looking at the keys. It won't be easy and it won't happen overnight, but when it happens, you will be doing almost automatically what so many supervisors only talk about. You will have mastered the skill.

DISCUSSION QUESTIONS

1. Why does the author claim that the five foundations are irreplaceable? Do you agree?

2. If a new supervisor concentrates only on incorporating the five foundations into his or her daily behavior, will this individual be a good supervisor?

3. Which of the five foundations would you give top priority? Which one would you give the lowest? Why?

4. List some reactions you would have if your supervisor practiced these five foundations with you.

Case Study

Request[1]

Mr. Big walked into his office yesterday morning and found a special letter in his in-basket. It reads as follows:

> Dear Mr. Big:
>
> Yesterday I received a big shock. My boss, Mr. X, told me he was preparing the necessary papers for my dismissal. I was so upset that I hardly remember what else he said.
>
> When I finally got around to asking him why, he told me that I was habitually late for work in the morning, that I had been warned a number of times, and that he would not tolerate lateness for any reason. I hate to go over his head to you, but I am desperate. It is true that I'm late about fifteen minutes two days a week, but let me give you some background.
>
> I was hired three years ago, after my husband died. I am forty and am the sole support of my three children, the oldest of whom is fourteen. My reason for being late is that I must get my three children off to school. It's not easy. This whole thing never bothered Ms. Y when I was in her department. In fact, she often complimented me and simply asked me to do the best I could about my lateness.
>
> The company has been good to me, and in appreciation I am really dedicated to this job. I work faster and more accurately and waste less time than anyone else in the department, despite the fact that I never receive credit and am not told how I am doing. I often work through coffee breaks and even part of my lunch hour to make up any time I owe the firm because of occasional lateness.
>
> Would you please review the situation for me?
>
> Sincerely,
>
> Jane Pitts

Assuming you are Mr. Big, how would you deal with this problem? It appears that Mr. X may not be practicing the five irreplaceable foundations. Should he be reminded? Should you intervene in behalf of Jane Pitts? Outline the steps you would take.

---

[1]Turn to page 265 to compare your thoughts with those of the author.

Creating a Productive Working Climate

After you have finished reading this chapter, you should be able to list the steps you would follow to create and maintain a productive working climate.

As a supervisor, your attitude is always showing. All the employees in your department have a special kind of radar that permits them to read and evaluate your disposition each day. It gives them a chance to size up and adjust to your present temperament or mood. If you drag into the office with a grouchy, negative attitude, your employees will get the signal and back away from you, going about their jobs with little enthusiasm and avoiding contact with you. If, however, you walk in with a positive attitude, the opposite can happen. They may pick up your mood, show more enthusiasm, and look for chances to communicate with you.

When you are positive, it is easier for those who work for you to be positive; when you show a sense of humor, it is easier for those who work for you to laugh; when you show confidence, it is easier for others to have a productive day. Your behavior and attitude affect the departmental pace, mood, climate, and culture.

THE DISCIPLINE LINE

The climate you establish is the atmosphere under which employees work—the mood of the working environment. It is also the degree of discipline you maintain. How much freedom do you give your employees? At what point do you draw the line? Many management specialists refer to it as the *discipline line*[1] and add

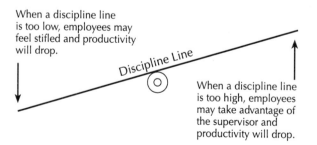

When a discipline line
is too low, employees may
feel stifled and productivity
will drop.

Discipline Line

When a discipline line
is too high, employees
may take advantage of
the supervisor and
productivity will drop.

[1]Some people prefer the term *authority line*. Your choice.

that supervisors must seek and find their own line based upon their leadership styles. The discipline line is the point beyond which employees know they should not push their supervisor; it is the control point. It defines what employees are permitted to do within the working climate without violating procedures, policy, and working standards.

A high, or permissive, discipline line permits maximum freedom because it calls for a minimum of control or supervision. For the most part, employees are expected to provide self-discipline. Such a line works best where employees need great freedom to be creative and no customer contact is involved. A commercial art studio is a workplace where such a line could be successful. Frequently a few employees tend to take advantage of such an environment.

A middle, or intermediate, line permits considerable freedom but maintains certain standards that relate to productivity. For example, in a retail store, bank, or airline office, high customer relations standards are maintained, yet the employees are encouraged to be relaxed and friendly. Dress codes are usually enforced.

A low, or tight, discipline line limits employee freedom. In some cases these restrictions are necessary. Tight discipline is appropriate, for example, when the company wants to protect employees or others. A low line would be required in an atomic energy plant, where safety is a paramount concern. Close supervision may be interpreted by employees as a way to limit their freedom.

> During her first few weeks as a supervisor, Billie permitted her discipline line to be extremely high and loose. She imposed no standards. When her supervisor complained that things were getting out of hand, she lowered (tightened) her line so drastically that her employees were confused and resentful. Billie learned the hard way that oscillating from a line too loose to one that is too tight, or vice versa, is an excellent way to destroy one's career as a supervisor. When it comes to standards, discipline, and control, *consistency* is the name of the game.
>
> The discipline line chosen depends on several factors: one, upon the work environment (art studio, bank, or atomic energy plant); second, upon the style of the supervisor; and third, upon the needs of the employees. New or untrained employees will need tighter supervision than seasoned employees. Within each environment many variations will occur. A supervisor, of course, could maintain a low, strong discipline line and still have a positive attitude and friendly atmosphere.

Once you find the right discipline line for the work situation, maintaining it will require daily attention. To illustrate, let's look at three hypothetical situations in the same work environment.

> Rick is currently running a rather tight department. His discipline line leaves little room for socializing and a narrow margin for error. The atmosphere is one of strict compliance. An experienced outsider observing the situation senses that the department might be slightly overcontrolled, overmanaged, and overstructured. The productivity and quality levels are *average*.
>
> Ron, on the other hand, operates a loose department. He sometimes gives his employees more freedom than they know how to handle. The work gets done, but because of excessive horseplay, occasional errors crop up that must be corrected. Ron feels that employees resent close supervision, so he stays clear except

when he feels it necessary to become more involved. The atmosphere is one of noisy relaxation. A trained observer senses an absence of direction. The productivity and quality levels are *slightly below average.*

Susan is following a middle-of-the-road philosophy. The discipline line is there, but it is not overpowering and restrictive. She tries not to be too permissive but consciously avoids overcontrol. As a result, she does a balancing act between the two. She strives to create a democratic climate in which employees have a degree of freedom but still welcome her leadership, if and when necessary. To the perceptive outsider, the atmosphere is businesslike, with more than average communication between employees. The productivity and quality levels are *above average.*

You will recognize that these examples represent the three classic climates: *autocratic, permissive,* and *democratic.* You can find, of course, many variations of each. Although it is estimated that the great majority of working climates fall into the democratic classification, in some situations either an autocratic or permissive climate is more productive. Consider the following three points about climate:

1. You must create your own departmental working climate.

2. The best climate is the one that generates the highest-quality productivity and relationships between employees and their supervisor.

3. Climates change according to the needs of the department and its employees.

COMPASSION VS. CONTROL

The inexperienced newcomer to supervision may think that it is impossible to demonstrate compassion and maintain a tight discipline line at the same time. Not so. Compassion for others can be communicated in *any* working climate. In fact, if handled in a sensitive manner, employees may accept a stronger, lower discipline line from a more compassionate supervisor. Some less permissive supervisors consistently demonstrate that they care deeply for their staff members. Compassion and tight controls on employees are not incompatible.

DEVELOPING THE RIGHT CLIMATE BY EXAMPLE

The example you set contributes more than anything else to the working climate in your department. The speed at which you work sets a tempo for others. The friendliness you show toward customers or fellow employees sets a norm for others. The energy and enthusiasm you put into your work are transmitted to those who work for you. Most of your employees expect you to set standards through your personal behavior. They observe your every move: how you answer the telephone, the speed at which you work, and the way you communicate. In other words, as a supervisor, you are always in the spotlight. You are the model.

One of your employees can afford a bad day, but you cannot; one of your workers can get by with a grouchy attitude, but you cannot; one of your subordinates can let down, but you cannot. You are the supervisor, and as such, you must consistently set the best possible example. It is the price you pay for your leadership role.

Handling Emergencies

The way you handle emergencies shows your real character more than circumstances do. If you lose your cool under stress, the security of those who work for you will be seriously undermined. Take Marcia as an example.

> Marcia was recently hired to manage a government office located on a busy street in a rough section of a major city. She had more than ten men and twenty women working for her, and she knew that she was being tested in many ways. She had not yet been accepted by the staff. One day an automobile crashed through the front window, caught fire, and created general chaos. Marcia handled the situation calmly, efficiently, and without losing her head. From that moment on, she was fully accepted as part of the staff.

Marcia's behavior under stress demonstrated her leadership and gave the staff the security it needed. As a result, the working climate became more relaxed and productivity increased. You cannot make up a fake emergency to enhance your image with your staff, but if one comes along, do not panic; follow procedures and involve others in decisions.

Employee mistakes may create some of these emergencies, and the way you react to them is important. Nothing is more deflating to the ego or more embarrassing than to make a stupid mistake in front of others. Yet we all occasionally do it. The way you react to such mistakes by your staff members will greatly affect the climate you are attempting to build. Take Morton, for example.

> Morton was the bank manager of a small branch office. He had been in charge only two days when Hazel, carrying a large, heavy tray of coins, slipped on the newly polished floor and spilled everything. After helping Hazel to her feet, Morton calmly got down on his knees and helped retrieve the many coins. He showed no anger, no disgust, no impatience; in fact, he asked one of the other women to take Hazel to the employees' room while he counted and verified her cash drawer. As a result, everybody relaxed and Morton was well on his way to establishing a healthy, productive working climate.
>
> Employees are sensitive to the way a fellow employee is treated, and when Morton built a good relationship with Hazel, he enhanced his relationships with the rest of his staff.

Absorbing Pressures

The way you handle pressures from above affects the working climate. Every supervisor is occasionally on the receiving end of certain demands from people in higher positions. When such a demand is made, you may react in one of these ways: You can pass the pressure on by calling a staff meeting and chewing everybody out, or you can absorb as much of the pressure as possible without passing it on. Here's the way Steve, a section manager in a large factory, reacted.

It was Steve's first job as a supervisor, and in his anxiety to accomplish many things in the first two weeks, he had neglected to have his staff do the necessary cleaning up. As a result, the section was dirty and messy. Predictably, a high-level manager made a routine inspection late one afternoon and reprimanded Steve privately—and emphatically—for the condition of his area. Although he was emotionally upset and was tempted to chew out his staff (after all, it was their fault), he absorbed the pressure and said nothing that day. The following morning Steve discovered his staff was busy cleaning things up. Apparently someone had heard the reprimand Steve had received and passed the word along. Steve never had to say a word to his staff. They respected his willingness to take a beating on their behalf without passing it on. From then on, Steve had little trouble keeping a clean and tidy department.

Communicating Changes

The way you react to changes and communicate them to your staff is critical to a productive working climate. Changes, as we shall learn in Chapter 22, constitute a challenge to the supervisor. In fact, organizational changes are the source of most pressures felt by management and nonmanagement alike. The better you are at adjusting to change, the easier it will be for your employees to accept changes and the more productive your working climate will be. Even more important is the manner in which you communicate forthcoming changes to your employees.

Doreen received word Friday evening after all of her employees had left for the weekend that her department would be transferred to an older, less desirable building. She took time on Saturday to inspect the new location and work out a tentative floor plan. She announced the change in a positive way Monday morning and asked employees for input on her plan. Before the day was over everyone had made a good adjustment, and some persons were looking forward to the additional freedom that would result from being more isolated.

How can you tell when you have created the ideal discipline line or working climate? High productivity and quality (measured by sales, production units, quality control reports, or service standards) and good employee-supervisor relationships are good indicators. The characteristics of a poor climate are complaints, human relations problems, absenteeism, employee rip-offs, hostility, errors, and a general lack of enthusiasm. Like a custodian controlling the temperature in a room, the supervisor should occasionally take readings and make adjustments.

The major reasons for the deterioration of formerly productive departments are neglect, failure to alleviate controllable pressures, and an inappropriate discipline line. A supervisor with a high, loose discipline line will have more problem employees when those employees lack self-discipline or lack work-related training. Many are unable to discipline themselves.

MONITORING YOUR DISCIPLINE LINE

You cannot maintain a good working climate without giving it some personal attention. You must work at it daily by contributing new ideas and lively comments, injecting a little humor to keep employees reacting in positive ways, inserting some deserved compliments to help motivate people, and, above all, communicating. Obviously, you must do a great deal of testing and experimenting before coming up with a satisfactory climate. Do not expect immediate results. Even after you have achieved a good climate, it is not easily maintained. Constant work is required. However, the supervisor who eventually does create and maintain an effective working climate can thereby establish good productivity records and enhance his or her personal progress. Here are some suggestions to keep in mind as you work toward this goal.

Advantages of a Low, Firm Line

Err on the side of strong leadership. A strong leader is one who provides the correct balance of control and freedom in her or his area of responsibility. Most employees prefer consistent leadership behavior whether strong or weak. Being able to predict a supervisor's reaction has a stabilizing effect on employees. Most employees cannot function well in an atmosphere devoid of leadership and direction. They want decisive leadership and work best in a predictable, controlled environment. The fewer rules the better in most situations, but the rules must be clear and set a firm, clear line that all perceive accurately.

> Joyce moved in as the new store manager quietly and in a warm and friendly manner, but she set a much firmer discipline line than her predecessor. Productivity (measured in sales) was up 20 percent the first month. Later, some of her employees told her what it was like to work under the previous manager: "I didn't feel like I was headed anywhere." "There was little satisfaction in doing good work." "Time goes much faster under your supervision." "If there is anything that frustrates me, it's a manager who doesn't lead."

Consistency Is the Key

Find the ideal climate for your department and then maintain it. Be consistent in the way you treat your employees and predictable in the way you handle your duties as a supervisor. Daily inconsistency keeps everyone on edge and holds productivity down.

> Raymond, an operations manager for a branch bank, set his discipline line on a daily basis. When he was in a light mood, he was extremely friendly and tolerant (raising the line); when he was in a serious mood, he was stern and demanding (lowering the line). In less than two months he had lost two employees, and two others had requested transfers. When asked why, one replied, "He expects us to adjust to his mood every day, and we never know just what to expect. He's inconsistent and unpredictable. It's worse than dealing with your own children." Another employee said, "Once you get used to the rules, he changes them in a capricious manner that leaves me disturbed and angry. I would prefer a less capable but more consistent manager."

Seek Feedback from Employees

One way to get feedback from your staff is to mingle a little with your employees during breaks. If the timing seems right, ask how things are going and then listen to the responses you receive. Be open to their feedback. If you are trusted, you may hear complaints or compliments. If you receive few complaints, you probably have the kind of climate you want; if you receive many complaints, things must be out of balance, and you should adjust your discipline line. It is easier to make small adjustments to a working climate than to make major repairs. If you listen to employee complaints and value their input you may receive information that leads to greater productivity.

Fine-Tune Your Discipline Line

Adjust your discipline line frequently and gently. Maintaining the right discipline line or climate takes sensitive maneuvering. The supervisor who overreacts one way or the other often must start from scratch. Here is a classic example.

> About three months ago, things were going well in Carl's department. Production was high. Morale was great. Apparently Carl had come up with the perfect climate, so he relaxed and became more permissive. He felt he could trust his staff. Two weeks later, things began to go wrong. Productivity dropped and mistakes increased. Carl, overreacting, moved in and tightened the discipline line harshly and emotionally, resulting in even lower productivity. Employees didn't want to work hard for someone who gave them freedom one day and took it away the next. Carl needed to learn that sudden, drastic adjustments to his discipline line can easily boomerang. The best policy is to take frequent soundings and make minor adjustments.

Maintain a Lively Climate

Lighten the climate with a sense of humor. It is easy for the supervisor, weighed down with many responsibilities, to become too serious about the job. When it happens, a cloud of gloom may settle over the department. The sensitive supervisor, seeing this situation beginning to develop, will break it up with a little fun or appropriate humor, and lighten up the mood. Take Odie's situation as an example.

> Odie operated a highly successful fast-food franchise. Most of his employees were part-time high school and college students. Knowing that he could pay only minimum wages but needed dependability and high performance, he did everything possible to make the work fun and status-building among the employees' peers, who were frequently customers. After the store was closed, his employees would play their favorite music over the P.A. system. His employees would dance and sing along—so did Odie. His comment to me was, "It is nothing more than a human relations safety valve that permits everyone to let their hair down harmlessly for a short period. It releases the pressure and helps me keep the working climate I need to be successful."

Keep Employees Challenged

Employ the "Chapman Attitude Principle," which states that employees, generally speaking, have more positive attitudes when they are busy. Idle workers usually become bored and eventually negative. By keeping employees busy through advanced planning and delegating, the supervisor will create a more positive working climate and reach higher levels of productivity. The most difficult job in the world is one in which an employee has too little to do. The effective supervisor will see that no such jobs exist under his or her direction.

Communicate Daily

The most disastrous thing you can do as a supervisor is to break off communications with your people. This breakdown usually happens when managers get so busy with reports, planning, research, and other activities that they stay hidden in their offices too long. Loss of communication—for any reason—will destroy morale and productivity faster than anything else. It is only through daily communication that you can measure the atmosphere and decide if you need to adjust your discipline line. Because of this concern, some supervisors force themselves to get away from their other responsibilities once each day for the purpose of casual communications with their employees. It is a sound practice.

Web Surfing on the Job Raises Tough Questions

Probably the single most important contributor to increased productivity in your company has been the personal computer. It is hard for many supervisors to imagine how they could ever complete their tasks without their computer. Production machines are run by them, important reports and records are created with them and filed in them. To be successful, the supervisor must be proficient in using the computer. If you are not, it is a good idea to seek out computer training classes. Continuing and professional education opportunities are readily available through local colleges as well as local libraries or high schools that offer adult evening classes.

One problem that has arisen with the computer in the workplace is use of the computer for personal business while at work. Employees sometimes use their computer to surf the Internet for their own purposes. Some use e-mail to send personal messages to friends and family. Employers everywhere are struggling with the question of how to control nonbusiness computer usage. A recent survey by Vault.com on Internet use revealed that 37.1 percent of 1,244 workers interviewed surfed nonwork-related sites "constantly," and 31.9 percent did so "a few times a day." About one-third of companies now use some type of tracking software that lets them monitor Internet use at work. Overuse can be reduced by making it clear that Internet use will be monitored for signs of abuse. Some experts urge employers to establish Internet-use policies that permit moderate use, particularly during nonwork hours.

Violations of workplace rules concerning computer usage can result in serious consequences for employees. Recently, for example, a school superintendent of a large midwestern school district resigned his position for unspecified violations of the school district's Internet policy. An article in the local newspaper reported that the county prosecutor's office filed a subpoena requesting the school administration turn over computers assigned to the superintendent, initiating criminal investigation into the matter.

Internet surfing on the job raises tough questions. As a supervisor, you must know your company's policies regarding personal use of computers and enforce the policy on abusers by following established disciplinary procedure. If your company has no Internet policy, employees may take advantage of this situation, and as a result, their productivity may decrease. If the decrease in productivity is unacceptable, the supervisor may be forced to take disciplinary action against the employee in order to correct the problem. An employee cannot, however, be held accountable for disobeying a rule that does not exist. In such cases where company policy on nonbusiness computer usage has not been established, policies governing lack of productivity or abuse of personal time become the basis for disciplinary action.

AN IDEAL CLIMATE ENCOURAGES SELF-MOTIVATION

The ideal working climate is one that creates self-motivation in workers. It is generally recognized today that in most work environments traditional motivational techniques do not work well. Supervisors get little response from most workers through pep talks, contests, pay increases, and traditional forms of counseling. In a large number of cases, a worker is either self-motivated or not motivated at all. The word *motivation* comes from the Latin word *movere*, which means literally, "to move." Machinery cannot move on its own. For example, for a clock to move it needs some motivating force, some energy source external to itself, like a wound main spring, battery, or other source of energy. On the other hand, movement or motivation is internal to living organisms. For example, we cannot motivate or force an orange to grow; it either grows or it doesn't. If we want to grow an orange we plant an orange seed, create and maintain the right kind of conditions including the best soil, sunlight, moisture, and temperature. Once the seed is planted we must wait for it to germinate. No amount of coaxing will motivate it to grow. Maintaining the proper environment may enhance the possibility that the orange seed will be motivated to grow but does not guarantee the orange seed will grow into a tree and bear fruit. As living organisims, our employees are not machines and their motivation is internal to them. Like the orange, the person chooses to move.

The contemporary supervisor is challenged to create an environment where, without prodding, workers will want to achieve. In short, employees "catch" motivation from the surrounding climate, a climate created primarily by the way the supervisor supervises. When an atmosphere of confidence and involvement is created, the worker feels good about his or her role and wants to reach out to achieve. Creating and holding on to such a climate is one of the most difficult challenges both new and experienced supervisors face. Research has shown that an environment conducive to internal motivation exhibits the following three characteristics:

1. Purposeful and meaningful work

2. Continuous learning

3. Accurate, timely, and specific feedback on performance

Let's look closely at each of these characteristics.

Purposeful and Meaningful Work

Supervisors must communicate to their employees that they consider them to be valuable to the company. Telling them is necessary but not sufficient. Here are some things the supervisor can do to create purposeful and meaningful work for their employees.

1. *Involve them in planning changes.* Many times employees are only informed or included in the change process at the implementation stage. When possible include your employees in change from the beginning; involve them in the planning stage of a change.

2. *Meet with employees as a group on a regular basis.* During the meeting dedicate a portion of time to seek their input and opinions on issues important to the department, not only when planning change but in solving problems and making decisions. Their input is especially important when the solution of a problem changes any aspect of an employee's work routine.

3. *Show them how their contribution affects the department's or the company's welfare.* In some cases the supervisor may be able to show how the company's products or services enhance the lives of its customers and society in general.

Sometimes employees are told that if they do not like what is happening they can quit. Do not send such a message unless you are prepared to deal with a negative reaction. Doing or saying things that devalue employee contributions quickly and thoroughly undermines the feeling of having purposeful and meaningful work.

Continuous Learning

A job that continually challenges the employee to learn is crucial to motivation. If a job is mastered easily it may become boring or monotonous to the one doing it. Motivating environments contain elements that require the employee to build new skills in order to complete the job. Here are some things the supervisor can do to provide learning opportunities.

1. *Engage in continuous improvement.* Encourage your employee to seek new techniques, new technology, or improvements to the existing work. Provide opportunity for employees to learn more about their job, company, or industry. Many companies provide in-service training on a variety of topics such as new computer software, financial planning, or supervision. The supervisor can set the example by personally engaging in training opportunities.

2. *Provide opportunity for education beyond the job.* Some companies provide tuition reimbursement for employees enrolled in college. Encourage the use of this opportunity and adjust work schedules to accommodate school schedules when possible. Supervisors who simply change a set work schedule that makes it impossible for an employee to complete a class begun under an old schedule undermines trust.

Employees can really get hooked on training and development at work. Well-trained employees who seek to keep their skills current are motivated employees.

Accurate, Timely, and Specific Feedback on Performance

Employees want to know how well they are performing. Feedback is the cornerstone of both growth and productivity. Many companies formally evaluate employee performance at specific times. Annual or semiannual evaluations are the norm. Probationary employees are often evaluated more often during their probationary period. Performance appraisal affects employees in important ways. The outcomes of the performance appraisal often influence pay raises, job security, promotions, and other important employment decisions. All these factors are extremely important to the employee. Supervisors doing appraisals should keep the following in mind.

1. *Do the appraisal on or before the due date.* The longer the appraisal is put off, the less effective it will be.

2. *Take time to cover the results of the appraisal with the employee.* The appraisal conference should be done in private, and each area appraised should be discussed thoroughly.

3. *Allow your employee receiving the appraisal to ask questions for clarification.*

4. *Provide a blank appraisal form to the employee at the beginning of the appraisal period.* Encourage the employee to study its contents and as time goes by discuss any ambiguities or questions that the employee may have regarding what behavior is being assessed and how that behavior gets rated. Employees should not be surprised or blindsided by the results of their appraisal.

5. *Encourage self-appraisal.* If the performance appraisal procedure allows, let your employees appraise their own performance and have them bring their appraisal to the conference. The supervisor completes an appraisal also, and during the conference, both appraisal perspectives and contents are compared and contrasted, often providing helpful insights.

A more thorough discussion of the formal appraisal is offered in Chapter 15.

DISCUSSION QUESTIONS

1. (a) Describe three ways in which management of your company offers its employees purposeful and meaningful work.
   (b) Describe three ways in which your management encourages continuous learning.
   (c) Describe three ways in which your management provides timely, accurate, and specific feedback on performance.

2. Give an example of a supervisor whose discipline line is either too firm or too lax, resulting in low productivity.

3. Do you agree that compassion and strong discipline are compatible? Defend your position.

Mini-Game

Climate

Objective

To gain insight into causes of poor employee morale and to learn ways to restore a productive climate in a demoralized department.

Problem

Supervisor Joe has just returned from a disturbing private conference with Mr. Big. He was told that his department productivity had dropped more than 20 percent in the past sixty days. Mr. Big didn't pull any punches. Joe must get employee morale and productivity back up. Joe is upset and feels that he has been considerate with his employees who are now letting him down. He knows that things have been going badly in the department. Productivity is down; morale is low; griping is high; mistakes have been too frequent. What should he do? After considerable soul-searching, Joe comes up with ten steps he might take to restore a healthy working climate in the department (see the following list). Joe wants advice to help him determine which steps would help and which might do more harm than good. (Readers not involved in group role playing are invited to go directly to the list.)

JOE'S LIST OF PROPOSED ACTIONS

1. Call a fifteen-minute departmental meeting. Release the productivity figures and make it clear that you expect immediate improvement.

2. Instead of a group meeting, take time to counsel each of the five employees on the matter privately. If an employee's productivity is down, be frank about it; if it is mediocre, discuss what can be done to improve it; if productivity is good, be complimentary.

3. Say nothing, but start tightening the department by your actions. Set a more disciplined climate without talking about it.

4. Start immediately to correct all violations or unacceptable behavior you spot through private conferences in your office. Be pleasant but firm. Supervisors must use language that tells employees what specific behavior is acceptable and unacceptable. Generalities do not change behavior. When making an assessment of another's behavior, back it up with specific examples.

5. Withdraw and act hurt until the employees feel sorry for you and, as a result, come around.

6. Start involving your employees in selected departmental problems that you previously handled yourself.

7. Have an off-the-job party at your home for all five employees.

8. Give each employee a written report of the productivity drop and ask for written feedback on what might be done to get back to previous productivity levels.

9. Go to Mr. Big with this list and ask him for suggestions.

10. Spend more time with employees, listening to their complaints, working beside them, having coffee with them during breaks, and generally circulating to improve communications.

Procedure

Break the class up into teams, each with four to six members. Each team then selects a spokesperson to summarize the team discussion. Have each team spend twenty minutes doing the following: (1) Eliminate those steps that might do more harm than good. (2) List the remaining steps and number them in order of preference. (3) If possible, come up with an action that the group prefers over any of those listed.

Once finished, each group should put its list on the blackboard. Take ten minutes to discuss differences. Everyone then votes for the list they feel will be most effective in getting productivity back up to the previous level. You win if you vote with the majority.

Postgame Discussion

Discussion should center on (1) differences among the answers of the teams, (2) whether any formula would actually restore high productivity, and (3) what caused the department to become demoralized.

The Shift to Total Quality Management

After you have finished reading this chapter, you should be able to explain the significance of TQM and apply its principles to enhance your department's productivity and your career.

A new word is circulating in the field of management today—the word is *paradigm* (pronounced para-dime). Experts define paradigm from different perspectives. Here are a few typical examples:

"A model or scheme for understanding the changes that have taken place in recent years."

"A new way of looking at things."

"A new framework for perceiving, thinking, and valuing a particular part of reality."

According to Joel Arthur Barker, author of *Future Edge: Discovering the Paradigms of Success*,[1] a paradigm is a set of rules that establishes or defines boundaries. Our paradigms are our stories of how our world works. The paradigm for describing how management works has changed. When we hear someone use the word *paradigm* it should remind us of the shift in the old way of looking at

---

[1]William Morrow and Company, Inc., New York, NY.

management. *Total Quality Management* (TQM) is a new way of looking at our work performance. It tells us that we are playing a new ballgame with new rules in the workplace. How we adjust to these changes will, to some extent, determine our success as supervisors.

THE THREE BASIC ELEMENTS OF TQM

Quality First

Although one must recognize that *quantity* (the number of products produced or customers served) runs a close second, under TQM *quality* is pushed up front because management understands that higher quality puts a firm in a better position to compete domestically and internationally.

Mrs. Kelly decided to open a small delicatessen in her hometown that would compete head-to-head with one that had been in operation for more than twenty years and had an excellent reputation. Was there room for two delicatessens in the same town? Most observers said she would last less than a year. But Mrs. Kelly adopted a new paradigm, the Total Quality Management (TQM) approach. She purchased the highest quality food and other supplies; she took more time in the preparation of all items on her menu; she (and her part-time help) gave better service. She focused her attention on customer needs and satisfaction, even to the point of free delivery at home when one of her customers was ill. Result? In two years her operation was thriving. Mrs. Kelly's higher quality standards gave her a competitive advantage.

Start with the Customer

In the past, many organizations—large and small—confined their quality efforts to the production of the best possible line of products. Quality control was an inside effort. Under TQM, quality control starts and ends with the customer or client. The strategy is basic: Make customers happier with your product or service and they will pass up your competitors and stand in line at your front door. Even if they must wait, they prefer your service and product.

> Against the advice of his friends, Hank bought the equipment and started a swimming pool maintenance service. His strategy was to make customers happier with his service even though he would use the same equipment and chemicals as his competitors. How did Hank accomplish his goal? If he heard one of his clients was going to have a "pool party," he would provide an extra cleaning before the party without notification or extra charge. He took time to listen to client problems even if they had nothing to do with his service. He continually checked and serviced all the pool heating and cleaning equipment to avoid surprise break-downs. Hank took the attitude that the customer always came first, and he took that extra step his competitors failed to take. How have things turned out? Hank now has three service trucks in operation and is the leading pool service firm in his community.

Employee Accountability

Under TQM everyone is accountable for their actions. Accountability means more frequent performance reviews, closer follow-up should a customer be unhappy, and almost zero tolerance when an imperfect product is placed prematurely in the hands of a client. In short, everyone must do their job and accept personal responsibility for doing it *right*. Employees who do not live up to quality standards are retrained, reassigned, or advised to seek a different kind of job.

> When Sylvia was hired and trained to do high-precision work in a high-tech factory she was amazed to discover that she would go through a weekly performance review for the first two months and a monthly review thereafter. The next thing she discovered was that quality standards had permeated the entire organization and that her successful co-workers took great pride in the part they played in turning out the best possible product. After surviving her probation period, her supervisor said: "Sylvia, we are pleased to have you aboard. We are also pleased that your productivity is above average without sacrificing quality. I consider you to be a quality employee working for a quality outfit. Although our standards are high and there is always some pressure involved, you will discover that there is a lot of job satisfaction working here and there are times when we relax and have a lot of fun."

The swing to quality while maintaining high quantity levels is the number one story in the world of business today. This change is primarily responsible for the success America is winning in foreign markets.

IBM AND GM LEARNED THE HARD WAY

You may have heard the story about a time when IBM was struggling. It had to downsize and adjust to the new way of doing business internationally. IBM had been recognized by most business leaders as the number one international company. The trouble was that IBM became too big with too many layers of management and, for some reason, stopped listening to its customers. The company was concentrating on producing its famous computers but was not always solving its customers' problems. Result? Some small computer firms (Apple, Microsoft, and others) slipped in and did a better job with customers. IBM was forced to recognize that its way of doing business (its paradigm) was outdated. It was operating under the wrong frame of reference. So what happened? IBM adopted a version of TQM—starting with the customer and working back. Today IBM is back and stronger than ever!

A similar paradigm shift took place with General Motors. GM took the U.S. automobile market for granted. Customers would always buy Chevies, Buicks, and Cads. Nothing would happen to its market share, so why change? But car buyers discovered that a few Japanese cars were more dependable, more fuel-efficient, required less service, and had dealers who were more responsive to customer needs. As a result, GM lost part of its market. What went wrong? Just like IBM, GM was not listening to customers. Result? GM designers got busy! They focused on customer needs and quality-made cars from production of subassemblies to final assembly and delivery. GM, like IBM, started to look at its own organization differently. GM today is starting to win back previous customers. Their version of TQM is taking hold.

As a new supervisor, it is imperative that you sense just where your firm stands as far as TQM is concerned. Is your company still in the talking stage? Are they in the middle of switching? Or have they almost completed the transition in adopting those phases of TQM that are appropriate to their future success?

Answering these questions will tell you just how much you may need to adjust your own attitude. To assist you in making this determination, please complete the following exercise.

QUALITY COMFORT ZONE SCALE

How comfortable will you be under the new rules that will come with Total Quality Management? Will you welcome the changes with enthusiasm? Will you take pride in working for a TQM firm? Or will you resist such changes and be more comfortable with an organization that does not set high standards of quality? To find out, read each of the following statements and place a check in the appropriate box to the right.

Statement	Yes	Not Sure	No
1. Are you willing to change from the old to the new even if it means a struggle to improve your attitude?	❑	❑	❑

Statement	Yes	Not Sure	No
2. Do you accept the responsibility of training your staff to work under the new quality standards?	☐	☐	☐
3. Are you prepared to accept accountability for implementing the TQM approach?	☐	☐	☐
4. Can you gear yourself to prevent problems from happening rather than picking up the pieces afterwards?	☐	☐	☐
5. Do you accept the premise that most people prefer to do quality work?	☐	☐	☐
6. Do you agree that there is always room for improvement in how you or your company does things?	☐	☐	☐
7. Can you accept the idea that treating customers "no worse" than your competitors do is unacceptable.	☐	☐	☐
8. Will you commit yourself to the principles and practice of TQM?	☐	☐	☐
9. Are you willing to frequently assess your performance as a supervisor without urging from others?	☐	☐	☐
10. Do you accept the premise that anyone can improve the quality of their performance without sacrificing quantity?	☐	☐	☐
11. Are you willing to have the quality of your performance measured by your superiors at any time?	☐	☐	☐
12. Do you agree you will be happier and more proud of yourself after you fully accept TQM and stick with it?	☐	☐	☐
13. Are you enthusiastic about setting up a TQM program for your department?	☐	☐	☐
14. Does the policy of putting "prevention" above "correction" appeal to you?	☐	☐	☐
15. Will TQM provide you with greater job satisfaction?	☐	☐	☐

Totals

If you came up with ten or more yes answers, your chances of finding TQM within your comfort zone are excellent. Seven or fewer yes answers indicates you are only mildly in favor of TQM. For every two not sure answers, give yourself credit for one yes answer.

No matter what commitment your employer makes to Total Quality Management, the commitment you make to yourself is the key to your future career success. If you are committed to getting your employees or team members to put customers first, producing the best product or service possible, and keeping improvements on a steady, consistent basis with frequent accountability, you are on the winning track. You will be playing the supervisory game under the best possible game plan.

DISCUSSION QUESTIONS

1. How would you explain the terms *paradigm shift* and *TQM* to a friend who has never encountered them before?

2. Which of the three basic elements of TQM do you favor? Why?

3. What changes do you feel would take place in the work environment of a corporation that adopts the TQM philosophy for the first time?

4. How would you go about increasing the amount of feedback you get from your employees concerning your performance as a supervisor?

Mini-Game

Philosophy

Situation

Mr. Big has returned from a two-day seminar in which the TQM philosophy was discussed in detail and his company (a retail, sales-oriented firm) has adopted it with 100 percent support from the CEO down. As a consequence, Mr. Big is introducing the philosophy to all of the departments over which he has authority.

Objective

Gain the support of all personnel in Joe's department to put TQM into operation.

Problem

In presenting the TQM plan to Joe's department, Mr. Big makes the statement that he wants to increase the quality of the way customers are treated by 5 percent and that, in his opinion, if this is accomplished sales will automatically increase 10 percent because happy customers return and bring others with them. Quality, to Mr. Big, means the manner in which customers are treated. He wants all customers to be treated *measurably* better than the way customers are treated by other retail stores selling the same products.

Ms. Y objects to Mr. Big's statement. She claims that to achieve a 5 percent increase in sales not only should customers be treated measurably better but the product itself must be measurably better. To Ms. Y it is the combination of both better service and better products that is necessary.

Players

Mr. Big and Ms. Y

Procedure

The person chosen to play Mr. Big is to argue that the manner in which customers are treated is all a retail store needs to improve because all retailers must purchase products from the same manufacturers and wholesalers. To a retail store TQM is 90 percent the way customers are treated.

The individual chosen to play Ms. Y is to argue that TQM means both a better product and better attention to customers. It is the challenge of retail store buyers to find and buy higher-quality merchandise at the lowest possible price. TQM to a retail store is 50 percent product and 50 percent the way customers are treated.

Postgame Discussion

Discussion should be centered around what constitutes TQM in this retail store. Those who work in a manufacturing firm or who service clients such as in a hospital or bank should discuss how TQM would benefit their customers.

The Effective Work Team

After you have finished reading this chapter, you should be able to (1) communicate the essential differences between a traditional department and a contemporary team arrangement, and (2) operate successfully with employees from diverse cultural backgrounds.

A major restructuring of organizations is taking place in the United States. Downsizing, thinning out of middle-management positions, and greater international involvements are in progress. These and other unsettling changes are necessary to enable firms to reach higher quality and productivity levels in their efforts to remain competitive. It is the challenge of the decade!

In the three previous chapters, you studied the fundamentals involved in creating good relationships as a *traditional supervisor*. You may not have been aware that everything you learned is even more applicable in becoming a *team leader*. In fact, if you think back, you will realize that everything you have absorbed, once put into practice, would make you a successful *coach*. This capability can be highly significant to your future because of the following trends:

■ A steady movement away from the traditional pyramid departmental structure to the circle or team arrangement.

- Increased empowerment, which means that team and departmental personnel are given more autonomy to make decisions, take action, and enhance their own roles.

- The changing ethnic composition of units, which is becoming more representative of all domestic and international cultures.

FROM THE PYRAMID TO THE CIRCLE

The traditional department with authority and responsibility held tightly by the supervisor is giving way to a new, more productive team approach. Study the comparisons illustrated in the figures on the next page.

TRANSITION DANGERS

In making the transition, it may help traditional supervisors to think of themselves as "boundary managers" instead of direct, forceful bosses. That is, a supervisor acts as a team "facilitator" and public relations agent, as well as a leader-supervisor. For example, spend more time coordinating productivity efforts

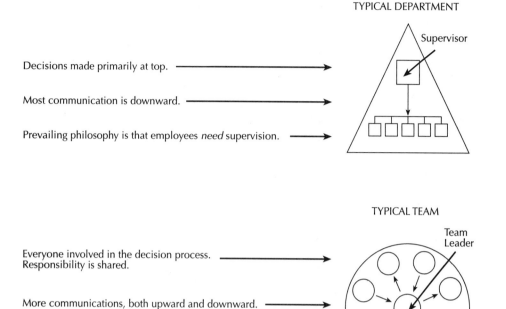

TYPICAL DEPARTMENT

Supervisor

Decisions made primarily at top. ⟶

Most communication is downward. ⟶

Prevailing philosophy is that employees *need* supervision. ⟶

TYPICAL TEAM

Team Leader

Everyone involved in the decision process. ⟶
Responsibility is shared.

More communications, both upward and downward. ⟶

Prevailing philosophy is that employees are capable of ⟶
managing themselves.

with other departments, obtaining resources the team needs, and negotiating conflicts inside and outside of team boundaries.

A team boundary is the sphere of responsibility or work area of the team. A boundary manager is needed when a problem transcends the team's boundary. The team hands the problem off to the boundary manager and he or she takes it from there. The sharing of authority once held only by the supervisor can some-times cause a leader to feel isolated and ineffective. Should this feeling arise, the leader might mistakenly return to the old style.

THE TEAM IDEA IS NOT NEW

Many books have been written about the change just presented. The team con-cept has been around for a long time and tried under many formulas. Naturally, some organizations are more suited to adopt the team approach than others. The basic trend, however, is gaining momentum. The supervisor of the future will be prepared as a team leader as much as a departmental manager. Why will this prepa-ration be prevalent? Because when *employees get swept up in a well-led team project, they become more involved. Personal involvement in decision making can produce higher levels of both quantity and quality.* As a result, everyone benefits.

When Dora accepted an offer from a more progressive firm, she was warned that as a supervisor she would need to absorb and apply the team philosophy en-dorsed by the new president. She accepted the challenge and immediately started to learn as much about the team approach as possible. Dora knew it would mean sharing the authority she previously enjoyed, more frequent communication, added patience so that each team member could be involved in major decisions, and a variety of other changes. In fact, she would need to revamp her behavioral patterns and style as a supervisor. For the first thirty days, things were bumpy and, on a few occasions, chaotic.

At times, Dora was tempted to fall back on her old command-and-control approach, but she resisted. She wisely recognized that she could be sending a mixed message to team members by oscillating between the two leadership styles. This inconsistency could cause confusion and lower productivity. Instead, she accepted suggestions from other team leaders (fellow supervisors), and everything started to come together. When asked by her superior how she was doing, Dora replied, "I still feel a little insecure and I still haven't been able to shed all of my previous habits, but all team members are responding and I am more excited about my job than ever before."

EMPLOYEE EMPOWERMENT

Empowerment is the key term when it comes to developing an effective team. Under the team umbrella you give employees more power to operate freely, more space to be creative, and more chances to contribute to productivity in *their own way*. Under the pyramid structure, it is the supervisor who draws the discipline line. Under the team structure, employees usually draw their own lines. When these freedoms mesh with reality, the employee is empowered to make the team more productive. In other words, rejoicing over the success of the team is more rewarding than making personal progress at the expense of others. Rewards are better when shared with others who have also made a contribution.

RULES OF THE GAME

What does one do to become an effective team leader? Here are a few suggestions.

- Delegate more authority and responsibility to all team members. Only in this way will they feel that they are involved and true members of the team.

- Encourage risk taking and experimentation. Within bounds, let members make mistakes without coming down hard on them. When mistakes happen, help every team member learn from them.

- Develop a *shared vision*. By being a good listener, you will be better able to help the team develop goals that every member wants to reach. Then make sure that the rewards are shared equally.

- Set the stage for team problem solving. You create a problem-solving atmosphere by taking the time to bring everyone close to the problem so that they can contribute to and accept the consequences of the decision.

- Invite self-expression and open discussion even if it involves conflict. This approach can eliminate feelings of resentment that often cause members to tighten up and cooperate only superficially.

- Run team meetings regularly in order to do the preceding activities as a team.

PERSONAL CHARACTERISTICS REQUIRED BY A TEAM LEADER

What are the personal characteristics of a successful team leader? We could talk about patience, having a positive attitude toward team operations, willingness to listen, flexibility, a desire to inspire, and many other traits. But ahead of those characteristics that come to mind quickly is the number one skill—*sensitivity*. It takes a light, delicate, and insightful touch to form a group of strangers, potentially from different cultures, into a viable, productive team. It takes a perceptive individual who understands group dynamics and can lead without pushing. Such a leader must have compassion for all people and a deep desire to help each individual reach her or his potential as a team member.

It is the ability to help members develop a *mutual respect* for the efforts of other members that can convert a work unit into a team. Some people refer to mutual respect as the glue that keeps a good team together—like the motto of the Three Musketeers: "One for all, all for one."

A personal characteristic that should be near the top of any list is a *sense of humor*. A team that cannot relax now and then is a team in name only. When a team achieves a goal, a "reward party" is in order; when a team suffers a defeat, some laughter is needed to enable everyone to learn from the past and begin again. A perceptive leader (or coach) knows that sometimes it is necessary to encourage relaxation to prepare for the next effort.

Building a work team is similar to putting a winning basketball team into competition. It does not happen in a few weeks. Sometimes it takes two or three seasons. When total empowerment is accomplished, the results are obvious. The total team power is measurably greater than that previously exercised by each individual player. It is this added dimension that creates a winner.

> At the beginning, Dora didn't fully understand all the benefits of empowerment. For example, she didn't sense that being involved with a winning team could increase the self-esteem of all players and that this, in turn, would increase their contribution in new, creative ways. She didn't realize that empowerment could convert a worker into a more dynamic participant who was willing to work for the team goal with more enthusiasm and dedication.
>
> With her new approach, Dora found herself communicating more frequently on an informal level, compromising more to accommodate team members who had demonstrated higher personal productivity. But most of all, she noticed a better learning climate emerging—everyone wanting to know how they might contribute more in different areas and what they needed to learn to make it possible. Then, when she looked over the productivity schedules, the bottom line showed that the new approach was working.
>
> "Wow!" Dora said to herself. "By giving up some of my control and authority, I have empowered myself along with other team members."

THE MULTICULTURAL TEAM

The movement from the pyramid to the circle and team empowerment becomes more intriguing when the international composition of many work units is introduced. The predominantly white male team of the past is being replaced with an enticing mix of gender, age, race, and cultural backgrounds, both domestic and international. Even now, it is not unusual to find five or more different cultures represented in a team of ten workers.

How does the team leader deal with this challenge? It is primarily a matter of attitude. If the leader views a multicultural team as an unwelcome challenge, problems will compound. On the other hand, if the leader perceives the new mix as an opportunity to utilize a larger pool of talent to further empower the team, relationships will be friendly and productivity will increase. Here are a few techniques that will assist those team leaders who prefer the positive view:

- Learn from one another. Interteam member relationships can be strengthened as each individual learns to appreciate and enjoy the culture of another. Free and open communication encouraged by the team leader will help this happen.

Some team leaders may think it inappropriate to ask new members from a different culture to discuss their backgrounds and work experience in a different environment. Done properly, however, such discussions could build stronger interpersonal relationships, as well as avoid needless misunderstandings. Each culture has differences that affect work behavior. Thus, when a team member knows how a member from a different culture "sees" the world, the give-and-take can be enhanced. For example, some cultures are more patriarchal than ours, making it natural for workers from these backgrounds to sit back and wait for the boss to give orders rather than move into team efforts on their own.

- A new team member—especially if her or his culture has not previously been represented—needs and should receive special support and training by the team leader. This extra effort by the supervisor can set the tone for other members, and everyone benefits.

- The leader should discover and value the special talents the new member brings to the team and see that those talents are made known and used, inviting collaboration between the seasoned members and the new individual.

- The team leader or supervisor plays an important role in helping those from foreign cultures learn team protocol. Until the procedures and courtesies normally practiced are accepted by newcomers, they will not find the work environment congenial. As a result, they will not make their full contribution to the team.

- Strong, productive teams are built around strong relationships that are mutually rewarding. That is, all members need to benefit from the presence of each team member. Should the leader discover that a misunderstanding or conflict exists, immediate counseling of those involved is recommended. A team is most effective when members are compatible and each relationship is mutually rewarding.

The more you explore the team concept, the more you will realize that not all teams work out. Some individuals who are excellent traditional supervisors can-

---

CULTURAL COMMUNICATIONS QUIZ

This exercise has been designed to help you measure your sensitivity regarding communications with recent arrivals to the United States from other cultures. Place a check under "true" or "false."

True **False**

1. There are more commonalities than differences among cultures.

2. It is good practice to notice and discuss openly with an individual differences among cultures.

3. It is considered good taste to learn and use a few words in the language of the other person.

4. Nonverbal communication can speak louder than words.

5. Most people from foreign cultures have more respect for authority than native-born Americans.

6. It is a good idea to ask those with cultural differences whether they wish to be praised in public or in private.

7. Workers from other cultures fear that their traditional values will be taken away.

8. It is a good idea to reinforce positive behavioral changes with compliments.

9. It is easier to understand English than to speak it.

10. Some persons from other cultures speak less English than they could because they fear making mistakes.

Total _____

The author considers all ten answers to be true.

---

not make the behavioral changes necessary to become the kind of leader required. Often it is better to work for a good traditional supervisor than to be part of a team with a weak, ineffective team leader.

CONTROL AND DISCIPLINE

In an advanced and experienced work team, members usually discipline themselves in order to achieve and maintain group acceptance. A team that normally operates in unison can exert peer pressure on an errant member. Often the leader can remain an observer. When this passive observance does not work, the leader needs to move quickly and quietly to confront the behavioral problem before the individual loses face by disrupting team progress.

ATTITUDE AND THE MULTICULTURAL TEAM

What is the most important factor in creating a successful, high-producing, multicultural team? Many would say it is the attitude of the team leader. Does the leader *want* a team made up of persons from diverse cultures, or is it being mandated by management? Is the leader free of prejudice, so that fair treatment is guaranteed? Does the leader bring to the surface the full potential of each member, so that long-term goals can be reached? Has the leader accepted the challenge inherent in forming a model multicultural team?

> When Dora took over the department in her new firm, she was not surprised about the mix of men and women or the different age levels. It did surprise her, however, to realize that she had one Asian, one Hispanic, two African Americans, and one Arab to work with. Obviously, her new company had an international flavor well beyond that of her previous experiences. Did the mix make Dora's job more difficult? At the beginning, yes. She had to remind herself that the most basic and important principle of human relationships is to treat everyone as an individual. It would be her job to ensure that each member received the full respect of all others. Building healthy, open, and compatible interpersonal relationships would be her goal.
>
> After a full month, Dora had learned more than the identities of the members of the team she had inherited. She discovered, for example, that it was the goal of the team that really brought them together. All she needed to do was work hard herself, teach others by drawing on her greater store of knowledge, communicate a lot, compliment a lot, and keep management apprised of the progress being made.
>
> When Dora discovered that the team concept was a top-priority goal of her new company and that all team leaders met in seminars on a regular basis, she was delighted. This environment would give her the support and skills she would need to survive as a leader in the future. All this activity confirmed that she had made the right decision to join her new corporation.

TEAMWORK

In order for teams to perform successfully, team members need to be aware of and practice the fundamentals of teamwork. First, the team should meet on a regular basis at a specified time. Teams that do not meet or miss meetings routinely do not perform well.

Research on team dynamics indicates three service roles or functions that team members must perform during their meetings. The service roles include (1) leader, (2) recorder, and (3) observer. Each role carries specific responsibilities that affect team dynamics. Except for the leader's role, having team members volunteer to fill each role is often more desirable than appointing someone who may not want it.

The Leader's Role

In most cases the supervisor or manager of the department fills the leader's role. In self-led teams the leader role may rotate among the team members. In both cases, the leader of the team assumes the following responsibilities:

- Ensures that team members perform task and maintenance functions, and reduces nonfunctional behavior.

- Assists the team in choosing and focusing on its tasks and goals.

- Encourages free expression and balanced participation.

- Helps team members listen to each other.

- Helps the team manage conflict.

- Communicates concerns of the team to the next level of management.

One person or leader does not easily accomplish all these outcomes. In an effective team, each team member shares responsibility for performing tasks and maintenance behaviors and for minimizing dysfunctional behaviors. In less mature teams the accountability for these behaviors falls on the leader. The following chart describes each of these behaviors in detail. Dysfunctional behaviors should be addressed immediately. Team members need to be confronted privately about their behavior when it jeopardizes the team. Clear expectations for what is expected and the consequences for failing to perform as expected should be explained thoroughly. If the behavior persists, the person may need to be formally disciplined or removed from the team.

The Recorder's Role

The recorder performs an important function for the team. Primarily the recorder is the historian for the team. The recorder is responsible in the following areas:

- Provides the team with written documentation of the ongoing discussion by recording comments on an easel or board for all the team to see.

- Asks for clarification of ideas or statements as necessary.

- May participate in group discussion, but primarily focuses on recording team members' discussion.

Team discussion frequently ebbs and flows. Depending on the nature of the topic, the discussion may prompt many ideas, thoughts, or suggestions to roll out quickly and randomly. The recorder is responsible for capturing key words or phrases during the discussion. This transcription allows the discussion to progress to other thoughts without losing what has been said or suggested. Some team members may require more "think time" than others in order to fully express their thoughts on a subject or idea. Having a written document in front of them provides the opportunity to refer to an earlier statement on the flip chart. An illuminating

TEAM BEHAVIORS

Task Behaviors

Beginning:
Proposing tasks, goals, or action; defining group problems; suggesting a procedure

Informing:
Presenting facts; giving expression of feeling; offering an opinion

Exploring others' ideas:
Asking for opinions, facts, and feelings

Clarifying:
Interpreting ideas; asking questions in an effort to understand or promote understanding; saying things in another way

Coordinating/ Summarizing:
Pulling together related ideas; restating suggestions; offering a decision or conclusion for group to consider

Reality testing:
Making a critical analysis of an idea; testing an idea against some data; trying to see whether the idea would work

Maintenance Behaviors

Peace-making:
Attempting to settle disagreements; reducing conflict; getting people to explore differences

Gate keeping:
Helping others to participate; keeping communication channels open

General agreement:
Asking whether a group is near a decision; testing a possible conclusion

Encouraging:
Being friendly, warm, and responsive to others; indicating an interest in others' contributions (by facial expressions or remark)

Compromising:
Giving up part of a personal idea to settle conflict; willingness to change to keep group together

Dysfunctional Behaviors

Aggression:
Lowering others' status; attacking the group or its values; joking in a nasty or hurtful way

Blocking:
Disagreeing and opposing beyond "reason"; resisting stubbornly the group's wish for personally oriented reasons; using hidden agenda to stop the movement of the group

Dominating:
Asserting authority or superiority to control the group or certain members; interrupting contributions of others; controlling by means of flattery or other forms of insincere behavior

Out-of-field behavior:
Making a display of one's lack of involvement; seeking recognition in ways not related to group tasks

Special interest:
Using the group as a vehicle for outside interests; putting one's beliefs and needs ahead of group needs

Source: Adapted from John McKinley, *Group Development Through Participation Training* (New York; Paulist Press, 1978).

thought might emerge that was missed the first time. Skills for a recorder include being a good listener and summarizer.

The Observer's Role

The observer is like a mirror that reflects team behavior back to the team members. The reflection is open for investigation. To accomplish this task, the observer:

- Provides the team with observations of its behaviors and processes.
- Makes comments that are group directed and does not refer to the participants by name in the feedback (at least not in early discussions).
- Reports observations at times specified by the leader.
- Sits where he or she can see most team members.
- Reports what he or she observed, not what he or she thinks occurred or should have occurred.

The observer should be alloted a specified amount of time during the team meeting to discuss his or her observations. The team may use a formal questionnaire for assessing team behavior. Numerous team climate questionnaires are available, but using one specifically designed for your team is often the most rewarding. A typical team climate questionnaire focuses on evaluating teamwork. Here are three examples of questions that might appear on a questionnaire. Your team can design its own feedback form and ask its own questions. Instructions direct each team member to individually evaluate the team's effectiveness in key areas. All individual scores can be averaged and compared to one another. All group behaviors are data for analysis.

After completing this feedback form the team discusses its scores. Goals for correcting weaknesses can be set. The team may also wish to celebrate its strengths and accomplishments.

Being a member of a fully functioning and effective team is highly rewarding. The cohesive team, effectively led, often outproduces the most productive individual working alone. Making and keeping a team effective requires the constant diligence of each member. Your team's behaviors collectively will determine

TEAM FEEDBACK FORM				
Category	Scales (please circle)			
	Unsatisfactory	Satisfactory		Excellent
Willingness to listen to one another's views:	1	2	3	4	5
Completes assigned tasks on time:	1	2	3	4	5
Balance of participation:	1	2	3	4	5

how effective your team actually is. Research has shown that teams exhibiting the following seven behaviors (or normative conditions) are most likely to be effective.

Seven Normative Conditions for Effective Teams

1. **Shared planning:** Group decides its goals and objectives through consensus decision making.

2. **Shared decision making through consensus:** Each member must be motivated to carry out the decisions of the group and agree that the following three conditions have been met.
   a. I have heard and understood all viewpoints expressed.
   b. My viewpoints have been heard and understood by all.
   c. I am motivated to carry out whatever decision the team makes.

3. **Shared leadership:** The special responsibility of the leader is to perform group task and group maintenance behaviors. Leadership is a set of behaviors, not an individual.

4. **Shared evaluation:** The group assesses the process of its discussions not just the product of them. The observer role provides feedback to the group on the process. The group must discuss this feedback.

5. **Two-way communication:** Group members actively listen to what is said and to what is not said, as well as attend to verbal and nonverbal behavior.

6. **Mutual trust:** Participants interact in ways that support the feelings of others as worthy persons, even at times of open disagreement.

7. **Voluntary participation:** Each person must accept responsibility for his or her own actions and for maintaining group conditions that support the personal integrity of the other participants.

Source: Adapted from John McKinley, *Group Development Through Participation Training* (New York; Paulist Press, 1978).

A leader must help the team address any problems it experiences. Try to be as specific as possible when describing the weaknesses of your team. You may wish to study more about team dynamics and the stages that teams go through as they develop. An excellent resource is the research of B. W. Tuckman and M. C. Jensen.[1] The leader of a group needs to hone his or her skills in team leadership. For some, these skills seem to come naturally. For the rest of us, study, practice, and help from others is necessary and desirable.

WHEN SHOULD THE NEW SUPERVISOR TRY OUT THE TEAM CONCEPT?

Some new supervisors will discover that they have joined an organization that promotes and supports the team approach. In these organizations, supervisors should, like Dora, make the transition as soon as it is comfortable to do so. For

[1]"Stages of Small-Group Development Revisited," *Group and Organizational Studies* (December 1977).

those supervisors who join firms that have had little or no experience with teams (as is often the case in small companies), the traditional or pyramid approach is recommended. This environment does not mean, however, that one cannot build a working and productive team within the pyramid structure. Many innovative supervisors have discovered that the difference between a department and a team is primarily the kind of leadership provided. You can be called a supervisor by an organization and still develop and lead a most effective team even though you receive little help and encouragement from above. If your style of supervision favors the team concept, move with confidence in that direction.

Mini-Game

Pyramid vs. Circle

Objective

To assist students in evaluating the advantages of the traditional style of supervision versus the team approach.

Procedure

Split the class in half. Assign each half the responsibility of convincing the other of the superiority of either the traditional or team approach to organizing employees. Allow for open discussion and debate. Both sides should focus on how the traditional approach or team approach relates to the following:

1. Employee motivation and empowerment

2. Quality and quantity of work

3. Supervisory responsibilities and challenges

4. Multicultural workforce

5. The organization's views about worker involvement in general

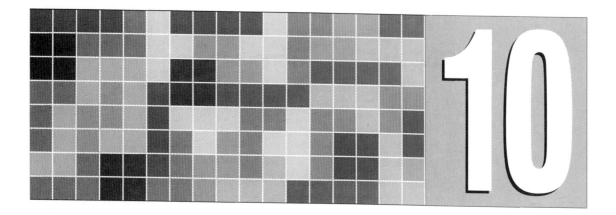

Communicating Privately

After you have finished reading this chapter, you should be able to (1) eliminate any fears you may have regarding private, one-on-one communications; (2) list the five conditions under which private communications can be effective; and (3) apply the techniques professionally to an actual situation.

"It's a mistake to try to teach the first-line supervisor to be a counselor," said Barbara Crane. "Counseling is for professionals only. In the hands of the regular supervisor, it could do more harm than good. Besides, the word *counseling* has a negative connotation. It sounds so psychological that it scares beginning supervisors off."

"I agree, Barbara," replied William Carroll, the director of human resources. "Although the words *counseling* and *private communications* can often be used interchangeably, we should reserve the word *counseling* for performance problems and disciplinary situations. It would be best to call all other one-on-one sessions *communicating privately*. The difference is important because in normal private communications, open, positive feedback should be encouraged."

The author supports the view of Mr. Carroll. But whether you are talking about counseling, interviewing, advice giving, guiding, or coaching, communication is a major tool in your kit.

The supervisor is charged with the responsibility of keeping all relationships with employees healthy and productive. The best method for supporting and improving relationships is to have a sound program and preventive maintenance based on good communication, fair treatment, and other widely accepted human relations practices. But no matter how good the maintenance program may be, any given relationship can become strained, hostile, indifferent, hurt, out of balance, or weak. If it does, the supervisor must diagnose the problem, prescribe the solution, and handle it as a team leader. The best remedy for a poor supervisor-employee relationship is counseling or talking things over. Private communication, initiated and conducted skillfully, can strengthen a weak relationship when nothing else works.

WHAT IS INVOLVED IN PRIVATE COMMUNICATION?

Private communication is a controlled, two-way conversation under optimum conditions. It involves sitting down in some private place and getting job problems out in the open without hurting each other by talking, listening, and trying to understand the other person's point of view. It involves working out solutions that people can accept. The structure of private sessions varies widely. Sometimes a long heart-to-heart talk is needed to clear the air. Sometimes a quick exchange will clear up a misunderstanding. Perhaps the supervisor does most of the talking; the next time, it may be the other way around. Private communication is more than a casual discussion resulting from an accidental encounter. It is a serious, two-way communication initiated by either the employee or the supervisor to deal with a problem or goal. The purpose is to increase productivity by solving problems and strengthening or repairing working relationships. It is not designed to solve personal or psychological problems. As a supervisor you are *not* a psychiatrist, a psychologist, or a professional counselor, but you can counsel employees in your department in order to create and maintain relationships affecting departmental productivity. All other kinds of counseling should be off-limits.

Private communication usually takes place under one of two circumstances: (1) when the employee voluntarily comes to the supervisor with a suggestion, problem, or grievance, or (2) when the supervisor intervenes to motivate an employee, correct a problem, or forestall a grievance.

The supervisor has the advantage when the employee initiates the discussion. For one thing, it means the open-door policy is working and confidence has been established. Even when the employee approaches in a hostile mood, the supervisor should welcome the communication because talking things over may be the only safety valve available. Most of the time, employees will approach the supervisor without hostility. The climate will then be relaxed and nonthreatening to both parties. These off-the-cuff sessions can do much to strengthen relationships further. The more the employee initiates counseling, the better.

Most of the time, however, the supervisor must initiate the process. Intervention by the supervisor is necessary when situations develop that are hurting the productivity of the department. Naturally, private communication is a sensitive procedure. It takes a good sense of timing, a smooth approach, and enough personal confidence to get things started. Because of the need for sensitivity, little of it takes place. The following statements express the problem:

> It's dynamite to move in on some of these sticky human problems. No, thanks. If time can't solve 'em, don't expect me to.

> I'm always available to talk things over with the employees in my department if they come to me, but I'm not going to rock the boat by going to them and stirring up more trouble. It's hard enough to keep the lid on this department the way it is.

> I work so closely with my people that I communicate constantly on an informal stand-up basis. If I called someone into my office and closed the door, he'd be too scared to talk.

For obvious reasons, many supervisors avoid private communication even when they know that interviews could solve problems and increase departmental productivity. The most common reason is fear of the unknown.

THE FIVE RS OF PRIVATE COMMUNICATION

The purpose of this chapter is to dissipate your fears about private communication and demonstrate that you can and should use the technique frequently and comfortably. It requires no magic. You can start right away without fear or misgivings if you understand and use the following principles. They are known as the five Rs of private communication:

> . . . the **R**ight purpose, the **R**ight time, the **R**ight place, the **R**ight approach, and the **R**ight techniques.

Once you learn these principles, private communication will become one of your most important supervisory tools.

The Right Purpose

Private communication as presented in this chapter should be used only for the specific purposes presented in the following list. The supervisor must not exploit the techniques to pry into employees' lives or for other nonbusiness purposes.

1. *To strengthen, maintain, or restore a working relationship between you and one of your employees.* The primary job of the supervisor is to keep relationships healthy, and private communication is the best tool for this task. It should be used, however, only when the break in the relationship has caused a drop in productivity. Let's look at Mr. K as an example.

   > Supervisor Joe asked Mr. K to work overtime on Friday night. In the process, Mr. K was not given a chance to reply that he had promised to take his son to a scholarship banquet. Afterward, Mr. K said nothing, but his attitude changed and his productivity dropped. In talking privately with Mr. K, Joe was able to find out what was wrong, apologize, and restore the relationship.

2. *To motivate employees to achieve greater productivity.* Private communication can sometimes help a new employee bring productivity up to standard or help more experienced employees increase their productivity. In other words, employees can be motivated to improve through the counseling process. Supervisor Joe's communication with Ricardo shows how private communication can work to motivate.

   > Ricardo had done an excellent job for four months as a part-time employee. Then he started arriving late, making mistakes, and otherwise interrupting the smooth operation of the department. Supervisor Joe moved in with a fifteen-minute counseling session. He discovered that Ricardo had been so involved with a personal problem that he had lost sight of his goal, which was to earn enough money to finish college. As a result of the discussion with Supervisor Joe, Ricardo was able to focus on his goal and his part-time job became important again. His productivity was soon back up to its normal level.

3. *To resolve personality conflicts.* Working relationships between two employees in the same department can sometimes deteriorate, causing emotional conflicts and a drop in productivity. In order to protect both the department and other employees, it is sometimes wise for a supervisor to move in with counseling. The following incident is a case in point.

   > Mrs. R had made the mistake of badgering Mrs. Q about her productivity, and Mrs. Q had reacted by sulking and letting her productivity drop below

standard. Supervisor Joe heard the rumble and invited Mrs. R to talk it over. The basis for the approach was that he was responsible for Mrs. Q's productivity and that Mrs. R (because of her maturity and ability) should take the initiative (with Joe's help) to restore the injured relationship. The repair work took time and required much outside support from Joe, but this approach worked.

4. *To discipline or terminate an employee.* Typically in an organization's disciplinary procedure, the first step is usually called a counseling session. Skillful counseling is the best possible tool to use in correcting employee violations of rules, procedures, or policies. It is a sensitive task to discipline others, but when it must be done, it requires a private setting to ensure that others do not overhear the discussion. Supervisor Joe used this technique effectively to correct one bad habit and enabled Mrs. Q to save face.

> Mrs. Q was socializing too much with other employees, overstaying her coffee breaks, and discussing nonbusiness matters over the telephone with other employees. Supervisor Joe was inclined to be tolerant until he noticed that her activities were affecting the productivity of others. Then he invited Mrs. Q into what became a twenty-minute counseling session. Joe stated his concerns quickly but was careful not to show any hostility. He also gave Mrs. Q a chance to defend some of her actions. The period ended with a positive exchange by both parties. After two weeks, Joe was pleased with the way Mrs. Q had curtailed her socializing.

Counseling is also the best approach when the supervisor must terminate someone. Companies are subject to federal EEOC laws and should adopt a disciplinary procedure. In cases where the company is accused of wrongful discharge or discrimination, the disciplinary procedure is reviewed by the courts. The company not having one is flirting with a lawsuit. A counseling session involving termination is never easy, of course, but when handled properly, it can substantially help the employee, the supervisor, and the company.

> Due to a cutback in staff, Joe was forced to terminate an employee some months ago. Rather than handle it on a cold, one-way basis, Joe took the time to discuss the situation at length with the employee in a counseling environment and then provided the individual with a good reference, as well as other assistance. The employee left the company in a better frame of mind, and, of course, Joe felt better too.

5. *Orientation.* Orienting new employees is an excellent time to engage in private communication. Many supervisors set up a formal orientation period with new employees during the first day on the job, at the end of the first week, and at the end of the first month to help them adjust more fully and make it through the probationary period successfully. It is imperative that the supervisor orient a new employee. Turnover rates, job-related accidents, and satisfaction are strongly correlated to orientation. The better the orientation, the higher the satisfaction and the lower the turnover and accidents will be. The supervisor should not delegate orientation to another employee nor assume that the company's human resources department has done the job. The supervisor is accountable for introducing new employees to co-workers, for showing them

around, for covering things such as where to eat, where the restrooms are located, when breaks are taken, starting and quitting times, when payday comes around, and so on. Company policies and procedures that affect the new employee's work should also be thoroughly covered during orientation. The supervisor should prepare an orientation manual containing pertinent information, frequently asked questions, and important phone numbers to call. The new employee can then refer to it as needed. The orientation process is discussed thoroughly in Chapter 12.

The Right Time

Because private communication is always a sensitive process, the timing (usually under the control of the supervisor) is vitally important to a successful outcome. If the timing is right, the results can be excellent. If the timing is wrong, little may be accomplished. Here are four suggestions that should help you choose the right time.

1. *Do not intervene until you are sure it is necessary.* Every employee has a few bad days or a temporary struggle with his or her attitude. Use private communication only after an employee's productivity has shown a downward trend over a period of time. You do not want to jump too early nor allow too long a time to elapse before confronting the situation. Premature intervention can do more harm than good.

2. *Do not initiate a counseling period when you yourself are upset, frustrated, or angry.* Counseling is a two-way affair, and if you use that opportunity to get rid of some inner hostility, it will kill any chance of a successful session.

3. *Remember that certain times of the day are not conducive to counseling.* Peak activity periods, just before lunch, and just before the end of the day (when employees may be anxious to get home or meet appointments) are not the most suitable. Also, try to avoid periods when the employee may be upset emotionally, unless the cause of the upset is the reason for the counseling.

4. *Do not set up a private communication session too far in advance.* If you invite an employee to meet you in your office at 2:00 P.M. when it is only 10:00 A.M., he or she has four hours to worry and get upset and probably will produce at a lower rate. In almost all cases, it is better to set a time with either a short gap or none at all.

The Right Place

Having the right place for private communication can be more important than you think. It is almost impossible to do successful stand-up counseling or to accomplish much in a noisy place with frequent distractions. The ideal situation, of course, is a private office. Some supervisors, however, must settle for less. One solution is coffee-break counseling, provided that outsiders do not interfere. Another alternative is to make arrangements to use somebody else's office or a vacant room.

The Right Approach

The major reason supervisors back away from problem counseling is that they are afraid of the first hurdle, the approach. They think about it and plan it, but not knowing how to take the first step prevents them from executing their plans. At least four primary fears cause this hesitation:

1. Fear of saying the wrong thing at the beginning, thereby causing an unpleasant confrontation.

2. Fear of invading the employee's privacy.

3. Fear of opening up a hornet's nest of other problems.

4. Fear of being disliked by the employee.

Most of these fears are not substantiated by fact. Employees like to talk to their supervisors, even about unpleasant matters. Employees do not always resent being disciplined, if it is done in the right way, and often admit that help was needed, even though they would not ask for it.

To get past these fears, supervisors need a formula or procedure to follow. The following procedure is suggested if you have a difficult employee problem to face:

1. Invite the person into your office or other designated place without advance notice, eliminating time to build fears and create a threatening climate.

2. Start the conversation quickly, and do not beat around the bush. Try saying something like this: "We have something important to talk about; we will both benefit if we get at it."

3. State facts only. Do not make accusations. Try to keep a calm, pleasant, subdued voice. Encourage the employee to talk. Do not rush.

As you develop your own formula, one that fits your personality, you will find that it is not difficult to launch even a potentially unpleasant session.

The Right Technique

The two basic types of private communication are *directive* and *nondirective*. Using the directive technique, the supervisor does most of the talking and draws a rather firm line on the direction the interview will take. Although the supervisor should use this approach in a gentle and quiet manner (constructive private communication ends when an argument begins), the employee should sense that advice or direction is being given. Communication in these sessions is mostly from the supervisor to the employee. This technique is usually considered best for the following situations:

1. When a violation of company rules or policies has occurred.

2. When mistakes need to be corrected.

3. When employee hostility (toward you, others, or the company) has reached a stage where it can no longer be tolerated.

Nondirective private communication is almost the opposite. The supervisor does less talking and encourages the employee to communicate more. It is a soft approach designed to bring hidden problems out into the open or to set a climate for free and constructive discussion on any matter important to the employee. The permissive, unstructured, or open type of counseling is often therapeutic and provides motivation for the employee. It is the only technique to use for positive communication when no problem exists; it is considered the best approach for the following situations:

1. When an employee appears to have lost her or his touch or positive attitude over a sustained period of time, resulting in lower productivity.

2. When you want to strengthen or restore a relationship.

3. When you feel you can motivate an employee to achieve greater productivity.

THE ART OF COMMUNICATING

Bert Decker, in his book *The Art of Communicating*, lists nine behavioral skills that constitute the key elements of better interpersonal communication.[1] As you read through the list, notice how much more than voice is needed in effective communications.

- Eye communication
- Posture and movement
- Gestures and facial expressions
- Dress and appearance
- Voice and vocal variety
- Language, pauses, and nonwords
- Listener involvement
- Using humor
- The natural self

MRT DISCUSSIONS AND THE NONDIRECTIVE TECHNIQUE

The mutual reward theory (chapter 5) functions well when the rewards are sufficient and well balanced between supervisor and employee because both parties come out ahead. The employee gains rewards from the supervisor, and the supervisor receives high productivity and subsequent recognition from superiors. When such rewards are insufficient or out of balance, or the wrong rewards have been provided, MRT counseling may be the answer. When a supervisor takes time to sit down with an employee and work out a sound, reasonable reward exchange,

---

[1]*The Art of Communicating: Achieving Interpersonal Impact in Business.* Crisp Publications, Inc., 1200 Hamilton Court, Menlo Park, CA 94025.

improved motivation is almost predictable. This kind of resolution can happen best under the nondirective approach because the employee is more apt to state openly those rewards that are desired. The two cases that follow illustrate the technique and the approach.

Jerry had watched Mildred's productivity deteriorate for three months. In addition, her co-workers were now complaining that she was not carrying her part of the workload. Jerry called Mildred into his private office and in a quiet, nondirective manner said, "Mildred, there are certain rewards I can give you as an employee. There are also rewards you can give to me as your supervisor. Would you be willing to discuss them?" During the next forty minutes they developed a practical reward exchange and outlined it on paper. Jerry was careful to agree to only those rewards that he could actually provide. He made certain that the rewards he requested from Mildred were reasonable. This arrangement turned out to be mutually rewarding. It was clear the following day that Mildred would quickly regain the motivation she had shown when she was first employed. By using MRT counseling, Jerry had rebuilt a relationship that improved productivity in his department.

Martin, a management trainee for a hotel chain, had been assigned to Sandra's department for thirty days as part of an extended training period. After he had been in the department two days, Sandra gave him a special assignment that involved some research and a written report. Although it was turned in on time, the report did not live up to Sandra's expectations or reflect Martin's high potential. Sandra decided to use the soft, laid-back approach of MRT counseling. After some small talk about a humorous incident that had occurred earlier in the day, Sandra said: "Martin, I realize you will be with me only for six more weeks, and I appreciate having you. I am a little concerned about your quality of work on the project you just completed. I want you to learn everything possible while you are here. Would you permit me to propose an arrangement whereby we both can benefit from your being in this department? For example, if you will write down three job-connected rewards you would like to receive from me this week, I will write down three rewards I would like to receive from you. We can then openly discuss them. Is it a deal?"

Twenty minutes later they had carved out a reward exchange that was easy for Sandra to implement.

MRT conferences offer an unusual opportunity to the leader who is willing to sit down and forge a simple reward-exchange system with an employee. It could be the most motivating technique in your survival kit.

For most situations, it is more effective to use the nondirective approach more than the directive one. If you find you are not using the nondirective approach more often, you may be using counseling primarily to put out fires, instead of considering it as a way to strengthen relationships, increase productivity, and prevent problems from developing. Generally speaking, the more you use the nondirective technique, the less you will need the directive one.

Of course, the way you use either approach determines its effectiveness. Here are some techniques that will help in both situations:

1. A quiet voice is more effective and less threatening than a loud voice.

2. A good way to dissipate the employee's hostility is to let him or her talk it out first. Do not interrupt.

3. When the employee is talking (perhaps defending some action), listen instead of planning your rebuttal.

4. Periods of silence in an interview can help the employee do some important self-evaluation, so do not rush to break in on him or her.

5. Free and honest communication is restricted when a time limit is imposed or implied.

6. Because most abuse coming from employees is directed to the system, the organization, or themselves, do not take negative comments personally.

7. The resolution of a problem is not the only sign of a successful counseling period. The mere act of achieving two-way communication is worthwhile.

8. Attempt to end all sessions on a positive note and, if necessary, schedule a follow-up meeting.

LINK ALL PRIVATE COMMUNICATION TO INDIVIDUAL GOALS

For maximum effectiveness, all counseling sessions should be tied to the employee's goals. The supervisor may be required to help the employee reestablish previous goals or establish new ones.

> Maggie, a registered nurse who supervised the maternity ward on the night shift, was having trouble with Marty, a vocational nurse in charge of cleanup procedures. Marty wanted to take over the RN's responsibilities instead of performing her own tasks. When Maggie discovered, through counseling, that Marty was taking college courses leading to RN certification, she modified her approach. She agreed to give Marty extra duties that would help in her advanced training, provided that she took care of her other, more mundane responsibilities first. This concession immediately improved the relationship.

Surveys made in large organizations show undisputed evidence that the further up the management ladder a person travels, the more time she or he must spend counseling others. Some company presidents spend up to 80 percent of their time in private communication with their executives. Without question, private communication is a tool the ambitious supervisor or team leader cannot ignore.

DISCUSSION QUESTIONS

1. What additional reasons might explain why supervisors are reluctant to initiate private communication sessions with their employees? What would you suggest to a supervisor who has this problem?

2. Some management and personnel people claim that young supervisors today find it more difficult to do counseling, especially for discipline or termination, than their older counterparts. Do you agree or disagree? Why?

3. Does frequent stand-up or informal communication between a supervisor and an employee eliminate the need for private communication? Build your case one way or the other.

Case Study

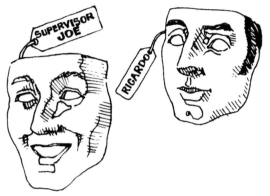

Technique[2]

Supervisor Joe is upset over the night watchman's written report (sent through Mr. Big's office) accusing Ricardo of goofing off on the job and of (on one occasion) having a woman friend at work with him. The situation is aggravated by the fact that Supervisor Joe recently defended Ricardo in front of Mr. Big, who had used him as an example when accusing Joe of being too soft with his employees. In checking further, Joe also discovers that the stockroom (one of Ricardo's responsibilities) is in poor condition. Joe concludes that Ricardo is taking advantage of him. He decides to have a serious talk with Ricardo this afternoon when he reports to work after his class at college. Joe is aware that Ricardo is highly sensitive, unpredictable, and sometimes explosive. He also recognizes that Ricardo has been a productive employee in the past and has high potential. His problem is deciding between the two counseling techniques.

Technique 1: Directive private communication. Under this firm approach, Joe would force an unpleasant confrontation by laying all the cards on the table in a stiff warning designed to shake up Ricardo. It would leave no possibility of misinterpretation. Ricardo would know exactly where he stands, and the session would amount to a first warning that could lead to termination if Ricardo's behavior does not change.

Technique 2: Nondirective private communication. Under this softer approach, Joe would try to avoid an unpleasant confrontation by talking things over easily and quietly, so that in the end Ricardo would discipline himself. Joe would try to listen more than talk; he would be sensitive to Ricardo's explanation. In this manner, Joe would gain better results in the end and avoid harsh words that would be mutually disturbing.

Which technique would you use? Why? If you select an alternative approach or a combination of the two, defend your position.

---

[2]Turn to page 265 to compare your thoughts with those of the author.

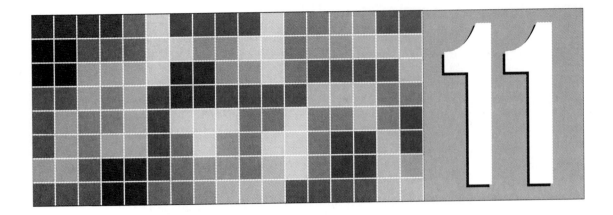

The Problem Employee

After you have finished reading this chapter, you should be able to use your skills to deal confidently with problem employees.

A problem employee is one who repeatedly violates a departmental discipline line, frequently causes disturbances among other personnel, or lowers productivity through some form of unacceptable behavior. Sooner or later, every supervisor must deal with such an employee. Problem employees can quickly destroy the effectiveness of a team. Managers and team leaders do not have the luxury of letting time take care of such individuals and cannot sweep the problem under the carpet.

Private communication is the answer, and the techniques covered in the previous chapter will come to your rescue. A skillful supervisor is often able to turn a problem employee into a superior employee by discovering the cause of the problem and coming up with the right answer. Sometimes, however, the best a supervisor can do is alleviate the problem so that everyone can live with it and productivity is not damaged. In some cases the only acceptable solution is to take corrective measures, which may end with the dismissal of the employee. Every case deserves individual analysis and treatment.

Diane, a single parent, was demonstrating an increasing amount of hostility toward her fellow employees—so much so that departmental productivity was measurably down. After two counseling sessions, the problem was narrowed down to an imbalance between home and career. Diane was unable to separate the two and, as a result, she was adding home problems to job demands. This behavior irritated co-workers, created customer complaints, and put unreasonable demands on her supervisor. Once the situation was isolated and discussed,

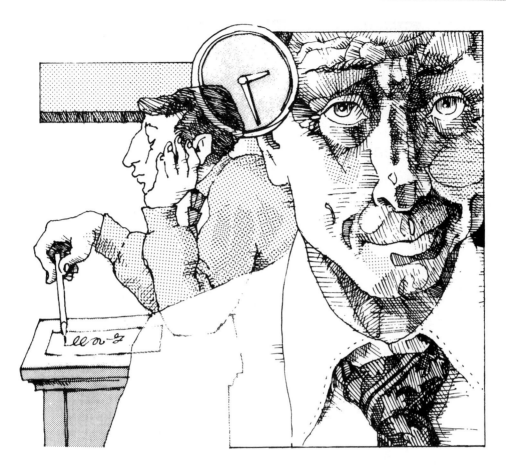

Diane was able to discipline herself to achieve a better home-career balance. She was no longer a problem employee.

Chris was a classic example of how the frustration-aggression hypothesis can create a problem employee. A recent graduate from an MBA program, Chris had set excessively high career goals for himself. As a result, he became frustrated over his slow progress; this frustration, in turn, resulted in aggressive behavior. For example, Chris would lose his patience in working with others and walk away in a huff. During staff meetings he would seek controversy and spill out his feelings. After two counseling sessions, Chris recognized his own problem and found employment in a new environment where his talents and education could be put to more immediate use.

A PROFESSIONAL PERSPECTIVE

What are some of the fundamental concepts involved? What are the mandated corrective steps? And, most important, how can you prepare now to handle such individuals?

First, you should keep the following five fundamentals in mind, so that you view the individual—and the problems he or she is creating—in professional perspective.

Expect Good Results

Have faith in your ability to resolve the problem and build a better relationship with the individual. You must initiate communication with the problem employee if the problem itself is to be dealt with openly and a solution reached. If you fear the process, you are already at a disadvantage.

Everyone Can Come Out Ahead

Accept the premise that you can find one solution that is best for the individual, you, and the firm. The only way you can achieve this elegant solution is through open, two-way communication. Your goal is to save the employee, keep him or her in your department, and convert the individual into a productive, nondisturbing member of your team. The more you anticipate good results, the more they are apt to occur.

The Nondirective Approach May Be Best

Recognize that heavy discipline at the beginning often intensifies an existing problem. Both you and the employee may have a tendency to be defensive. If you create a threatening climate, the employee may become emotional. The problem employee becomes more of a problem and a solution becomes impossible. Another reason a heavy hand at the beginning can backfire is that heavy discipline can, perhaps through misinterpretation, cause other employees to feel uncomfortable.

Waiting Is Usually a Mistake

The longer one waits to correct unacceptable behavior, the more explosive the interview may become. Most supervisors who delay taking action permit the behavior of the problem employee to get under their skin, where it festers until the supervisor can no longer deal with it objectively. The sooner you deal with a problem, the less emotional you will be.

> Jason tolerated Rosemary's disruptive behavior for six weeks without saying a word. Each time she violated his discipline line, his dislike for her increased; each time she was insensitive to customers and co-workers, he became more frustrated. Finally, one morning he reached his tolerance level, invited her into his office, and exploded. The moment the interview was over, Jason knew he had made several mistakes. His relationship with Rosemary worsened, and he could not see any chance in the future to restore it. He had a guilty feeling about his behavior, and he knew it had hurt his relationships with her co-workers. He was ineffective for the rest of the day. As a result, Jason resolved to deal with such problems in the future as soon as they surfaced.

Protect Yourself

Accept the fact that a single problem employee can cause your downfall as a supervisor. The following case illustrates this fundamental.

Some co-workers did not think that Marge was ready for her promotion to operations officer of her busy savings and loan establishment. But management thought differently, and their confidence in her seemed justified, at least during the first months. A serious cloud appeared when Susan, a teller, became a problem. It started when Susan violated the acceptable dress code; it intensified when she became sullen with some customers; it became intolerable when it affected the productivity of others. Although Marge had no experience in handling such a situation, she knew she had only three alternatives. She could delay action, she could go to her boss, or she could initiate a one-on-one talk today. She decided on the last and immediately called Susan into her office.

Marge was careful not to create a threatening climate. She did not overplay her hand, but she quickly led into the problem and made it clear that she was in charge and was going to stand her ground. Although she experienced some difficult moments, eventually some healthy two-way communications took place. Susan decided that the work environment in a savings and loan institution was not for her, and one week later she resigned. Susan departed without hostility, and Marge had solved her problem. From that moment on, all of her employees seemed to respect her more, and productivity increased. Best of all, management was most complimentary. Her immediate supervisor said, "We were monitoring the situation carefully and sensed that your future depended upon how you handled Susan. We are extremely pleased."

OBJECTIVITY REQUIRED

Even if you accept these fundamentals and practice them, solving employee problems will not be easy. Many, however, are less difficult than they appear. One reason is that an employee may become a problem in your eyes but not in the opinion of others. The employee is irritating you but not co-workers or other management personnel.

Roger had a solid reputation as a superior manager, but he became irritated with Tony, a management trainee, the first day Tony was assigned to his department. Roger thought Tony was too aggressive. He immediately disciplined Tony in unfair, unprofessional ways—not his usual attitude. Then, by chance, he overheard two of his regular employees defending Tony. Roger took stock of himself, admitted he had been unfair, and made a complete turnabout. As a result, he built an excellent relationship with Tony. What he had interpreted as aggressiveness was assertiveness that others appreciated.

Your discipline, or authority line, is essential for employees not only to respect you but also to keep their productivity at a high level. Discipline must be maintained at all costs. But the supervisor must be careful to treat all employees fairly and consistently. Maintaining productivity leaves no room for personal vendettas between a supervisor and an employee.

The supervisor must protect his or her discipline line in quiet, effective ways or eventually lose the respect of those who must live with it. To permit one employee to cross the line is to lose the respect of those who still honor it. When the supervisor loses authority, productivity can drop drastically.

Joel had been able to maintain a relaxed, comfortable discipline line for almost six months. Not a single employee was taking advantage of him. Then

Victoria, who was having personal problems, started testing the line from all directions. She not only challenged traditional procedures she had previously honored, but she started to make complaints to Joel's boss. The conflict came to a head when she challenged Joel openly on a procedural matter in a staff meeting.

Joel initiated a long interview the following day to discuss her recent behavior in relationship to departmental productivity. The atmosphere was tense until, near the end of the interview, the conversation turned to Victoria's career goal, and Joel stated that he would like to help her reach it. Eventually a kind of trade-off took place: Victoria promised to be more sensitive to Joel and to departmental objectives, and Joel agreed to do what he could to prepare her for her career goal without favoring her over others. The compatibility contract lasted until Victoria earned a promotion, six months later.

EXPLORATORY INTERVIEWS

The purpose of the exploratory interview is to lay the problem on the table in a nonthreatening manner. Both parties should have an equal chance to communicate; both old and new facts should be introduced; if possible, the roots of the problem should be revealed. *Sometimes the exploratory interview can do it all.*

Sally took Jennifer out to lunch to discover, if possible, what was causing her hostility. She found a private place, made certain that the environment was relaxed, and then introduced the subject. The discussion that followed showed that Jennifer thought Sally had been unfair to her and that her resentment had created a barrier between them. As a result, she had violated the departmental discipline line to show her independence. When Sally convinced Jennifer that the unfair treatment had not been intended, they both agreed to start from scratch. The exploratory interview had solved the problem. No further action was necessary.

Construction superintendent Rich had received two reports that Betty, the woman who did cleanup work in the completed buildings, had violated safety regulations. He called her into his mobile office and quickly introduced the subject. It turned out that Betty was uninformed about the safety regulations and had not been aware that she was breaking them. When he received no further complaints, Rich figured the exploratory interview had corrected the problem.

If an employee's behavior is not appropriate, the reason may be caused by inadequate training. Be sure to check to see whether the employee knows how to perform correctly before taking disciplinary action.

CORRECTIVE INTERVIEWS

When the exploratory interview tells the supervisor that the problem is deep, a follow-up is indicated. Such a follow-up can take one of two forms. In cases that show evidence that firm rules have been broken, the supervisor initiates a series of corrective interviews. In cases where the human relations problems are complex, one or more noncorrective follow-up discussions may be necessary to resolve the problem. The decision to conduct follow-up interviews can be made during the exploratory interview or later. The supervisor can discuss it with the employee in advance or use the wait-and-see approach. Each case requires individual analysis. Sometimes the exploratory interview is interpreted by the problem employee as a warning; sometimes it is not.

Assume that during an exploratory interview you suspect that a problem employee is violating a rule, but you have no evidence. Later, however, you discover the evidence. At that point you set up corrective interview 1.

Corrective interview 1. The purpose of this first follow-up step is to verify the violation and warn the employee. Verification means *critical documentation.* Although required documentation varies among organizations, basically it should include (1) a specific description of the violation; (2) the name of the violator, the date it occurred, and the date of the corrective interview; and (3) the written acknowledgment or rebuttal of the employee. A corrective interview 1 is, in effect, a documented first warning.

Corrective interview 2. This interview need not take place unless a further violation is reported. If a second incident (even a different violation) is reported, the second interview should take place with the same documentation procedure. This meeting becomes a second warning.

Corrective interview 3. This interview is necessary only if a third violation occurs. The procedure will vary according to each organization (and legal counsel) but generally will include (1) a third person (upper management person, representative from the human resource department, or staff lawyer); (2) a review and presentation of previous documented warnings; and (3) notice of termination. Whatever the procedure, the supervisor should permit two-way communication and attempt to show the employee that he or she has been treated fairly. The rights of the employee must be protected at all costs.

When this procedure is followed carefully, most employees will improve their performance or submit their resignation voluntarily before corrective interview 3 takes place.

FACING DISAGREEMENT OR CONFLICT

As a supervisor, you may run into a conflict with an employee, a peer, or your own boss. Four steps will help guide you through such an experience so that the best solution is found and both you and the other party maintain a healthy relationship.

Step 1: *Don't put the other person down.* It is important to preserve the integrity and self-respect of all parties. In a heated discussion, it is easy to say something demeaning. To avoid this trap, keep your focus on the issue, not the person.

Step 2: *Search for common ground.* Try to see things from the other person's perspective so that you can discover a basis to resolve the matter. In order to better understand the other person's position, you must listen with empathy and be flexible.

Step 3: *Do not expect behavioral changes.* The purpose of resolving conflicts is to find agreement on what must be done, not whether a behavioral change is required of you or the other party.

Step 4: *Compromise is not throwing in the towel.* The goal is to find the best solution to improve productivity (reach agreed-upon goals), not to discover who might be right or wrong. Thus a compromise—especially after an open discussion—can be the best solution for both parties and the company.

Agreeing to a compromise does not mean you have given up your individuality. It simply means you understand the situation.

NONCORRECTIVE INTERVIEWS

Assume that during an exploratory interview you discover a deep-seated human relations problem. Perhaps a personality conflict between two co-workers is damaging productivity. Maybe one employee's attitude is so negative that it is hurting the productivity of others or causing customer complaints. Possibly a conflict has arisen between you and the problem employee. Situations of this nature call for one or two follow-up interviews.

Noncorrective follow-up 1. A single exploratory interview will not solve most human relations problems. It takes time to dissipate misunderstandings and misinterpretations. When an exploratory interview reveals hostility between the supervisor and an employee, for example, the conflict may never be solved. But holding one or two follow-up interviews is more effective than trying once and giving up.

Jane was disturbed to discover that Carol was upset and hostile toward her. About all she was able to accomplish during the exploratory interview was to listen and let Carol get her inner anxieties and frustrations out in the open. Three

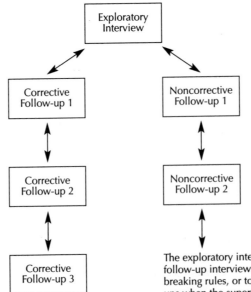

The exploratory interview leads to corrective follow-up interviews when an employee is breaking rules, or to noncorrective follow-ups when the supervisor hopes to resolve interpersonal conflicts.

days later Jane conducted a follow-up interview that was less volatile, with more of a two-way discussion. At this stage both individuals admitted to some mistakes and misinterpretations. The relationship was beginning to be rebuilt. Later Jane initiated a third interview in which mutual rewards were discussed. Eventually the relationship was fully restored, and all hostility dissipated.

Noncorrective follow-up 2. As just illustrated, more than one follow-up interview is often necessary to solve a human relations problem. The process of restoration is not easy or fast. In most cases, some give-and-take is necessary to build a new foundation for mutual respect. Normally some behavioral changes must take place on both sides in the interim between interviews. The supervisor should not expect to be able to solve all human problems, but in most cases the combination of good exploratory techniques and one or more follow-up interviews is an excellent way to ensure harmony and high productivity in a department.

SOLVING PROBLEMS: AN ONGOING PROCESS

Give the interview process a chance to work. Inexperienced supervisors sometimes become discouraged if they do not see immediate results. Resolving conflicts, helping others change their attitudes, and dissipating hostility take time. Remind yourself that although the process does not always work, it works often enough to be worth your effort. Even if you fail, you will have had the satisfaction of trying.

When Your Image Is Being Tested

Your image as a supervisor is important. A problem employee can cause a great deal of conversation both inside and outside your department. If you wind up with such an employee, you can rest assured that others will be watching how you respond. The nonproblem employees on your staff will be watching even more closely than management. Studies show that most co-workers have a lower tolerance of problem employees than supervisors expect. Your employees want you to solve the problem to make life easier for them. Obviously, the supervisor who has enough leadership ability to solve the problem will enhance her or his image in all directions.

When the Employee Is Unable to Reach Standards

You may have to learn to live with certain low-level employees. You may discover one or more employees in your department who do not, and never will, live up to your expectations. These individuals do not influence the productivity of others or cross your discipline line, but they contribute less than other workers. For example, you may have a mature employee who has seniority but cannot adjust quickly to dramatic changes, or an employee who refuses to communicate but produces better than average work. Such employees can make your job as a supervisor more difficult, but they are not troublemakers.

Sometimes counseling will strengthen these employees; sometimes it won't. When you have done your best to change their behavior, you must continue to be positive with these employees without letting them pull you down or hurt your leadership ability.

When Chemical Dependency Is Involved

To maintain and increase productivity, supervisors need to be alert to the possibility of chemical dependency (including alcohol abuse) among employees. Tolerating abuse/addiction is not in the best interest of the employee, the supervisor, or the organization. So how do you handle suspected dependency problems?

First, know your organization's policy and conform to it. Second, learn enough about dependency to recognize when a problem might exist. Third, always consult your superior before you begin any form of intervention. Fourth, have a third person present should a discussion with the employee take place.

As a supervisor, you are the key person in terms of monitoring job performance. It is up to you to provide documentation of failure to reach standards. Should such documentation show a possible dependency problem, it is time to consult a superior and bring in a professional. Procrastination is not the answer.

It might help you to view a dependency case as getting around the bases in a ballgame. You reach first base when you recognize that a problem exists, document your observations, and schedule a discussion with the employee. You arrive at second base when you create an open atmosphere for the discussion of reasons for nonperformance and let it be known that you will support bona fide efforts to correct it.

You get to third base when the employee recognizes the jeopardy his or her job is in, takes responsibility for the problem, and commits to improving performance. You reach home plate (and score) when the employee seeks professional help from either internal or external sources and undertakes treatment.

Keep in mind that you are probably more important to your organization than the problem employee in question, so do not let the individual destroy you. It means you must deal with the employee in legal ways so that both you and the organization are protected. If you need backup assistance, do not hesitate to ask for advice and support from your supervisors. As a beginning supervisor, you are not supposed to know all the answers, so do not let personal pride keep you from seeking support. In dealing with problem employees, it can be a serious mistake to act prematurely on your own.

When Sexual Harassment Occurs

Sexual harassment is behavior of a sexual nature that causes a person to be uncomfortable. In most cases, sexual harassment is more than a single incident. Rather, it is a deliberate pattern of behavior pursued over a period of time.

Sexual harassment violates the law and inhibits work performance. Victims can be male or female, a manager or subordinate, a vendor or customer. It is the responsibility of the supervisor or team leader to create and maintain a working environment where no form of harassment from any source is permitted. The following steps are recommended:

1. The topic of harassment should be discussed openly in a staff meeting, and the supervisor should state the legal parameters and encourage complaints from any individual.

TYPICAL FORMS OF SEXUAL HARASSMENT		
Verbal	**Visual**	**Physical**
Telling risque jokes	Wearing suggestive attire	Touching, making physical contact
Asking for sexual favors	Staring at someone's anatomy	Standing too close
Commenting on one's sexual anatomy .	Flirting nonverbally	A too lengthy handshake
Pursuing an unwanted relationship	Not wearing undergarments	Hugging or kissing
Paying unwanted compliments with sexual overtones	Sitting in a revealing position	

2. Upon receiving a complaint, the supervisor should listen and record the specific conditions under which the alleged harassment took place.

3. The supervisor should then take up the matter with the director of human resources or another superior for verification and possible action.

4. In counseling an individual who may be guilty of sexual harassment, the supervisor is advised to have a third-party specialist present.

5. The individual who initiated the complaint should be advised on the action taken and encouraged to return should any further harassment occur.

When a Reduction in Staff Is Mandated

Sometimes a nonproblem employee must be released because of a cutback in personnel. In such cases, the supervisor must work closely with the department of human resources to make certain that no age or other type of discrimination is involved. Releasing a good employee may be the most difficult action a supervisor must take. Everything possible should be done to assist the individual in finding another position of equal or higher status.

This chapter has been designed to give you the confidence, techniques, and procedures that will help you either prevent employee problems or handle them gracefully and legally when they emerge. If you can handle problem employees effectively without turning to your superiors for help, you will not become their problem employee.

DISCUSSION QUESTIONS

1. In what specific ways might a new supervisor build sufficient personal confidence to deal with a problem employee on a one-on-one basis?

2. Assuming that the supervisor is a skillful communicator, would you give counseling a 50–50 chance to convert a problem employee into a superior one? Defend your answer.

3. If a problem employee resigns voluntarily between corrective private communication sessions 1 and 2, has the attempt failed? Explain your views.

Mini-Game

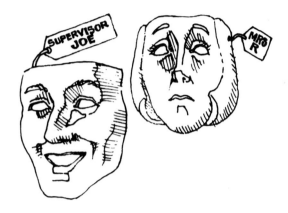

Confrontation

Objective

To evaluate the nature of conflicts between traditional supervisors and assertive employees.

Problem

The relationship between Supervisor Joe and Mrs. R has deteriorated. Mrs. R is hostile, taking pot shots at Joe in conversations with co-workers, openly confronting him in staff meetings, and generally being disruptive. The situation is hurting the productivity of the department and rendering Joe ineffective. Readers not involved in role playing should study and evaluate the conflict between Supervisor Joe and Mrs. R on page 272.

Players

Supervisor Joe and Mrs. R.

Procedure

The players rehearse their own roles over and over, until they are deeply into the characterization. Neither party is to communicate with the other. Mrs. R is to enter Joe's office determined to come out ahead; Joe is equally determined to resolve the problem to his satisfaction. After a ten-minute confrontation—no holds barred—both individuals are to relax and switch roles, each playing the other.

Postgame Discussion

Discuss the nature of such conflicts and the possibility of dissipating them through the interview process. What might Joe have done to eliminate the problem in the first place? Is Mrs. R justified in her assertiveness?

Role of Supervisor Joe

You are disturbed by Mrs. R's hostility. You recognize that she is extremely capable and a high producer. You recognize that she may become a supervisor eventually, but first you feel she should "pay her dues," as you did. She is criticizing you before your superiors and showing disrespect for you and your position among co-workers. You recall a constructive talk with her sixty days ago when you stated that you would give her the training she needs to become a supervisor, which you feel you have done. You do not feel her impatience is justified. In the next few minutes you intend to listen carefully and keep an open mind, but under no circumstances will you bend your discipline line. You would be happy if Mrs. R moved to another firm.

Role of Mrs. R

You feel your assertiveness is justified because Joe has you boxed in. He refuses to recommend you for a higher position outside his department. He does not appreciate your high productivity and generally fails to understand you. You recall a meeting sixty days ago when he promised to help you win a promotion to supervisor in another department. He has not fulfilled this promise. He seems to feel you should "pay a price" to him before he will go to bat for you. You have no intention of being subservient. Because you have an outstanding record within the department, you feel that any pressure you put on Joe is justified. As you enter his office, you intend to listen and keep an open mind, but if Joe doesn't handle things to your satisfaction, you intend to resign on the spot.

Staffing

After you have finished reading this chapter, you should be able to incorporate the suggestions into your management style, resulting in fewer personnel mistakes and thus creating a more cohesive and productive team or department.

As a new supervisor, Virginia set out to hire a qualified replacement for an employee who had left. Without any background in interviewing, Virginia selected an individual with a persuasive personality but also with psychological problems. Further investigation would have revealed that the applicant had been a problem employee in all of her previous jobs. Virginia lived with the situation for six months. Finally, after the human conflicts created had rendered her so ineffective that Virginia's own job was on the line, the individual resigned on a voluntary basis. Inexperience had caused Virginia to hire a problem rather than solve one.

As a manager, you may or may not become deeply involved in the staffing process. Some managers have complete control over who is hired or transferred to their departments; others are assigned new employees from the human resource department, with or without refusal power. The more your role as a manager involves you in the staffing process, the more important this chapter will be to you.

EMPLOYEE TURNOVER

In some respects, the lower the personnel turnover in a department, the better. Employee stability and high productivity often go together. But frequent personnel turnover is a fact of life. No matter how effective you become as a

supervisor, now and then a key employee will shock you with a resignation. A promotion or lateral move that is good for the firm can create a problem for the supervisor.

Mary was pleased that management had selected Carla to supervise a newly created department. It was a high compliment to Mary, who had trained Carla as her assistant. But the decision would mean screening, employing, and training a replacement. Other factors were involved. Which of her current staff could best fill Carla's shoes? Would now be a good time to reorganize the entire department? How could she turn the vacancy into an advantage?

Personnel changes present major challenges to all supervisors—challenges that must be approached with sound planning and vision.

THE STAFFING PROCESS

The workforce is changing. The number of working single parents has increased and will continue to grow. People are living longer; therefore, employees are concerned with elder care. New fathers, as well as mothers, see the value of bonding with new babies and want time off for this purpose.

Staffing includes much more than simply filling a vacancy. It also involves determining long-term personnel needs, orientation and training, transfers and reassignment, rotation, performance evaluation, and terminations. The moment a vacancy or personnel change becomes a reality, experienced supervisors ask themselves these questions:

- Is the function performed by the employee who is leaving absolutely necessary?

- Could the tasks be divided among other employees?

- What skills are missing among the staff?

- What kind of new person will contribute to greater productivity?

- Is someone being trained to eventually take my job as supervisor?

The goal of every supervisor should be to hire, develop, and maintain the most cohesive and productive staff possible. It is not a goal easily reached.

Preparation for the Interview

It is impossible to hire the best available applicant for a given job unless the skills and duties required are known ahead of time. If a printed job description is available, it should be carefully reviewed and brought up to date. If not, the competencies required should be written out by the supervisor. Only with such data at hand can the best match between applicants and job be achieved. Here are four additional tips:

Tip 1: Federal and state civil rights laws must be upheld in hiring decisions. Sex, race, and age have nothing to do with how an individual will perform and cannot play a part in the selection process. You must seek and hire the best-qualified person for the job. Disabled people should be considered equally by focusing on what they can do and how they can contribute to productivity.

Tip 2: The practice of first come, first hired should be avoided. You can not find the best applicant without taking the time to discover what the market has to offer.

Tip 3: Screening written applications and interviewing should be done studiously. The more one rushes the process, the more subjective one becomes and the more mistakes are made.

Tip 4: As an interview approaches, review the competencies you seek in an applicant (a competency is a skill that can be observed or measured); have a list of questions you intend to ask that will tell you about the applicant's prior related experiences; know what information you need to provide each applicant regarding the organization and the job—both advantages and disadvantages; and have a pad available for taking notes.

INTERVIEWER'S SELF-ASSESSMENT EXERCISE

This exercise is designed to help you prepare for an interview with a prospective employee for your department. Circle the number that best reflects where you currently fall on the scale. The higher the number, the better. In those areas where you rate yourself a 3, 2, or 1, strive for measurable improvement over your past techniques.

1. I analyze job requirements before beginning the selection process.	5	4	3	2	1
2. I study the qualifications of applicants in light of the job requirements.	5	4	3	2	1
3. I begin each interview by establishing a relaxed climate conducive to good communication and use open-ended questions to draw out essential information.	5	4	3	2	1
4. I avoid preconception, personal bias, and prejudice.	5	4	3	2	1
5. I adhere to equal employment opportunity guidelines.	5	4	3	2	1
6. I record key points.	5	4	3	2	1
7. I provide information about the job and the organization and answer the applicant's	5	4	3	2	1
questions.	5	4	3	2	1
8. I make selection decisions on the basis of job requirements.	5	4	3	2	1
9. I document my selection decisions.	5	4	3	2	1
10. I let all candidates know the outcome of their interview at the appropriate time.	5	4	3	2	1

Total _____

A score between 40 and 50 suggests that you probably conduct successful interviews. A score between 30 and 40 indicates some significant strengths, as well as some improvement needs. A score below 30 calls for a serious effort to improve in a number of areas. Make a special effort to improve in any area where you scored 3 or less, regardless of your total score.

Interviewing Techniques

Interviewing a prospective new employee is a form of counseling, and the five Rs outlined in Chapter 10 (pp. 101–106) apply. Generally speaking, it is a good idea to follow these additional steps:

Step 1: Put the applicant at ease so that you can get the most realistic view of how the applicant would perform on the job to be filled.

Step 2: Encourage the applicant to talk through appropriate questions so that you will learn about her or his potential ability to contribute to your department.

Step 3: Provide the applicant with an opportunity to ask questions.

Step 4: Verify the data on the application form, especially those pertaining to training and skills.

Interview Questions

Listed here are some typical questions that interviewers often ask job seekers. Their purpose is to generate a dialogue so that a decision can be based on as much information as possible.

- Why do you want to work here?
- What are your skill levels?
- What can you contribute?
- Why should we hire you?
- Why did you leave your last job?
- Do you have any weaknesses?
- Tell me about yourself.
- Tell me about a time when you had to:
    - solve a problem quickly
    - make a decision
    - deliver bad news
    - make an unexpected change
    - meet a deadline
    - organize an event

Care should be taken to ask the same questions of all applicants so that each individual is given the same opportunity to communicate and, from your point of view, more objective comparisons can be made. Questions of a highly personal nature or those that will embarrass or confuse the applicant should not be used. Do not ask questions that are discriminatory in nature. For example, questions about religious affiliations are not proper. For a complete list of questions you should not ask contact your local Equal Employment Opportunity Commission (EEOC) office and request information. The material they provide is free of charge and indispensable (see the EEOC Guidelines for Managers and Supervisors found at the end of this chapter).

Employment interviews are normally divided into two approaches. One is a guided pattern (directive); the other is less structured or unguided (nondirective). For an inexperienced interviewer, a guided pattern is often best. For example, a novice might consider using the following Job Qualification Checklist. The fictitious word CASSI is designed to help the supervisor remember to rate all five categories in each interview.

JOB QUALIFICATION CHECKLIST		
	Yes	No
C COOPERATIVENESS (Will the applicant make an effort to work well with the staff?)	___	___
A ATTITUDE (Does the applicant have a good work attitude? Does he or she really want to produce?)	___	___
S SKILLS (Does this person have all the specific skills to match the job opening?)	___	___
S STABILITY (Is the applicant seeking a permanent or interim job?)	___	___
I INTEREST (Has the applicant expressed high interest in the job?)	___	___

Although no system is perfect, any guided pattern has the advantage of providing at least some objectivity. Of course, the interviewer must ask the right questions so that the characteristics stated in the Checklist surface.

Ending the Interview

It is important to terminate the interview in a friendly manner, without making a false commitment. A suitable closing comment might be: "We will make a decision this Friday. If you do not hear from us by next Monday, we still appreciate your interest in our organization and we will keep your application on file."

Even under ideal circumstances, a final choice is difficult to make. It is usually advisable to talk to a superior—especially if two or more candidates appear to be equally qualified.

ORIENTATION AND TRAINING

All of the time and energy devoted to finding the best available candidate can go down the drain if the newcomer is not made a full member of the team. Chapter 14 provides suggestions in accomplishing this goal. The following suggestions can also be helpful:

- See that the new member is introduced personally to all members of the staff.

- Check out the use of any equipment the new employee will operate.

- Assign a regular employee as a sponsor to answer questions and help the new employee adjust.

- Make sure that basic department rules and company policies are understood.

- List and discuss specific responsibilities.

- Follow up at the end of the first day or shift to see whether the new employee has questions to be answered or whether any adjustments need to be made.

As mentioned in Chapter 10, studies have shown that poor orientation leads to higher turnover rates and worse, to industrial accidents. Some supervisors prefer a checklist to follow. A typical form is printed on the next page.

A supervisor should monitor the progress of a new employee until she or he has become a relaxed, full partner in the team and is making satisfactory progress toward maximum productivity. If additional training or counseling is required to reach this goal, it should be done quickly. With help, most new employees can make a complete adjustment within one week.

STAFF SHIFTING AND ROTATION

Moving staff members into different roles for both training and motivational purposes is an excellent practice and can measurably improve departmental productivity. Sometimes the employment of a new staff member precipitates such action. Even without personnel turnover, rotating employees from job to job is a good idea in many work environments. Employees who are allowed to stay in the same job too long often fall into a low productivity rut. When given a new challenge, their attitudes improve and they make a bigger contribution. Frequently a simple job exchange can help both employees because the more experience one obtains, the better prepared one becomes for future advancements—including that of supervision. In rotating or shifting employees, the following rules may apply:

Rule 1: Discuss proposed changes ahead of time with all parties involved.

Rule 2: Avoid forcing new assignments, especially if the individual is insecure about having the ability to perform in the proposed role.

Rule 3: If necessary, provide additional training.

Rule 4: Give all staff members a fair chance.

Rule 5: Avoid changes unless they are beneficial to both employees and the department as a whole.

Rule 6: Compliment those who make adjustments gracefully.

Advanced planning accompanied by personal counseling is the key to staff shifting and rotation. Spur-of-the-moment decisions can often do more harm than good.

SUPERVISOR'S ORIENTATION CHECKLIST

The new supervisor who has not been provided with more sophisticated materials by the firm may find this checklist helpful. It is divided into eight parts.

Tour of Workplace

- ❏ Office
- ❏ Cafeteria
- ❏ Parking
- ❏ Supply room
- ❏ _____
- ❏ _____
- ❏ _____

Completion of Paperwork

- ❏ W-4 form
- ❏ Insurance papers
- ❏ _____
- ❏ _____
- ❏ _____

Introductions to the Following People

- ❏ _____
- ❏ _____
- ❏ _____
- ❏ _____
- ❏ _____
- ❏ _____

Orientation Packet

- ❏ Operating manuals
- ❏ Profile of the firm
- ❏ Health plan
- ❏ Behavior standards
- ❏ _____

Copy of Job Description or the Giving of Task Assignments

- ❏ Discussion
- ❏ Answering questions
- ❏ Safety precautions
- ❏ Who to go to when help is needed

Follow-up Arrangements

- ❏ Next day or shift?
- ❏ Week later?
- ❏ Monthly review?
- ❏ _____
- ❏ _____

Special Attention

- ❏ Lunch?
- ❏ Coffee?
- ❏ End-of-day review?
- ❏ Compliments?

Delegating Orientation Responsibilities

- ❏ Can you delegate?
- ❏ Should you delegate?
- ❏ To whom?

_____

Transfers

When a supervisor senses that he or she has a problem employee, the first thing that often comes to mind is a transfer to another department within the same firm. In exceptional cases, such as an irreconcilable conflict between a supervisor and an employee, an in-house transfer may be feasible. Perhaps it will give the individual a new, fresh opportunity; perhaps she or he will be happier under a different management style. But to initiate a transfer as a ploy to get rid of a problem employee who you know will give the next supervisor a similar problem is not professional. If the request comes from a nonproblem employee, it is another matter. It is possible, for example, that some time in the future an employee of yours will ask for a transfer so that she or he will be free from your style of supervision. If it happens, do not take it personally. You cannot be expected to have the kind of style that will please everyone. In such cases, a transfer might be advantageous to all the parties involved.

Justifying a Larger Staff

You will hear certain supervisors complaining about departmental workloads.

- "There is no way to catch up around here."

- "The more we do, the more they pile it on."

- "Too much work—too few people."

Sometimes such complaints are justified. Often they are not. Only when all employees—and the supervisor—are working close to their productivity potentials and the workload continues to increase should a supervisor take an overload problem to his or her superior. In doing so, the following suggestions are made:

- Demonstrate your overload position with facts. Quote comparative labor cost figures with a similar operation.

- Compare today's heavier workload with that of past periods in an objective manner.

- If you cannot justify hiring a full-time employee, consider someone part-time.

Whenever a supervisor seeks to increase her or his staff, management will automatically pry into the operation with a sharp eye. Only when such scrutiny produces a well-run department is such a request given serious consideration.

THE PART-TIMER

Federal legislation defines a part-timer as an employee who works less than 1,000 hours per year (17 1/2 hours per week). Organizations generally view a part-timer as an individual who works twenty-nine hours per week or less. The average is about twenty.

Part-time jobs normally have these characteristics:

- Wages are typically lower.

- Only the basic or required benefits are provided.

- Some organizations use part-timers as a pool from which to select full-timers.

- Part-time jobs usually offer less job security.

- Part-timers give many types of organizations flexibility and lower labor costs.

THE CORE-RING APPROACH

To determine the best mix of full-time versus part-time workers, organizations are turning to the core-ring approach. As illustrated, core employees constitute the full-time, regular workforce. They are the heart of the organization and usually receive comprehensive benefits.

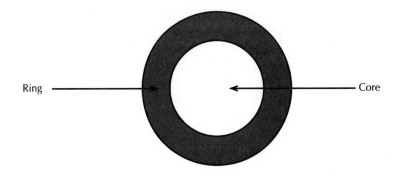

Part-timers, on the other hand, make up the outer ring of employees. Typically, they do not earn pensions, participate in profit-sharing plans, or receive paid vacations. Some sources estimate that more than 25 million part-timers participate in the labor force.

POPULARITY OF PART-TIMERS

Some experts claim that full-time, core employees are paid for eight hours of work but actually work closer to six or seven. This discrepancy is because it may take ten minutes or more for them to get ready to work, two fifteen-minute breaks are required, and often employees start getting ready to leave before the end of their work day. In contrast, part-timers employed for four hours may actually work at top performance for almost the entire period.

Part-time workers can be divided into three classifications: (1) full-time students who seek "peak period" jobs for approximately twenty hours per week to help with educational expenses, (2) housewives who seek part-time work so they can devote more time to children, and (3) retired people who wish to supplement their retirement incomes.

Many supervisors claim that part-timers are a welcome challenge when it comes to weaving them into the general mix of employees. They like the enthusiasm, energy, and flexibility they bring with them. Others claim that the high turnover rate of part-timers negates their advantages. All agree that it takes additional time and energy from the supervisor to convert part-timers into productive members of a work team.

THE ART OF SCHEDULING

Flex-scheduling, peak periods, and the need to customize "job hours" for people with special skills is an increasing challenge. Most supervisors, especially those who utilize part-timers, often prepare weekly printed schedules and post them on a bulletin board. Once printed and posted, the schedule becomes set. Changes are permitted only under exceptional circumstances.

Obviously, restaurants, fast-food operations, retail stores, and organizations that are open extended and irregular hours are presented with the greatest challenge.

> Frank operates his highly successful cafe with five full-timers and twenty part-timers. To simplify his scheduling, Frank posts a weekly schedule listing the hours to be worked by each employee. If a part-timer needs to be absent for a shift, it is the employee's responsibility to get a replacement from the total list of available part-timers provided, with telephone numbers, by Frank. Frank claims his system works 95 percent of the time and requires a minimum amount of supervision.

Like Frank, most organizations, using their computer capabilities, develop and execute work schedules and patterns to meet their own peculiar needs. Although some supervisors delegate this function, they recognize that the responsibility remains with them and that some flexibility is necessary to keep motivated employees.

SUPERVISOR'S RELATIONSHIP WITH THE HUMAN RESOURCE DEPARTMENT

Supervisors who work for large organizations that have professional human r esource departments (personnel and training) have a big advantage when it comes to staffing. Most of the work of recruiting, testing, interviewing, orientation, training, and terminating is done for them by professionals. In some cases, all the supervisor needs to do is accept or reject a possible staff member sent for consideration.

It is important, however, that the supervisor do everything possible to maintain good relationships with human resource experts. Fostering such a relationship includes the following activities:

1. Informing human resource and training specialists on the exact skills and competencies you need for maximum productivity.

2. Accepting the fact that human resource departments do their best to attract the most qualified applicants. (Employment people cannot change market conditions.)

3. Abiding by equal opportunity laws and other legal restrictions.

4. Paying compliments and offering feedback to those who get the right people properly trained to you.

5. Making sure the new hire is oriented into her or his particular work area. Remember orientation should be done by the supervisor and *not* delegated to anyone else.

All employment decisions including hiring must follow Equal Employment Opportunity (EEO) guidelines. EEO laws are enforced by the Equal Employment

EQUAL EMPLOYMENT OPPORTUNITY (EEO) GUIDELINES
FOR MANAGERS AND SUPERVISORS

You must protect the rights of your employees and your employer under current EEO legislation. The following guidelines suggest a positive way to do so.

1. EEO legislation is complex and is constantly being tested and interpreted in the courts. Be alert for changes. When in doubt about how to proceed, seek the advice of your legal or equal opportunity affairs representatives.

2. Create and maintain an atmosphere within your organization that demonstrates you are aware of equal opportunity policies and SUPPORT THEM.

3. Refuse to permit discriminatory acts of any type by anyone in your unit. Racial slurs, jokes, and sexual harassment are offensive and have no place on the job. Even seemingly small incidents can make people *uncomfortable* and lead to charges of discrimination and subsequent investigations.

4. Analyze the positions you supervise to insure the qualifications required of the people who fill them are based on bona fide job requirements.

5. Be sure nondiscriminatory practices are being followed in all recruitment and hiring activities involving you.

6. Look for possible inequities in pay, job assignments, special projects, training, and promotional practices in your jurisdiction and correct them.

7. Fully implement your company's affirmative action plans and, wherever possible, lend your expertise to their development.

8. Make an effort to support and assist qualified females, minorities, and handicapped persons to advance within your organization.

9. Document any disciplinary action you take. Also, carefully document your reasons for selection, termination, transfer, promotion, or other personnel action. Be sure your documentation is adequate to support the action. If there is any doubt, check with a higher authority.

10. Do not retain unsatisfactory performers for any reason. Make every reasonable effort to help them meet standards and document these efforts. Then, if they can't do the job, terminate them or move them to a position they can do adequately.

Source: Reproduced with permission from *Guide to Affirmative Action: A Primer for Supervisors and Managers,* by Pamela J. Conrad and Robert B. Maddux. Published by Crisp Publications Inc., 1200 Hamilton Court, Menlo Park, CA 94025.

Opportunity Commission (EEOC). The supervisor must become acquainted with how EEOC impacts the organization and the supervisor. Employment decisions that ignore or violate EEO guidelines may result in costly litigation fees. Your human resources department can help explain these guidelines to you. The following chart will help to familiarize you with some basic EEO guidelines.

DISCUSSION QUESTIONS

1. Are the advantages of job rotation within most departments worth the effort? If so, why do the majority of supervisors avoid the process?

2. If you were a supervisor for an organization that assigned new employees to your department without giving you the opportunity to interview or reject applicants, would you make an attempt to change the procedure? If so, how would you go about it?

3. In addition to reviewing the material in this chapter, what might a supervisor do to obtain additional information and insights into staffing problems and interviewing techniques?

Case Study

Staffing[1]

In a regular staff meeting, Mr. Big announced that the company has acquired a new account that will increase business. The new business will require the hiring of two new employees within the next six weeks. Mr. Big expects you to be involved in the staffing process. You will interview and select from a short list of applicants provided to you by human resources. How will you prepare for the interview? What criteria will you use to select the best applicants?

[1]Turn to page 265 to compare your thoughts with those of the author.

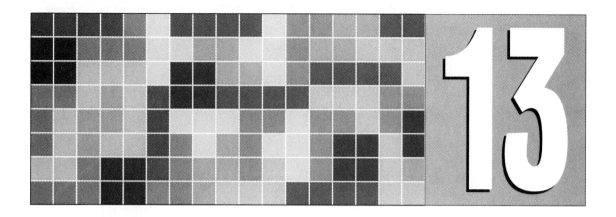

Delegation

After you have finished reading this chapter, you should be able to (1) list five reasons why supervisors don't delegate responsibilities and duties often enough, (2) describe the conditions under which a supervisor should delegate more, and (3) describe in specific terms how to do it.

"For Pete's sake, Harry, turn some of that stuff over to your employees and relax a little."

"Good grief, Sally, it's ridiculous for you to kill yourself doing such routine work when you have nine people in your department who need the experience."

"Come off it, Frank. You'd have plenty of time for more important things if you'd delegate some of those jobs you shouldn't be doing in the first place."

Sound familiar? Yes, it's easy to tell others to delegate and it's true that most supervisors should delegate more, but most of us have to learn the lesson the hard way. Take Dee as an example.

Dee was a new, young, capable, and highly enthusiastic manager. She had five full-time and three part-time employees. Despite advice from all sides, she could not learn to assign responsible work to others. Instead of delegating more, she simply pushed herself harder. Dee was so eager to be a successful supervisor that she was blind to what was happening. One of her best friends told her to manage more and do less. Her boss took her aside and gave her a heart-to-heart talk about the problem, but with little success.

Then one afternoon Dee passed out on the job and was taken by ambulance to a local hospital. The diagnosis was complete exhaustion. Dee hadn't received

the message from her friends or boss, but she heard it loud and clear from her doctor. He put it very simply: she had to learn to reduce her workload.

Delegating can, of course, mean many things to many people, but primarily it involves turning important work over to someone else. It means giving others the authority to do an assignment, with expected results mutually understood but keeping the responsibility yourself. It means having sufficient faith in others to let them do important work for you.

Training directors for large organizations are in an excellent position to analyze and compare how supervisors delegate. Here are three penetrating comments.

"When it comes to delegating, most inexperienced supervisors make two big mistakes: (1) they fail to do it skillfully, and (2) they fail to delegate enough. Delegation of duties is difficult to put into practice."

"The problem with delegating is that most supervisors know they *should* do it and most *think* they do it, but few *really* do it and those who do often go about it awkwardly."

"Lin could have been an excellent team leader, but she wanted to do too much of the work herself."

Delegating responsibilities and duties to others is a must. Unless you learn to do it often and skillfully, your future as a manager may be seriously limited.

FAILURE TO DELEGATE

Why do some supervisors fail to delegate as much as they should? The four basic reasons are all psychological in nature.

No Faith in Subordinates

Many supervisors do not see enough potential for success in the people who work for them and, as a result, never give their employees important and difficult assignments. Sometimes this kind of withholding happens because the supervisor has been burned in the past by poor performance; sometimes it is caused by unrealistic standards set by the supervisor. Most supervisors, however, simply lack confidence in the performance possibilities of employees. Unfortunately, this lack of confidence often results in poor performance when the supervisor is forced to delegate. To delegate successfully, you must have confidence in the results you anticipate and transmit this feeling to the employee.

Fear of Superiors

Every time you delegate important work to others, you risk failure and possible criticism from your superiors. You lay your personal reputation on the line, which is as it should be. If you are not sufficiently secure in your job and with your company to risk a few failures, then you should not be a supervisor in the first place. Fear is a powerful emotion that can tie you up in knots and cause you to be too cautious. You must conquer fear before you can delegate freely and effectively.

Desire for Personal Credit

Some supervisors with a strong need for ego fulfillment try to do all the important work themselves so that they will receive personal credit from their superiors. In taking this narrow perspective, they fail to see that by relinquishing personal credit to their employees they can (through motivation of individuals) increase productivity, which in turn will improve the reputation of the department. It is shortsighted for a supervisor to want personal credit when departmental success will ultimately be more beneficial.

Misjudgment of Time

Many supervisors are also shortsighted about time. They refuse to take time to delegate responsibility today to free themselves for more important work next week. Time is the supervisor's most important commodity. If you refuse to delegate because doing it properly takes too much time, you are guilty of poor planning. Skillful delegating saves time.

Questions to Ask Yourself

Before turning your desire to delegate into an action plan, consider the following questions:

- Have you clearly identified the work that you should delegate?
- Have you chosen the right person? Does the employee want to do the new task?
- Knowing you keep the responsibility, how much authority to make decisions are you willing to grant?
- What standards of performance will it take for you to be satisfied?
- What obstacles (if any) exist? How can they be overcome?
- Are you willing to spend the time required to train the person so that he or she produces at an acceptable level?
- Do you have an employee who has asked for more authority?

WHEN AND HOW TO DELEGATE

When should the leader delegate? You might wait forever for the perfect time to delegate, but some delegation should take place under the following conditions:

1. When you need more time for work that only you can do, especially planning responsibilities that will contribute more to departmental productivity than the job being delegated.

2. When delegating will help involve employees, improve their morale, and cause them to work closer to their potential.

3. When it will not show undue favoritism or seriously damage relationships with other employees.

4. When you are willing to take the time and effort to do a skillful job of delegating.

5. When you are under pressure and must relinquish some responsibilities in order to protect your physical and mental health.

How can you delegate skillfully? Everyone agrees that surfing, sky diving, and water skiing take skill, but few people acknowledge that the same is true of delegating. Yet delegating has its own special procedures. If you follow the following steps, you will greatly improve your skill in delegating.

Select the Task Carefully

Make up a priority list of assignments you might delegate. For a job to qualify for this list, it should be taking too much of your time, should be rather low in responsibility compared to your other duties, and should be motivating for your employees. Do not just delegate those tasks that you are bored with and that you are sure your employee will find boring also. Once you have your list, start from the top and delegate one task at a time. Try to spread them out over all your employees until you sense you are reaching a saturation point.

Select the Person Carefully

Consider all factors involved before selecting the person to whom you will give a specified task. Which employees have too much or too little work to do? Does any particular individual need a special challenge? Will the individual you select accept it with enthusiasm? Does the person have the training and talent to execute it well? How will co-workers react? Will it increase departmental productivity? Obviously, you must know your employees well if assignments are to fit the special needs and talents of each.

Prepare All Individuals for Change

Because sudden unannounced changes can disturb people and hurt productivity, announce your decision carefully in order to protect your relationships with all employees and to give the employee receiving the assignment all possible assistance. In most cases a group announcement is best so that everyone is informed, misunderstandings are minimized, and an opportunity to ask questions is provided. In delegating, you must be concerned with the feelings of all employees, not just those of the person to whom you are delegating.

Turn Over the Assignment

Consider the following steps in turning over new responsibilities to an employee:

1. Meet in private, where you will not be interrupted.

2. Allocate sufficient time to delegate carefully and thoroughly.

3. Go over the new job step by step. Illustrate or demonstrate whenever possible.

4. Ask the employee for verbal feedback on all details presented to eliminate future misunderstandings.

5. Give the employee an opportunity to ask questions.

6. Compliment the employee on previous work and transmit your confidence in the way she or he will perform the new responsibility.

7. Set a time and date for follow-up; however, it is often best to find out how the employee is doing before the due date.

8. Monitor task progress, but soon let the employee do the task without your interference or control.

Provide Follow-Up

Soon after delegating, make yourself available to answer further questions and provide additional training. Questions similar to these often facilitate communications:

- How are you doing on the new equipment?

- How do you feel now about your new assignment?

- Do you need any help I have not provided?

- Do you have any suggestions for me or other employees?

To delegate without follow-up is to ask for trouble and disappointment. You can delegate authority—power to get things done—but not your responsibility. The final responsibility for results is shared by all employees, but the supervisor must take the greatest percentage. If you learn to delegate frequently and skillfully, you will eventually worry less, feel less pressured, have more time to plan and organize, build better relationships with your employees, and motivate greater productivity in your department.

DELEGATING AS PART OF A LARGER PLAN

To become more efficient and make better use of your time, you must do both a departmental and a job analysis. That is, you must step back and look at how your department is operating to reach your productivity goals; you must then analyze all positions (including your own) to see how they can blend in better with the total operation. As you do this analysis, consider the following:

Discontinue low-priority tasks or nontherapeutic time wasters. As with most situations, a few little things will not contribute to productivity or employee morale and can be eliminated. The same is true with time wasters that do not contribute to a happy working environment or your own positive attitude.

Delegate more of what is left. To free yourself for more important tasks, set up a running policy (utilizing the techniques presented in this chapter) of continuous delegation so that employees' abilities expand as you become more effective as a supervisor.

Be more efficient at what you do. Here Chapters 14–20 will come into play. As you prioritize your work and improve your own job skills, you will cut down on the time devoted to various aspects of your job. If such time and task management requires additional training on your part, enroll in whatever program will help. Ask your superior to recommend worthwhile training. Seek a mentor—a person who can personally coach you.

What will you do with the time you save? Here are three suggestions: (1) spend more time improving relationships; (2) start solving problems before they occur; and (3) do even more departmental planning.

DISCUSSION QUESTIONS

1. Draw up a profile of an individual who, because of certain personality traits, might not be able to delegate and therefore should not be a supervisor.

2. Would most employees be happier and produce more if they were given more authority by their managers? Why or why not?

3. Why do so many supervisors use the lack of time as an excuse for not delegating? How would you convince such a person that spending time now can save time later?

4. Describe a task that your supervisor could delegate to you that would reduce her or his workload and provide you with the opportunity to learn.

Mini-Game

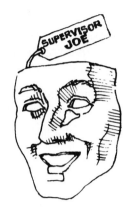

To Delegate or Not

Objective

To provide simulated practice in delegating.

Problem

Supervisor Joe has taken a close look at himself and his department and has decided that he *must* delegate more of his duties to his employees for the following reasons: (1) He has been working 60 hours a week for more than six months. (2) The pressure of trying to get everything done has put him on edge with some of the staff. (3) He has not been sleeping well because of worry. Last night he spent three hours formulating the following list of responsibilities he might delegate to his five employees:

1. *A weekly report that takes fifty minutes to prepare.* This report could easily be delegated to Mrs. R, but it would reveal certain departmental figures that have not been revealed to employees in the past. Nothing about the data is secret, but Joe feels he might lose control if everybody knows what goes on.

2. *A weekly job that Joe has always enjoyed doing.* Mrs. Q would love to do the job (she would probably do it better than Joe), but Joe wants to keep it because it keeps him closer to his employees and facilitates communication. This job usually takes about one hour.

3. *A routine weekly stock or supply room count that takes an hour and a half.* Joe has delegated this job before, but he always ends up taking it back because the grumbling from the employee disturbs him more than doing the job himself. Besides, sometimes the count is wrong, and he ends up doing the job himself anyway.

4. *Sending, via a computer connection, a fifteen-minute report to the computer center each afternoon at 4:00.* Joe has refused to delegate this task because, if it is not done accurately, he will be reprimanded by Mr. Big. Mr. K would be able to do the job and not be overloaded.

5. *A weekly (30 minute) delivery job of a special report to top management.* Joe has kept this task to do himself because it gives him a chance to have a cup of coffee and play a little politics with middle (and sometimes top) management executives.

6. *A routine meeting each month, which many supervisors already delegate to a subordinate.* It would be excellent training for Mr. G to have this assignment. Joe has kept it to himself, however, because he is afraid that something will happen at the meeting that he won't know about.

Procedure

Have the class number off from one to five to form five small groups. Each group selects a group leader. Each group is to find a quiet location where they can discuss Joe's list of six tasks that could be delegated. Which should be delegated first? Which last? Each group should assign a priority number from 1 to 6 to each possibility. The leader of each group should try to get complete agreement on the allocation of priority numbers within a fifteen-minute period. The following factors should be taken into consideration: Try to (1) save Joe as much time as possible, (2) relieve him of menial tasks, (3) improve departmental productivity, (4) train others for future supervisory roles, and (5) improve Joe's image as a supervisor. Once each group has completed its priority list, the results should be recorded on a master schedule on the blackboard.

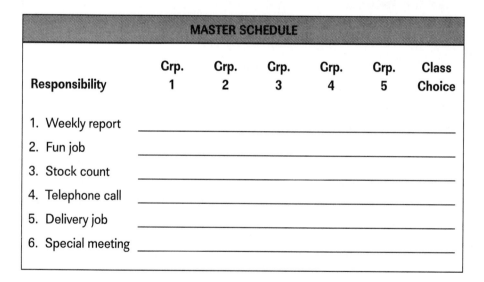

	MASTER SCHEDULE					
Responsibility	Grp. 1	Grp. 2	Grp. 3	Grp. 4	Grp. 5	Class Choice
1. Weekly report						
2. Fun job						
3. Stock count						
4. Telephone call						
5. Delivery job						
6. Special meeting						

After each group has recorded its choice, the points should be added horizontally and the total put in the last column under "Class Choice." The lower the number, the higher the priority given by the class.

Postgame Discussion

Should Joe delegate all six possibilities? Which, if any, should he keep to himself? What other factors should he take into consideration?

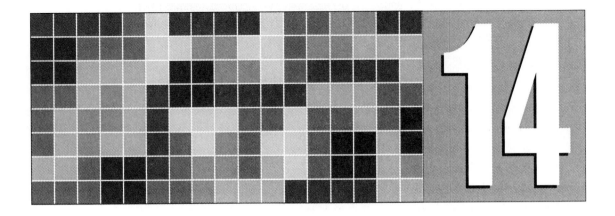

Use Your Knowledge Power

After you have finished reading this chapter, you should be able to apply the four-step teaching formula to earn the respect that comes from being an excellent on-the-job instructor.

A leader has three sources of power. First, considerable power goes with the job itself. It is called *role power*. It must be used wisely. The second source is *personality power*—using your personality to encourage greater productivity and accomplish other tasks. The third source is the most underestimated of all—*knowledge power*. You may not have viewed it this way in the past, but teaching your staff new ideas, skills, and competencies gives you prestige (and power) in their eyes. This chapter will assist you in making the most of your knowledge power.

Employees usually take pride in learning something new and doing it well. When you make learning possible, you earn their respect and build enduring, productive relationships. As a supervisor, you have daily opportunities to use your knowledge power.

The supervisor is frequently the only person who teaches the many skills that new employees need to learn: how to operate machines, complete forms, understand procedures, work skillfully with difficult customers or patients, complete reports, maintain equipment, and so on. Permanent employees need to learn how

to operate new generations of equipment, follow changing procedures, and perform tasks more effectively. On-the-job training never stops.

HOW TO TEACH BY NOT TEACHING

You can become an outstanding on-the-job instructor without employing any of the formal methods we usually associate with the traditional classroom teacher. All supervisors are models, and to a surprising extent your employees will adjust their behavior to the model you set. They will learn a great deal from you without your knowing it. But they also need specific help from you, and you want to provide this help in your own style without being labeled a "teacher." Instead of saying to a new employee, "Let me teach you how to do this," it might be better to say, "Let's figure out how you can do this quickly, comfortably, and correctly." Instead of saying to a regular employee, "Let me teach you to do it right the first time," it might be better to say, "Let me show you how I do this, and then you can figure out the best way for you to do it." It is one thing to be an effective classroom teacher; it is something else to be an effective on-the-job instructor.

YOUR ATTITUDE TOWARD TEACHING

What is your personal *attitude* toward sharing your knowledge with employees? Are you willing to set aside enough time to do it professionally? Do you desire to build a good reputation as a patient, caring instructor? *Are you more like Marvin or Mary?*

Marvin accepts a new employee into his department regardless of how much experience the individual has. When assuming his teaching role, he is patient, positive, and thorough, even if the learner is slow to catch on. As a result, Marvin develops a cohesive, productive, and loyal staff. His patient teaching attitude is admired and respected, especially by those from other cultures.

Mary consistently complains that new employees should have learned more in school. She shows little patience in teaching others. As a result, her staff makes more mistakes and personnel turnover is high. New workers are often forced to go to co-workers for help they need. Mary's negative attitude toward teaching others creates problems instead of solving them.

THE FOUR-STEP PROCESS

For years professional instructors have followed the four-step teaching process that is best used in practical on-the-job situations. You may wish to view this process as a baseball game, in that you have four bases to cover before you can score. In other words, you (the instructor) will take the employee (learner) around four bases, one at a time. What follows will show you the moves you should make, the dangers you face, and the signals you should follow.

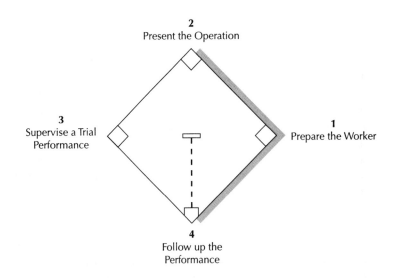

2
Present the Operation

3
Supervise a Trial
Performance

1
Prepare the Worker

4
Follow up the
Performance

First Base: Prepare the Worker

Because it is difficult to learn until one is psychologically and emotionally ready, your first responsibility is to help the new employee prepare for what you will teach. Here are four tips:

Put the learner at ease. Give the employee time to adjust to you as a person before you move into teaching the job itself. Find out a little more about the employee, make small talk, and try to put the person at ease. Make the effort to establish a relaxed learning climate. It is time well spent.

State the job you are going to teach and find out what the employee already knows about it. Do not waste time (or insult the employee) by teaching something he or she already knows. You may discover that a quick review is all that is necessary.

Motivate the person to learn the job. Give the worker some reason to learn. You might suggest that it could help the individual earn the respect of others, or you might talk about the personal satisfaction and pride that can come from learning something new. Make it sound exciting. Your job as a teacher will be much easier if the worker wants to learn.

Place the worker in the correct learning position. Just as a baseball player must have the right stance to hit the ball, it might be best for the worker to be at your left side instead of your right or to stand instead of sit. Determine the best physical position for the learner in each job you teach and be certain that he or she is located properly before you start. Attention to this factor will make the job easier for both parties.

Second Base: Present the Operation

Preparing the worker is comparable to reaching first base, and now you are ready to try for second. The following suggestions will take you there with little difficulty:

Describe, illustrate, and demonstrate one important step in a task at a time. Do not give so much information at once that the learner becomes confused. This careful instruction is not easy to do because you know the job so well that it is hard for you to remember how long it took you to learn it.

Tell the worker how to do the job, speaking clearly and slowly. Use simple words. If you must use a technical term, be sure to explain what you mean.

Whenever possible, follow up with an illustration. Take out your pencil and sketch the process; it need not be a work of art to convey the message. Show the learner by actually performing the job yourself, one step at a time. Be sure that you perform in complete detail so that your actions are easily observed.

Stress each key point. Determine and then stress the one key point in each step of the operation as you go through the process. This emphasis will help the learner recall each step later by remembering the key points, and the process will thereby become easier. When a given job takes more than five steps, this procedure becomes increasingly important.

Instruct clearly, completely, and patiently, but do not give the worker more than can be mastered. The greatest error that most supervisors commit is trying to teach too much too fast. They overestimate their teaching abilities and the employee's learning ability. If you try to teach too much at one time, you will only confuse the learner, and you will have to start over. Break the total job into separate steps and present them in sequence. Do not start the second step until the first has been mastered. If necessary, permit a lapse of time between steps. Focus on teaching the material thoroughly, even though time is at a premium.

Third Base: Supervise a Trial Performance

Give the new worker an immediate opportunity to do the job on a trial basis following this three-step procedure:

Have the learner do the job so that you can correct errors quickly. Few new workers perform jobs perfectly the first time, and the only way to spot errors is to have the worker try out the process under your direction. Of course, errors should be pointed out and corrected quickly without showing impatience.

Have the employee explain the key points of the job. It is important that the key points learned in the second step be repeated verbally by the learner during the first performance. Explaining each one makes it easier to remember.

Make sure the worker understands. It is vital that the learner understand why it is best to do a job in a certain way and why the job is important to the total efficiency of the department. Give the employee the opportunity to ask questions.

The idea of this third step is to continue until *you* know the learner knows. If necessary, continue the dry runs until the skill is mastered.

Home Base: Follow Up the Performance

Tell the worker where to go for help. If you are not easily accessible to the new worker, find a co-worker to help the employee achieve and keep a high level of productivity. In short, appoint a co-worker who will be compatible with the new employee and willing to help when needed.

Check frequently to see if all is going well. Take time to check with the worker as well as the sponsor. Nothing can replace your own interest during the employee's first critical days of learning.

Taper off coaching so that the worker does not feel oversupervised. After a certain point, the employee deserves the satisfaction and freedom of going it alone. Stepping back will provide the worker with the confidence needed to assume further responsibility at a later date. Oversupervising can destroy initiative. Pull away when your job performance standards have been met.

If you successfully follow these steps, your chances of success will be greatly enhanced. The new worker will know how to do the job, will do it right the first time, and you will have the confidence to be a long-term, productive member of your department. You will have begun to establish a solid relationship with the new worker.

If you have tried the four basic steps and still feel that you have failed in your efforts to train a new employee, the cause could be one or more of the following three errors:

1. *Failure to devote enough time to training.* You must allow sufficient time to do the teaching job properly, even if it means putting aside some of your other responsibilities temporarily. It will not be easy to do, but the long-range productivity of your workers will prove that you have spent your time well.

2. *Failure to follow the system step by step.* The system provided in this chapter takes time, but it works. If you skip a step, the system will break down.

3. *Failure to show enough patience with the slow learner.* Few new workers will be as smart as you would like them to be. Some may learn more slowly than em-

ployees you have trained in the past. When you must teach a slow learner to do a job, you must slow your own pace or the results will be most disappointing. Cover each of the four bases with special patience and consideration, even if it means taking twice as much time as you had devoted in the past. Keep in mind that slow learners can become excellent producers once they master the job, so the extra time you devote will not be wasted.

DELEGATING TRAINING RESPONSIBILITIES

Professional educators frequently admit that the best way to learn to do something well is to teach it. At times you may wish to delegate the training of a new employee to a regular employee who fully understands and practices the four-step process effectively. By delegating you will give recognition to the regular employee, provide excellent training to the new employee, and save yourself time. It may be wise, however, for you to retain the follow-up responsibility to make certain that the employee you selected as a coach does the job correctly.

GROUP INSTRUCTION

As a supervisor, you may be invited to make a presentation to other supervisors and your superiors. You can prepare for the event by making one or more group presentations to your own employees. Follow the same basic steps you use in individual instruction. That is, prepare the group (audience), present the new material (knowledge), gain involvement through questions, and summarize (follow through) by repeating the goal of the meeting.

As you follow these basic principles, you might also consider the following:

1. The more visual aids (keeping them simple) you prepare in advance, the more confidence you will have in your presentation and the more effective you will be.

2. Generally speaking, lecturing is the least effective teaching method, so strive for as much group interaction as possible.

3. Cover your subject carefully by outlining your instructions from start to finish.

Training never stops. As long as you must cope with an ever-increasing number of changes, you must accumulate new knowledge and pass on what you have learned to those who work for you. Everyone, including your superiors, finds it stressful to keep up with changes both in the environment in general and within the organization in particular. You will need to train yourself to deal with the impact of change, which means you will need to learn new ways to perform responsibilities. The greater the changes, the more you must learn; the more you learn, the more time you must spend instructing others and preparing them for change.

Changes manifest themselves in different ways: new procedures, new techniques, new generations of computers, new skills, and new ways of dealing with problems. As changes occur, you should occasionally search for new ideas and procedures to put into your own personal "knowledge bag." You should continue to educate yourself through both self-instruction and formal course programs. When you learn something that will improve the productivity of your department, you should pass it on, using the four-step method, to your staff.

Use your knowledge power wisely.

DISCUSSION QUESTIONS

1. Assume that you are going to start training a new employee on your computer system tomorrow. How would you implement the four-step system?

2. From your experience as a nonsupervisor (learner), do you feel that supervisors, generally speaking, are good instructors? Cite examples to support your view.

3. How can supervisors or team leaders train themselves to spend sufficient time on quality instruction that will earn respect from all employees? Be specific.

Case Study

Training[1]

Mr. Big has become increasingly disturbed over high personnel turnover, low productivity, poor quality standards, and the increasing number of mistakes made by new employees in all the departments under his management. As a result, he has designed a new orientation plan based upon the premise that the quality of on-the-job training has not been up to standard. The supervisor will be totally responsible for the implementation and success of orientation.

The new plan specifies the following:

1. The four-step teaching method is mandated.

2. At the end of two weeks, the new employee and his or her supervisor will meet in Mr. Big's office for a short evaluation and progress report.

3. Those supervisors who receive high marks from new employees will receive, as a reward, a one-time three-day weekend.

How do you respond to this plan? Do you feel the supervisor has been given a proper role in the plan? Will it reduce turnover, increase productivity, and curtail mistakes? What negative side effects might it generate? Is the plan too ambitious? Would Mr. Big have time to follow through on all evaluations?

Is Mr. Big being too heavy-handed in his approach?

---

[1]Turn to page 265 to compare your thoughts with those of the author.

The Formal Appraisal

After you have finished reading this chapter, you should be able to apply the techniques (1) to improve noticeably the next time if you have already done a formal appraisal, or (2) do a better than average job on your first formal appraisal.

In most sizable organizations, supervisors appraise each individual in their departments every six months or once a year. If you have been on the receiving end of such an appraisal, you probably still remember the supervisor, the printed instrument, the interview, and the results. The purpose of this chapter is to prepare you to administer such evaluations for the first time or to help you improve upon the way you have handled them in the past.

Appraisals give you an opportunity to improve your counseling techniques. They permit you to apply the five Rs of counseling you learned in Chapter 10. As such, they should be viewed as a positive experience—something you can learn to do well now that will stand you in good stead as you move into higher management roles.

APPRAISAL INSTRUMENTS

You cannot accomplish an appraisal without using a form or rating sheet that, after the interview is over, becomes a documented record. There are almost as many different appraisal instruments as there are organizations that use them. Few, if any, fully satisfy the people who designed them or the managers who use

them. Almost any form, however, can be used effectively if the supervisor's attitude toward it is positive.

Two examples of appraisal instruments are provided in this chapter. Study them closely and think about how the form could serve you when appraising an employee's performance.

APPRAISALS AND MBO

An important relationship links formal appraisals with management by objectives (MBO) philosophies. For example, your superior (evaluating you as a supervisor) might tie your appraisal to the success you have had in reaching the objectives you submitted at an earlier time. If you have made excellent progress toward the goals approved earlier, chances are good that you will receive a positive report. Other factors that may be considered include human relations skills, dependability, and the ability to handle problem employees.

In a sense, a formal appraisal is a form of accountability. You are asked to account for your past performance based upon certain standards that are included on the rating sheet. In a majority of organizations, salary increases, bonuses, and other forms of compensation are tied to the performance rating. Results are therefore critical to those being appraised.

APPRAISALS AND CAREER PLANNING

It is inevitable and fortuitous that going through the evaluation process frequently causes employees to review their own career progress or master plans. More than anything else, an appraisal tells you how you are doing and whether you should make adjustments to your long-term career path. It is a time of self-evaluation.

As a front-line supervisor, you will want to tie your appraisals to the future planning of your employees. If they receive weak appraisals, what can they do to make improvements before the next period arrives? What self-improvement projects might they undertake to eliminate deficiencies?

> Mrs. Petronzio was the director of a convalescent home with a staff of thirty-six. This year, for the first time, she was required by new management to do appraisals on all employees. She viewed the new responsibility as a challenge that could increase staff productivity and spent considerable time reading about appraisal techniques and getting acquainted with the form.
>
> Her first appraisal was with Maisie, a vocational nurse, who was highly dependable and capable of taking over any position that did not require the presence of a registered nurse. Mrs. Petronzio rated Maisie excellent in every category but cooperativeness because, in recent months, Maisie had become irritated with others in a variety of situations.
>
> Under Mrs. Petronzio's gentle probing, Maisie admitted that she was frequently upset over the poor attitudes and performance of registered nurses who were paid substantially more than she. When Mrs. Petronzio suggested that Maisie could qualify as a registered nurse with special training at a local college, she was interested. Eventually she undertook the program. Not only did Maisie receive an excellent rating in all factors the next time around but, after three years of training, she became a registered nurse—something that might not have occurred without the formal appraisal interview.

BENEFITS TO MANAGEMENT

Who benefits from these formal performance review programs? Why are they used so often? Are they truly helpful to employees?

Management has good reason for supporting the program and insisting that all people (including themselves) be measured occasionally under a standardized procedure.

1. It is the best way to make sure that the high-production employee is identified and recognized and that the low-production employee is located and counseled.

(Text continues on page 162.)

SHORT-FORM APPRAISAL*

EVALUATION OF WORK PERFORMANCE

QUANTITY
of Individual's Work

LOW	LESS THAN ACCEPTABLE	COMPLETELY ACCEPTABLE	MORE THAN ACCEPTABLE	HIGH

SUPPORTING COMMENTS: _____

_____

_____

_____

_____

QUALITY
of Individual's Work

LOW	LESS THAN ACCEPTABLE	COMPLETELY ACCEPTABLE	MORE THAN ACCEPTABLE	HIGH

SUPPORTING COMMENTS: _____

_____

_____

_____

_____

CONTRIBUTIONS
to Work Group's
Performance

LOW	LESS THAN ACCEPTABLE	COMPLETELY ACCEPTABLE	MORE THAN ACCEPTABLE	HIGH

SUPPORTING COMMENTS: _____

_____

_____

_____

_____

SIGNATURE OF EMPLOYEE _____ PREPARED BY _____

Manager's Signature _____ Human Resources approval _____

*Supporting comments must be specific and must include examples of performance that have been demonstrated to be in harmony with the rating.

LONG-FORM APPRAISAL*

PERFORMANCE EVALUATION AND
DEVELOPMENT PLAN
General

Name: _____   Date of Evaluation: _____

Date Hired: _____   Division and Dept.: _____

Job Title: _____   Evaluating Manager: _____

Time in Present Position: _____   Reviewed By: _____

The purpose of this evaluation is to:

1. **Set Goals.** The manager and the employee establish mutually agreed-upon goals for future progress and development.

2. **Inform.** The manager and the employee communicate openly and honestly about performance.

3. **Develop.** The manager and employee identify actions the employee can take to enhance his or her development at HP.

4. **Evaluate.** The manager and the employee evaluate results based on pre-established goals and performance measures.

I.   POSITION OBJECTIVES AND MAJOR RESPONSIBILITIES. Summarize specific responsibilities of the job.

_____

_____

_____

_____

_____

_____

II. ACCOMPLISHMENTS AND/OR IMPROVEMENTS: What specific accomplishments and/or improvements has this individual made since the last review? What progress has been made toward meeting established performance goals?

_____

_____

_____

_____

_____

_____

*Reproduced by permission of Hewlett-Packard, Inc.

Please consider the employee's demonstrated performance and mark the circle which most clearly describes that performance.

EXCEPTIONAL: Performance consistently far exceeds expectations.

VERY GOOD: Performance consistently exceeds normal expectations and job requirements

GOOD: Performance consistently meets expectations and job requirements.

ACCEPTABLE: Performance usually meets expectations and minimum requirements for the job.

UNACCEPTABLE: Performance is below the minimum acceptable level.

WORK QUALITY: The reliability, accuracy, and neatness of work produced.

○ Exceptional   ○ Very Good   ○ Good   ○ Acceptable   ○ Unacceptable

_____

_____

_____

_____

_____

_____

WORK QUANTITY: The amount of volume of work turned out.

○ Exceptional   ○ Very Good   ○ Good   ○ Acceptable   ○ Unacceptable

_____

_____

_____

_____

_____

_____

JUDGMENT: The ability to make well-reasoned, sound decisions that affect work performance.

○ Exceptional   ○ Very Good   ○ Good   ○ Acceptable   ○ Unacceptable

_____

_____

_____

_____

_____

_____

INITIATIVE: The combination of job interest, dedication, and willingness to extend oneself to complete assigned tasks.

○ Exceptional   ○ Very Good   ○ Good   ○ Acceptable   ○ Unacceptable

_____
_____
_____
_____
_____
_____

TEAMWORK: The working relationship established with fellow employees in the working environment.

○ Exceptional   ○ Very Good   ○ Good   ○ Acceptable   ○ Unacceptable

_____
_____
_____
_____
_____
_____

DEPENDABILITY: The reliance that can be placed on an employee to persevere and carry through to completion any task assigned. This also applies to attendance and punctuality.

○ Exceptional   ○ Very Good   ○ Good   ○ Acceptable   ○ Unacceptable

_____
_____
_____
_____
_____
_____

PERFORMANCE SUMMARY: _____
_____
_____
_____
_____
_____
_____
_____
_____

III.   DEVELOPMENT PLAN: What specific action can you suggest to help the employee improve his or her performance? How can you, as manager, help?

_____

_____

_____

_____

_____

_____

_____

_____

IV.   NEXT YEAR'S GOAL STATEMENTS: Establish with your manager goals that may include new and better ways to carry out job responsibilities, as well as plans for personal development. Stated goals should be included as basis for next formal performance evaluation.

_____

_____

_____

_____

_____

_____

_____

V.   EMPLOYEE COMMENTS: Each individual evaluated is encouraged to add any comments to this review. If additional space is needed, attach a separate sheet.

_____

_____

_____

_____

_____

_____

_____

_____

I am signing this evaluation to indicate that my manager and I have had a discussion of the above comments.

_____   _____

      Date   Employee Signature

2. Properly administered by the first-line supervisor, the system builds a stronger working relationship between the supervisor and the employee and thus helps improve performance.

3. The policy produces a more objective basis for salary increases and promotions.

4. A formal system, though never perfect, will provide better and more uniform treatment of individuals by supervisors than having no system.

5. Employee reviews provide organizations with the help they need to maintain and improve *quality* as well as *quantity* standards.

Management, however, is the first to recognize that the key to the success of the appraisal system is its administration. For this reason, supervisors are being given more and more training to make the system work. (It is also why you are reading this chapter.)

BENEFITS TO EMPLOYEES

It is easy to see why management endorses a good appraisal system that is properly administered, but what about its benefits to employees? Do they really come out ahead? In the great majority of cases, the answer is yes for the following reasons:

1. The procedure clarifies what is expected of the employee.

2. It provides a system of recognition and prevents employees from being ignored or lost.

3. It forces the supervisor to speak up or shut up on negative matters, thus creating a more objective and open relationship with the employee.

4. The rating helps the employee pinpoint weak areas so that improvements can be made.

5. It forces periodic communication between the supervisor and the employee.

These reasons are all good. Why, then, are rating systems unpopular with many supervisors and employees? Many employees complain every time their review period comes along, and some supervisors dread the process just as much. If the process is so beneficial, why do supervisors and employees react this way?

USING A POSITIVE APPROACH

Supervisors usually take one of two positions when it comes to formal reviews. Those who choose the first position see the value in the process and turn it into a positive tool. Their employees look forward to it. Those who take the other position refuse to see the purpose and fight the process most of the way. Their employees resent the procedure as much as their supervisors do. In other words, you as the administrating official determine the success or failure of any rating system; you can look forward to every review situation or you can try to avoid it.

How you handle the procedure will determine whether your employees consider it an opportunity or a disagreeable chore.

The positive approach pays off for professional supervisors because they use the merit rating system to improve productivity in their departments. They take advantage of the procedure to build better relationships with their people. They make it a vehicle to get raises and promotions for their better employees. Here are some suggestions to help you turn formal reviews into a positive rather than a negative force.

Accept the System the Way It Is

You are a supervisor, not the owner of the firm, a CEO, or a human resource director charged with responsibility for the program. If you spend your time complaining and trying to change the system, you won't have enough time left to make it work.

Do Not Take the Easy Way Out

With all your other responsibilities, you may be tempted to back away from an honest appraisal of your people by giving them a better rating than they deserve, sometimes referred to as the *error of leniency*. Employees know how they perform better than you do and may lose respect for you if you are too soft or permit intimidation. Most employees want an accurate evaluation and may feel short-changed and disappointed if you do not give it to them. On the other hand, be sure to be fair. A minimal rating or a grudgingly given high mark may leave the employee feeling unappreciated. Motivation to produce can drop dramatically if employees sense that you are not objective. As you complete the rating form, try following these suggestions:

1. Remember that you are appraising the employee's work, not his or her personality. Base your evaluation on objective data such as production figures, competence, attendance records, or mistakes.

2. Avoid basing your evaluation on the potential of the employee rather than on actual performance. Evaluate what the employee contributed to the department's productivity, not what he or she is capable of contributing.

3. Base your evaluation on the employee's average performance during the period covered, not on isolated examples of extremely good or bad work. One good or bad day, week, or month shouldn't necessarily result in a corresponding high or low rating.

4. Avoid the *halo effect*. In other words, rather than permit one prominent quality (good or bad) to influence your rating of other factors, include all important productivity factors.

5. Avoid the error of central tendency, in which you select the middle rating on all factors. Supervisors can fall into this trap when they are in a hurry or want to play it safe because they do not want to accept the responsibility of justifying a high rating or a low rating.

The modern approach to performance appraisal differs from the traditional approach in both emphasis and content. Some of the distinguishing characteristics follow:

- The salary-wage interview is often separated from the performance improvement interview so that salary does not dominate the discussion.

- The performance appraisal is future-oriented instead of focusing on past results.

- Emphasis is placed upon the establishment of work objectives that can be achieved by the next evaluation period, not on criticism about past performance.

- The basic idea is to develop a supportive climate and improve the relationship between the supervisor and the employee through nonevaluative listening, nondirective counseling, and performance feedback.

Always Discuss the Rating Openly with Employees

Different organizations follow different procedures. Some require that employees evaluate themselves first and then let the supervisor react. Some require the supervisor to rate the employees first and then let them react. Some leave it up to the supervisor.

Regardless of the system (and each has advantages), you should openly discuss the rating with the employee, explaining and, if necessary, defending your position on all factors rated. Try to establish two-way communication in which the employee has a free and fair chance to present his or her case. An employee rating without an unhurried discussion may be in compliance with the system, but it is a mockery of its purpose. Important employment decisions are based on documented performance. Pay raises, promotions, transfers, keeping one's job when a layoff is coming are serious matters and often determined by one's performance. Supervisors need to know how to appraise performance and how to conduct the appraisal conference so that the appraisal is accurate. If your company has a training program on this topic, take advantage of the opportunity and attend. Many times local colleges put on seminars related to management or supervision, and performance appraisal is generally included as a topic.

USING THE APPRAISAL FORM

The two parts to the performance appraisal are "Content" and "Process." Let us consider content first. The content is the appraisal form itself. A typical form, like the ones in this chapter, includes its purpose, instructions on how to fill it out, and where copies are to go. It contains the behavior categories being assessed, and the ratings scales by which performance is measured.

The supervisor should give the employee a copy of the form at the beginning of the rating period so they both may refer to it from time to time. Together they can focus on defining the categories of behavior. For example, the employee may need a more complete definition or clarification of exactly what behaviors the

FORMAL APPRAISAL EXERCISE

This scale is designed to help you improve your performance appraisal interviews and discussion with employees. Circle the number that best reflects where you currently fall on the scale. When you have finished, total the numbers circled in the space and then go through the scale a second time, placing a double circle around the number you intend to reach on your next appraisal.

	ALWAYS (10,9,8)			SOMETIMES (7,6,5,4)				NEVER (3,2,1)		
1. I let the employee do most of the talking.	10	9	8	7	6	5	4	3	2	1
2. I make an intense effort to listen to the employee's ideas.	10	9	8	7	6	5	4	3	2	1
3. I am prepared to suggest solutions to problems and development needs but let the employee contribute first.	10	9	8	7	6	5	4	3	2	1
4. My statements about performance are descriptive and specific, not judgmental.	10	9	8	7	6	5	4	3	2	1
5. I reinforce the positives in performance, as well as seek ways to improve below-standard performance.	10	9	8	7	6	5	4	3	2	1
6. I try to encourage the employee's ideas about expanding performance.	10	9	8	7	6	5	4	3	2	1
7. I invite alternatives rather than assume that there is only one way to approach an issue.	10	9	8	7	6	5	4	3	2	1
8. I use open-ended, reflective, and directive questions to stimulate discussion.	10	9	8	7	6	5	4	3	2	1
9. I am specific and descriptive when I express a concern about performance.	10	9	8	7	6	5	4	3	2	1
10. Know I want my employee to succeed.	10	9	8	7	6	5	4	3	2	1

TOTAL _____

A score between 90 and 100 indicates that you should be leading successful discussions. A score between 70 and 89 indicates significant strengths plus a few improvement needs. A score between 50 and 69 reflects some strengths, but a significant number of problem areas as well. Scores below 50 call for a serious effort to improve in several categories. Make a special effort to grow in any area where you scored 6 or less, regardless of your total score.

supervisor sees in the category labeled "Dependability." Of the many behaviors that could fall into this category, those behaviors the supervisor thinks fall in this category need to be communicated to the employee during the rating period, not just at the end when employees receive their performance appraisals. If the supervisor does not convey clear behavioral expectations of "Dependability," then employees have to guess as to what the supervisor thinks dependability is; they may guess wrong. Supervisors may find it necessary to include the employees in defining terms.

The rating scale should also be considered carefully because it has serious pitfalls. In our example notice that the rating scale goes from:

○ Exceptional   ○ Very Good   ○ Good   ○ Acceptable   ○ Unacceptable

Most supervisors find it easy to explain the differences between "Exceptional" performance and "Unacceptable" performance because they are the extremes. But many experience difficulty explaining the difference between, say, "Acceptable" performance and "Good" performance. Trouble brews when an employee asks what exactly they have to do to move from the lower rating of "Acceptable" to the higher rating of "Good." If the supervisor cannot tell employees what they must do to improve, one may wonder exactly how the supervisor arrived at that rating in the first place.

CONDUCTING THE APPRAISAL

The second part of the performance appraisal is the "Process." The process is how the performance review or conference is conducted. It is the *who, what, where, how, and when of the appraisal.* Many employees complain that their appraisal is completed by their supervisor and merely handed to them for their signature without a personal or private review conference. The employee is left out of the process entirely. Leaving the employee out is a big mistake. As mentioned earlier, performance appraisals have enormous effects on employees, and they expect and deserve a professionally conducted review. This process takes time and a professional review would have the following characteristics:

Who does it? One's immediate supervisor is usually the person who is in the position to observe directly the performance of an employee. Employees are skeptical of a review done by someone who does not see their work.

What is done? During the review, the supervisor allows time for questions and an opportunity for the employee to provide input into her or his final rating. This process takes open two-way communication. The supervisor needs to listen and be open to changing his or her rating during the discussion. Hurry through the formal appraisal and it will not accomplish its purpose. To rush the procedure is to destroy it. You must *make* time to do it properly.

Where is it done? The appraisal is a confidential matter between the supervisor and employee. It should be done in a quiet, private place.

How is it done? The review meeting deserves time, giving the employee the opportunity to thoroughly discuss her or his performance. The talk-listen ratio should be balanced or in favor of the employee, meaning that the supervisor should do most of the listening and the employee most of the talking. You must be sure of your ground when you rate an employee in a way that will affect the individual's future. When you must give an unsatisfactory rating, make sure you follow these steps: (1) have all the facts at your disposal; (2) discuss the problem with the employee; (3) take your decision to both your superior and the human resource director; and (4) be ready to recognize an improvement in productivity if and when it happens.

When is it done? Do not be late giving the appraisal. Late appraisals may cause a delay in a raise, promotion, or other important employment decision for the employee. Do it on time or before the last possible due date. If appraisals are routinely late in coming the employees may conclude that performance does not matter to the supervisor and may result in lower productivity or job dissatisfaction. Do not convey to the employee that once the regular appraisal is over, no further help or counseling will occur until the next time. If the appraisal was positive, the employee may feel you will ignore future problems. If it was negative, he or she may feel that you will not be available for more help until the next appraisal session. Good follow-up procedures are essential to the success of the system.

USING THE APPRAISAL PROCESS AS A POSITIVE TOOL

The first time an employee is formally appraised can be extremely important to both the individual and the organization. Take extra time to (1) explain the purpose and procedure, (2) go over the form in detail so that no misunderstandings remain, and (3) make sure the employee has an opportunity to ask questions and to feel at home with the procedure.

Introspective self-evaluation is the primary purpose of any appraisal program. It is not a tool to embarrass, intimidate, dispose of, annoy, or harass an employee, but rather to help the employee gauge his or her progress and future with the company. Geared to the needs of the employee, the system cannot fail; geared exclusively to the needs of the organization, it becomes suspect and loses its value.

Many appraisal systems seem overcomplicated with too much detail. Even so, try to work within the system by following the instructions carefully. Follow the necessary red tape without griping. The system depends on you to make it effective.

Sometimes you may be so enthusiastic over an outstanding appraisal that you either make or imply a promise that you cannot keep in a reasonable length of time. Nothing destroys morale more than a broken promise. Therefore you must protect everyone by making only clear statements that cannot be misinterpreted.

To fairly judge, measure, or evaluate the performance of another person is a sensitive, difficult process. Realizing that it is never easy to separate performance from personality, accept all available help to keep the procedure from backfiring and causing serious human problems. The suggestions presented will help you stay on the right track, but they cannot remove the responsibility of the ultimate rating decision from your shoulders. You are the only one close enough to the employee to have all the necessary facts and data, who can provide the quality counseling that must accompany the process, and who can translate the theory into reality.

DISCUSSION QUESTIONS

1. If you were the owner of a firm with fifty employees, would you initiate a formal appraisal program? Would you tie pay raises to the results? Would you develop your own instrument?

2. Can you explain why so many supervisors dread formal reviews? Does their attitude keep them from doing a good job of reviewing? Why is it so difficult to judge or evaluate others?

3. Do you agree that employees should complete their own appraisal forms and then let the supervisor react and make changes before submitting the forms to the human resource department?

4. Recall the details of your last performance appraisal. How was it handled? What could have been done to improve it, to make it more accurate and beneficial to you?

5. Often supervisors and employees remark that categories of performance are vague, that their definitions of performance are unexplained. For example, review the Short-Form Appraisal and define what exactly is meant by "quality of individual's work." Explain the difference between "less than acceptable" and "completely acceptable" in one's quality of work.

Mini-Game

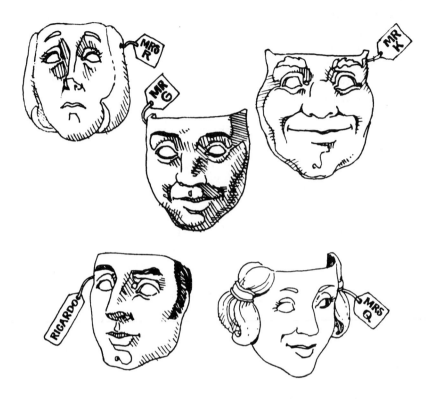

Option

Objective

To discover the advantages and disadvantages of two different approaches to formal appraisal of employees.

Problem

Ms. Y and Mr. X are in complete disagreement regarding the best way to appraise their employees. Mr. Big, tired of the conflict, decides to let the five employees in Supervisor Joe's department resolve it.

Procedure

Everyone in the class or seminar reads the following material. The five players then discuss the advantages and disadvantages of each approach from their point of view as employees being appraised. After the discussion, they vote on the approach (that of Ms. Y or Mr. X) they prefer.

Ms. Y's Technique

Ms. Y prefers the nondirective, soft approach. She likes to sit down in a non-threatening manner, and quietly discuss and settle on the rating of each factor without any advance preparation from either party. She feels that when employees fill out their own appraisal forms in advance, they tend to defend each rating they give themselves, and the interview may turn into an argument. Her approach is to ask the employee what rating she or he feels is right. If she agrees, they move on quickly; if not, they talk it over. Ms. Y frequently gives in, but she argues that her concession is not a "whitewash" job. She believes that through open discussion, employees sense their own shortcomings. Other pressures are not necessary. Her ratings are consistently higher than those of Mr. X.

Mr. X's Technique

Mr. X takes a more directive, hard approach. He follows the procedure of giving the appraisal instrument to each employee a few days in advance, asking that it be completed and brought to the interview at the scheduled time. In the meantime, he spends considerable time completing the same form independently. The interview consists of comparing forms and adjusting differences. When Mr. X feels he is right, he takes a firm stand and presents all possible data to back up his lower or higher rating. He does, however, make some adjustments when justified. He is always complimentary on high ratings, strives to be fair, and takes time to tie the procedure to long-term career plans.

Postgame Discussion

Which supervisor would you prefer to rate you? Why? Discuss how each technique might be improved or how a combination of both could be more effective.

Managing Yourself

"The fault, dear Brutus, is not in our stars, / But in ourselves
that we are underlings."

WILLIAM SHAKESPEARE
1564–1616

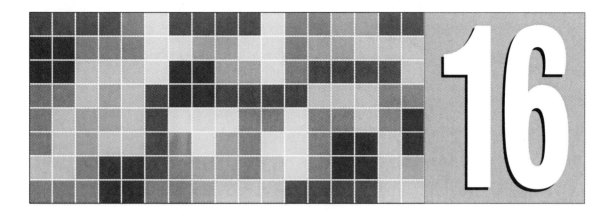

Learning to Concentrate

After you have finished reading this chapter, you should be able to apply the techniques that could double your ability to concentrate in disruptive environments.

Most beginning supervisors discover that their new and demanding responsibilities cause them to move, physically and mentally, in too many directions at the same time. Under these conditions, it is easy to start operating off the top of your head. When this sort of behavior occurs, it is a signal that you are not doing enough thinking or concentrating. Result? Confusion, frustration, and possibly a drop in departmental productivity.

WHAT IS CONCENTRATION?

Concentration is being able to focus your mental attention on a chosen project while you temporarily ignore matters of less importance. Concentration is devoting your mind exclusively to one problem until you have the best solution you are capable of reaching. Concentration is also getting the full message from a chapter you are reading in less time.[1] The nice thing about concentration is that it is a mental discipline anyone can learn.

---

[1] Are you concentrating to the best of your ability as you read this book?

ELIMINATING DISTRACTIONS

To accomplish a job that involves thinking, it is often necessary to isolate your-self from the many distractions most front-line supervisors face. These distractions include interruptions from employees, customers, superiors, emergency problems, repair tasks, filling in for an absent employee, and, of course, the telephone.

Freida makes it a practice to arrive at her desk thirty minutes ahead of her team of employees each morning. "I need to get away from telephone calls, em-ployee interruptions, and normal noise to improve my concentration. Thirty min-utes before the gang arrives is worth an hour when the shift is under way."

George, foreman of a construction crew, stays on site for an hour or so after everyone else has left. "I need some quiet time to plan for the next day. I con-centrate on having all the supplies ready for the crew when they arrive so that we can get off to a fast start. And, of course, it is a mistake to read blueprints un-less you have 100 percent concentration."

Hank has found a park bench near his noisy office where only the birds and the breeze can be heard. "When I have a knotty problem or need to concentrate on a report that is due, I often take my briefcase and head for my second office. On rainy days, I simply wait until I get home that night."

Isabelle divides her job as a supervisor into two categories. "First, I have my work time, which is devoted to tasks, counseling employees, keeping everyone informed, and making routine decisions. Then I have my mind-time responsibilities, which include doing work schedules, setting goals, making big decisions, and doing some creative thinking. Work time (90 percent) occurs under all kinds of conditions; mind time occurs when I step back to a quiet place where I can view the operation from a distance."

CONCENTRATING TO LEARN VS. CONCENTRATING TO MANAGE

Anyone can improve his or her power of concentration. Those with college degrees have obviously had opportunities to increase this power by mastering study habits and techniques. This practice gives them a slight advantage. But a big difference distinguishes concentrating to learn from concentrating to solve real work problems. For example, supervisors have so many immediate tasks to perform that when they concentrate on a major problem they must walk away, quickly concentrate, and then return to the remaining tasks. They do not have the luxury of sitting in a library where the environment is conducive to concentration.

People who have trained their minds to do analytical thinking—especially when numbers and formulas are involved—seem to have the edge when deep concentration is required. These same people are often good at goal setting and planning because they *like* to figure things out. This ability does not mean, however, that those with a different background cannot learn to concentrate at a level sufficiently high to be effective. All it takes is practice and a few simple rules.

When Martin accepted the position of manager with a chain restaurant, he didn't fully realize how much planning would be involved. A high school dropout, Martin never focused his mind on anything for more than a few moments. How did he survive? His superior told him to always isolate himself for thirty minutes each work day and do nothing but develop a written priority list of duties to perform that day. Slowly, through mental discipline, Martin learned to plan ahead. Along the way, he also learned to concentrate in other areas.

BARRIERS TO CONCENTRATION

In the busy, sometimes hectic, field of work, it is never easy to take time away from other responsibilities in order to concentrate on a special project. Many barriers keep supervisors from what we might term pure thinking. Some of these barriers are physical; others are psychological. Check those in the following list that frequently keep you from concentrating.

- Telephone calls

- Interruptions by employees or co-workers

- Noise

- Preoccupation on another matter

- Lack of training in how to concentrate

- Low tolerance of frustration

- Lack of motivation

- Procrastination

- Fatigue or stress

- A "to-heck-with-it" attitude

THE EFFECT OF PERSONALITY

Due to many factors, particularly the influence of personality, some people find it easier to concentrate than others. Some actually enjoy the process. Bill and Hazel provide us with an excellent example.

Bill and Hazel operate a successful quick-stop reproduction and printing operation. You seldom see Bill because he is in the back office, thinking through problems and planning ahead. His training as an engineer and computer programmer has given him unusual powers of concentration that fit his quiet personality. Hazel, on the other hand, works out front, doing a superior job with customers. She loves people and makes the most of her outgoing personality. Obviously, the division of work between Hazel and Bill is ideal. But last year, Bill had open heart surgery and Hazel found it necessary to take over his work in addition to doing her own. By the time Bill returned, things were a mess. "What did you expect?" said Hazel. "I can't deal effectively with demanding customers and concentrate at the same time."

WEARING TWO HATS

Few supervisors are fortunate enough to have another person to do their concentrating. Most must wear two hats. One is used to deal with daily operational tasks (working with customers, dealing with production factors, etc.), and the other (a concentration hat) is used for planning purposes. With desire and training, Hazel, in our previous example, could learn to do both, as is the case with almost all supervisors.

TIPS ON HOW TO CONCENTRATE

In assuming your responsibilities as a new supervisor, learning to wear both hats effectively is important. Here are a few tips that will assist you in wearing your concentration hat.

Limit your time. It is not how much time you spend concentrating that is important, but rather how intensely your mind is focused while you are at it. Experience shows that when you limit yourself to a certain amount of time for concentration purposes (say, thirty minutes instead of an hour), you accomplish more.

Matt, a supervisor in a machine shop, has a difficult report due each Friday morning. For years he has devoted a full afternoon on Thursday to completing the report. Then he discovered that if he allocated only two hours each Thursday afternoon (always in a quiet front office where no one could reach him), he could complete the report in half the time with fewer mistakes. In discussing this change with his superior, Matt said, "Apparently, when I limit my time, I concentrate better."

Divide and conquer big projects. When facing a major project like preparing an annual report or budget, it is often a good idea to divide the work into smaller parts. Short, intense periods of concentration make more sense than trying to concentrate for an extended period of time when mental fatigue can set in.

> Sylvia wanted to write an orientation manual for her corporation, but every time she sat down to put her thoughts in order, an interruption occurred and she would become frustrated and give up. Then, with permission from her superior, she tried a different approach. She left work early each Friday afternoon and went straight home, where she devoted two solid hours of concentration to the project. By spreading out the work, Sylvia was able to complete the work in six weeks. Her superior was most complimentary when she turned in the finished project.

Visualize the benefits. Concentration is aided when the rewards that come from a completed project are pictured in advance. Such visualization (imagery) can provide more motivation than was previously present.

> When Polly's divorce was final, she had to decide whether to do her own income tax or pay a professional. To keep expenses down, Polly decided to do it herself. To provide motivation, she pictured herself on a skiing trip with the money she would save. Always good with figures, she discovered she enjoyed the process because it gave her a better view of where her limited income was going. It also gave her an annual ski trip.

Project a professional image. Managers who learn to concentrate on setting goals, establishing priorities, and completing special projects communicate a more professional image to upper management. They demonstrate they can come through when clear thinking and decisive decisions are necessary.

> Roberto had the reputation of being a happy-go-lucky supervisor who got the job done but was not interested in a higher position. When he turned thirty, Roberto decided to go back to finish his college degree so that he could give his career a boost. In doing so, he learned how to concentrate, and after he submitted a few new projects, management took a second look at Roberto as middle management material.

Getting it done. Procrastination is the postponement of an important project without a good reason. It is, in effect, backing away from the periods of high concentration necessary to get something accomplished.

> Raymond discovered that self-talk was his best method to get into a mood in which he could concentrate. He would say to himself: "Here you go again, backing away because you are too lazy to concentrate. Get it done now so that you will feel better this weekend."

EIGHT STEPS TO SUCCESS

The next time you need to concentrate on a major problem or project, follow these simple steps:

1. *Isolate yourself.* Find a location where you are free from interruptions and excessive noise. Once you arrive, make yourself comfortable. Relax enough so that other matters leave your mind. You are then ready to concentrate.

2. *Review the situation.* If you are concentrating with the help of a computer, bring up all facts and past history. If you are working away from a computer, have all available data with you, including printouts. Study the data.

3. *Give yourself a time limit.* With full concentration, fifteen minutes is a long time. Attempt to beat the time allotments you have used in similar situations in the past.

4. *Outline what you intend to do and get started.* Most people think better with a pencil in their hand.

5. *List all options.* Review the various possibilities and strategies that might improve the situation or solve the problem.

6. *Weigh and decide.* Thinking means tossing possibilities back and forth in your mind until you come up with the best approach or solution.

7. *Make a decision or complete the project.* Whatever has required your concentration now needs to be stored in your memory bank for present implementation and future use. Concentration almost always produces something of value.

8. When you find yourself procrastinating on an important project, take action. Organize your day to allow some period of time for the project and work on it for the entire time allotted. Just do it! "The job never started takes the longest to finish," as they say.

The chapters ahead deal with mind-time factors that will make you an effective supervisor or team leader now and lead you in the direction of a more significant role in the future. *Why not use what you have learned about concentration in this chapter to get the full meaning of the chapters that lie ahead?*

Thinking[2]

Lisa and Lester are discussing how some students get better grades than others even though they spend less time preparing for examinations. Lisa states: "I think it is simply a matter of concentration. Many bright students do poorly because they never learn to concentrate. Of course, there is a big difference between learning to concentrate to retain information and solving problems out in the real world."

"Here on campus we concentrate to learn, pass tests, and earn a degree," replies Lester. "Students who never learn to concentrate are disadvantaged in real life because they don't focus their minds on problems and create plans for the future. The purpose of a college education is to teach you to think and concentrate. Nothing more, nothing less."

"I'm not so sure," replies Lisa. "Concentrating on campus is simply learning to store knowledge so that we can pass exams and move on to something else. In the real world, you deal with tough problems and difficult decisions in a work environment that is hectic. To be honest with you, I think a noncollege person can learn to concentrate on the job as well as a college grad. I agree that college teaches one to think, but as far as concentration is concerned, I don't believe there is much carryover from campus to the workplace. Concentration comes first, thinking next."

Do you agree with Lisa or Lester?

---

[2]Turn to page 266 to compare your thoughts with those of the author.

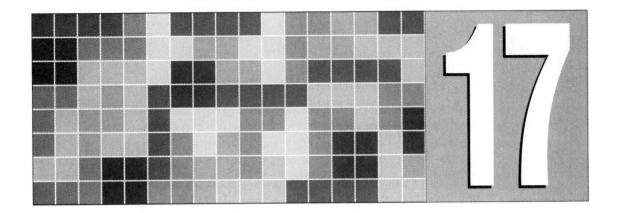

Establishing Goals and Planning

After you have finished reading this chapter, you should be able to (1) write out the planning formula covered in the chapter, (2) describe each part in detail, and (3) adapt it to your own work situation.

"It's great to be a lowly employee instead of a supervisor because you can report to work without thinking. You know, just stumble in and let the job grab you instead of you grabbing the job. Let the supervisor do the planning, scheduling, and thinking. After all, she's getting paid for it. Let her see to it that you have a productive day."

This quotation may not express the best possible employee attitude, but it contains enough truth to cause the supervisor to ask some pointed questions. If the supervisor doesn't give the department direction, who will? If she or he doesn't organize, plan, schedule, and pick up the loose ends, where will such leadership come from? If the supervisor doesn't provide the employee with a good day, who is to blame?

Some fairly basic differences separate the positions of employee and supervisor. The employee can become involved in the activities of the department without worrying over where the department is going. The employee can relax without having to fit what he or she does into a total plan.

The worker can achieve job satisfaction without sweating out reports, plans, figures, purchases, statistics, comparisons, and so forth. The supervisor, on the other hand, must constantly look at the overall picture. Are all employees properly assigned and fully productive? How is the department doing in comparison with others? How much increase in productivity might be expected in the next six months? What cost factors can be eliminated or reduced?

THE IMPORTANCE OF PLANNING

The role of a supervisor is a far cry from that of an employee. You cannot just let things happen but must *make* them happen. You must control a multitude of factors, deal with countless emergencies, and pick up a variety of loose ends, constantly directing and guiding the activities of others. No matter how many details must be faced, no matter how frantic the pace, you must stay on top of the situation and in control.

Nobody likes to work for an unorganized supervisor.

How can you do all these things? By *being an organized person with a definite plan.*

Managers must occasionally pull themselves away from the trees so that they can see the forest. They must learn to concentrate (see Chapter 16) so that they can develop significant, appropriate, and practical goals. The degree to which a manager is successful in seeing the big picture will determine the long-range success that he or she will enjoy.

The Gantt Bar Chart

Henry L. Gantt, an early management consultant, recognized that any sound plan is made up of a number of interlocking projects (smaller plans) that are dependent upon each other and must be molded together under a time limitation. He designed a bar chart showing the relationship of time to various subprojects in a master plan. Assume that you are the owner of a restaurant that needs remodeling, but you do not wish to close down. You might construct a Gantt-type chart like the following one to show how the restaurant could be remodeled one section at a time.

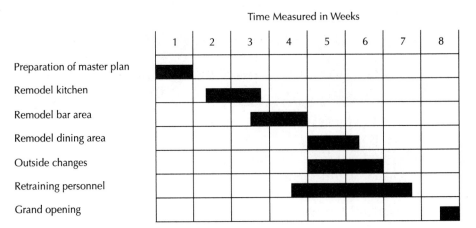

Restaurant Remodeling Chart

Network Analysis Plan

Production engineers often design highly sophisticated plans when a new product is to be manufactured. A plan that stresses an awareness of each step in a production path is called *network analysis*. A chart clearly identifies each step (some operating simultaneously) in an entire project—one that might take months or years to complete. For example, Program Evaluation Review Technique (PERT) is a well-known system that the U.S. Navy used to save almost two years on a missile project.

MASTER CALENDAR

Effective managers who set project deadlines for themselves frequently use calendars. Such deadlines act as reminders and facilitate productivity. Calendars can also be used for pending business appointments, staff meetings, conventions, and so on. Some managers prefer large calendars that can be displayed in their office as a reminder to all staff members. Others prefer pocket varieties that can be used both at home and on the job. Managers use their preferences in individual ways.

FORMULA FOR SUCCESSFUL PLANNING

Beginning supervisors do not need highly complex systems to handle their responsibilities, but they can benefit from a simplified one. The following formula serves this purpose.

$$MO + DP + SP = DS$$

Put into words, it means the following: MO (management objectives) plus DP (department plan) plus SP (small plans) equal DS (department success). Each symbol in this formula will take on a special meaning as you continue toward becoming a more organized supervisor.

MANAGEMENT BY OBJECTIVES

All supervisory planning should start with top management objectives (MO or TQM). They are the broad goals of the company that you sometimes find stated in employee handbooks or in annual reports to stockholders. Management objectives, or goals, can be expressed in terms of service standards, sales volume, profit pictures, or similar criteria and will change from time to time. Sometimes the supervisor may have a small voice in forming these broad objectives, but most of the time the supervisor must take responsibility for goals handed down from higher management and must then relate the operation of the department to the company goals. In so doing, the supervisor should ask these questions:

1. What are the current objectives of my company?

2. How might my department contribute more to reaching these objectives?

3. Is my department doing anything not in conformity with these goals?

Departmental Plans

Obviously management objectives are never reached unless they are implemented with actual productivity within reach of the smaller divisions making up the organization. So DP is added to the formula because a department cannot contribute significantly to management objectives without a plan of its own. At this point is where you come into the picture.

You should develop your own departmental plan, gear it to broad management objectives, and then communicate it to your own employees.

Departmental plans can take many forms, so you may receive considerable help from your manager in building your plan. She or he may ask you for a monthly, semiannual, or yearly written plan, provide the necessary forms, and give you a model to work from. On the other hand, if your manager does not ask you for a plan, you may prepare one exclusively for your own purposes. In either case, you should do the following:

1. Make your plan workable because an impossible goal does not motivate.

2. Make your plan flexible so that you can adjust to changes beyond your control.

3. Include all elements or factors over which you have control.

4. State the expected increase in productivity (tangible, sales, or service) in clear terms. Always include previous figures for comparison.

5. Tie your plan to management objectives.

A workable departmental plan is not easy to develop. It will take time, effort, and some communication on your part, but without it you have no direction. The kind of plan you develop will depend upon many variables that cannot be discussed here. Your employees should be involved in the formulation of the plan because they will be expected to help accomplish it.

Let's assume that you now have a developed departmental plan. It contains the broad objectives you hope to reach in your department in the next six months or year. It states the things you hope to achieve so that your department will show growth and improvement and will make its maximum contribution to the company as a whole. If you can accomplish these goals or come close to them, your reputation as a manager will be greatly enhanced. Once you set these goals, you have committed yourself. Management may not hold you firmly to them, but managers will probably refer to them from time to time.

MODEL

Six-Month Plan

- Develop a more effective orientation program for new employees.

- Make better use of FAX equipment. Delegate responsibility to an assistant.

- Institute a weekly staff meeting to improve communications and morale.

- Achieve a 5 percent increase in productivity with one less employee.

- Establish a computer bulletin board communications network.

- Initiate individual communication sessions for each employee to enhance motivation.

- Coordinate this plan with a formal appraisal program.

- Update computer software to enhance the tracking of in-process inventory.

Small Plans

We now come to the next part of the formula, the SP, or small plans. You cannot, of course, reach the goals of your overall plan unless you make it work by dividing it into little plans that are achievable on a daily or weekly basis. In short, you need a continuous supply of small plans or goals to augment your major departmental plan. Many experienced supervisors develop a daily checklist (tied to departmental plans), which they follow as closely as the situation permits.

> "While driving to work in the morning, I organize my day by making up a list of things to do. When I get to my desk, I write this list on my calendar pad and assign priorities. I then spend the rest of the day trying to check them off. It works for me."

> "I never leave work, even if I'm late, until I have a priority list of things to do when I show up the next day. This list makes it easier for me to leave my problems at work and gives me a good starting point the next day. I'd recommend it to the beginning supervisor."

> "For the last twenty years, I've made it a practice to show up fifteen minutes early every morning so that I can organize my daily plan. I find I can sort things out more clearly this time of day."

Small daily plans eventually add up to the successful completion of overall departmental plans. The daily checklist is an excellent practice and is strongly recommended for both the new and the experienced supervisor. The key to such a list is setting up the right priorities and following certain rules. (Setting priorities will be discussed in Chapter 18.) It must be emphasized, however, that the only worthwhile goals are *reachable* goals. For that reason, small, short, and immediate goals make sense. Some supervisors divide their small plans into daily and weekly classifications. A weekly goal might include something that takes more than one day to accomplish, such as changing a basic procedure, training a new employee, or contacting a series of customers. A daily goal might include taking someone to lunch, counseling with an employee who seems unhappy, finishing a report, or similar activities.

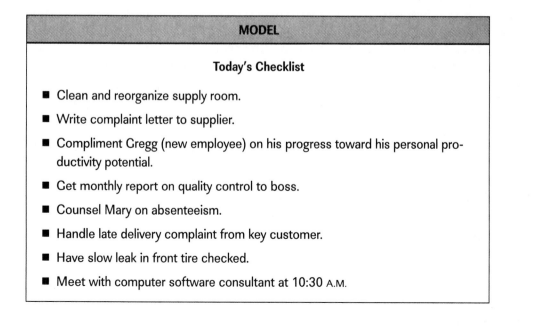

MODEL

Today's Checklist

- Clean and reorganize supply room.
- Write complaint letter to supplier.
- Compliment Gregg (new employee) on his progress toward his personal productivity potential.
- Get monthly report on quality control to boss.
- Counsel Mary on absenteeism.
- Handle late delivery complaint from key customer.
- Have slow leak in front tire checked.
- Meet with computer software consultant at 10:30 A.M.

DEPARTMENT SUCCESS

Department success is a combination of many factors and personal characteristics, but *being an organized person* is certainly one of them. It is especially true of supervisors because only those who can organize a small department can organize a larger operation. The sooner you demonstrate to your superiors that you have the ability to organize yourself and your department, the sooner you will start your climb up the organizational ladder.

As a way to review, let's now apply the formula to a single case involving JoAnn, a young bank manager. She has been a manager for only a short time and has been charged with the responsibility of opening up a branch in an enclosed shopping center. How might the formula apply to her?

Management objectives (MO). JoAnn works for a statewide banking operation that has four basic goals at this point: (1) to trim overhead expenses; (2) to maintain profits; (3) to improve the image of the bank through a higher quality of service; (4) to improve the cultural mix of employees and bring more women into top management. JoAnn feels strongly that her small branch (only nine employees) can contribute to these companywide objectives.

Departmental plans (DP). A few weeks before she opened her branch, JoAnn was required to submit a plan for the first six months of operation. It was based to some extent on what other new branches of the same size and in similar situations had experienced. It included the following: (1) the date when she anticipated that the operation would become profitable; (2) deposit and loan figures she hoped to achieve, stated monthly; and (3) a customer relations plan that she hoped would satisfy all clients, especially those business organizations in the shopping center that would depend heavily upon her bank.

Small plans (SP). JoAnn has her own system when it comes to small-action plans or goals. Each weekend (usually at home) she develops a few weekly goals. She writes them in her appointment notebook. They include goals such as (1) special public relations efforts through calling on a few key clients, (2) getting reports to the head office in better shape and before deadlines, (3) planning a short staff meeting, and (4) performing a training job that needs to be done. But JoAnn does not let it go at that; she also uses a daily goal system. Every morning when she arrives and opens the bank (she tries to beat everyone else by twenty minutes), she sits down and writes on her desk calendar the smaller things she wants to accomplish before she goes home. Often there are deadlines or time orders for these priorities. Some of these goals she has thought about enroute to work, so it takes only a few minutes to write them down. She may add one or two during the day, but she makes an effort to check them off as she goes. Again, this activity is a private matter. On days when she completes all her small goals, she has a great sense of satisfaction. Sometimes, of course, she must postpone a few goals until the next day because a hectic pace prevented her from attending to them.

Implementation of the formula, simple as it may be, can convert a disorganized, unsuccessful supervisor into an organized, successful one. If JoAnn desires to move into a higher position at a later date, she is smart to adapt the formula to her own style.

Here are some final tips that will help you put it into operation:

Keep your departmental plans simple. A departmental plan is simply a proposed blueprint, or map, for the future. An ultrasophisticated plan may look pretty, but it may not be workable. Keep it simple and attainable.

Organize yourself on a daily basis. Most supervisors need a simple procedure to follow each day in order to accomplish first things first and follow through on other activities. The daily checklist is a worthwhile tool.

Achieve results through people. Your departmental plan and your daily checklist are useless unless you put them into action through people. You must develop your human relations skills to make your plan work.

Be a do-it-yourself goal setter. Create a sense of urgency. Assert yourself by creating objectives for your unit. Do not wait for your superior to encourage you. Communicate that you are already an organized person with an upper management future.

SUPERVISORS AND COMPUTERS

Some years ago supervisors could "get by" without using computers by claiming that they could do what needed to be done by themselves or they would exclaim, "Wait until the bugs are worked out of them and then I will get involved." Those days are gone forever! Today the front-line supervisor needs to be computer literate in almost all supervisory roles. Would-be supervisors who fail to learn computer systems or take advantage of management information systems (MIS) while still on campus may find themselves on the outside looking in; those who are *already* supervisors may find themselves back in nonsupervisory positions.

Why the emphasis on computer savvy?

Supervisors must rely on instant information to make decisions. Sophisticated MIS changes occur regularly. The quantity and quality of data, as well as the speed at which it can be obtained, must be used to advance productivity. In short, supervisors must utilize computers to stay in the information and communications "game."

Computerized information systems are reshaping many organizations. Traditional departmental boundaries are giving way to information networks available to all; even more important, the computer facilitates decentralization in organizations with little or no loss of control. The pace of business leaves no room for debate. The supervisor who does not play the "computer" game with enthusiasm is heavily handicapped and will eventually lose out to those who do. Fortunately, most future supervisors are already computer literate. Later, as they move into higher management, they are likely to find themselves traveling on an airplane using a laptop computer with access to messages and information anytime, anywhere—an indispensable part of their effectiveness.

SOFTWARE PACKAGES TO HELP SUPERVISORS

To illustrate how the supervisor of the future can make maximum use of the computer, all we need do is review the basic software packages currently available.

Word Processing: Word processing allows a busy supervisor to be his or her own secretary. For example, a bulletin may need to be written (with graphics), edited, and posted in a hurry. No problem with a word processor.

Spreadsheets: This software allows the supervisor to turn the computer's memory into a large worksheet in which data formulas can be tested. For example, a supervisor might want to discover what hiring a new employee might do to profitability. A few moments on the computer and the answer is on the screen.

Database Management: These programs make it possible to obtain and review information from a larger base to make comparisons.

Graphics: This capability allows a supervisor to display information in the form of charts or graphs that can be used in short departmental meetings and other forms of communication.

Networking: Programs that interface permit the transfer of data to and from other supervisors and managers. The impact of networking on interorganizational communications is already being felt.

KNOWING ABOUT PERSONAL PERFORMANCE CONTRACTS

Your superior may wish to work out a personal performance contract (PPC) with you, or you may wish to work out one for yourself and submit it to your superior as a surprise. A PPC establishes future goals for which an individual becomes accountable.

In simple terms, a contract is a written agreement between an employee and his or her manager that forecasts accomplishments *to be achieved* within a specific time period. Where possible, benefits should be tied to accomplishments.

Here are the normal steps taken in the development of a PPC:

1. Write out the specific needs or goals to be accomplished.

2. List the top three objectives that become the essence of the contract.

3. Gain the approval of your superior.

4. Develop an action plan so that both parties will know what the employee will be doing over a given time frame.

5. Emphasize the self-development aspects of any contract.

6. Conduct reviews to ensure steady progress.

7. Remember that any contract is a two-way street. Whether the employee reaches her or his goals may depend upon your contribution to the contract.

The full significance of the formula and the whole idea of planning may become more meaningful to you after you read the next two chapters, which are designed to help you put your plans into operation.

DISCUSSION QUESTIONS

1. Do you agree that when supervisors prepare their own written plans (with little or no pressure from management), they are more likely to translate the plan into motivating goals?

2. In what ways will an organized plan affect the productivity of your employees?

3. How might you involve your employees in the planning and organization of a department plan? What affect does participation in planning have on motivation?

4. Could a supervisor "overplan"? That is, be too concerned about what is to be done when, by whom, and completed on a certain date? What affect could overplanning have on employees' productivity? Why?

Case Study

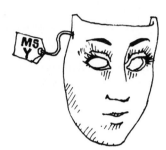

Planning[1]

Mr. Big is a strong, almost obsessed proponent of personal planning and organization. He uses an elaborate system of daily, weekly, and long-term goals for himself. He uses a personal computer at home for both personal and business purposes. He believes that organization is the best form of personal discipline and that goal setting is the most motivating thing a person can do. Each night, before he leaves work, he writes all of his goals for the following day on a desk pad. He spends some time each weekend at home setting goals. He always submits a complex plan to his superiors, and always on time. He gets satisfaction from checking off a written goal when it has been accomplished.

Ms. Y is also a strong believer in goal setting and good organization, but her approach is flexible and unstructured. She does not follow any specific formula, and she never writes anything down. Rather, she keeps a changing master plan in her mind. She constantly revises it when driving on the freeway or while relaxing at home. She claims that it takes too much time to prepare a written plan, that upper management ignores most of the plans submitted, and that changes make them obsolete almost immediately. She also believes that too much structure keeps one from being creative and flexible.

Do you support Mr. Big or Ms. Y? Defend your position. Would you recommend a compromise?

---

[1]Turn to page 266 to compare your thoughts with those of the author.

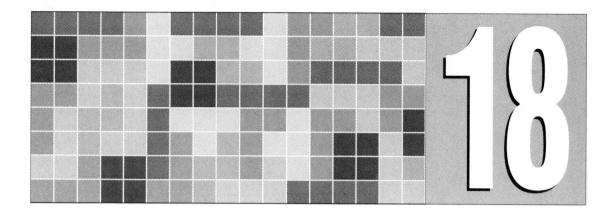

Setting Priorities

After you have finished reading this chapter, you should be able to accomplish one of the following: (1) noticeably improve your priority alignment as a supervisor, or (2) noticeably improve your educational and personal daily priority alignments as a nonsupervisor.

Priorities are a vital part of any plan. In one respect, they *are* the plan. They indicate what you feel is most important and what can be temporarily ignored. Obviously, people who are good at setting up priorities accomplish their plans or goals more easily and efficiently than those who are not.

In putting a plan into operation, you need to concentrate on doing the most urgent tasks first. Just because a particular task is assigned to you first does not mean it should be handled ahead of other things; just because you didn't have time to do something yesterday does not mean it should have top priority today.

GOALS, OBJECTIVES, AND PLANS

A wise person once said, "A goal is a dream with a deadline." So true! Setting a goal is the first step in achieving the goal. To illustrate, let us say that you are at point A. Point A is the actual state of affairs where you are at present. Let us say that you decide point A is no longer satisfactory and you wish to make changes. Think of the changes as a journey from point A to point B. Point B is the desired state of affairs, how you want things to be. Point B becomes your "Goal." The

actions you take to move to point B become your "Objectives." Getting to a goal may take many objectives. Those things that impede your progress to the goal are called "Obstacles."

Reaching goals often involves overcoming tough obstacles. It certainly includes planning. Planning is essential to reaching almost every goal. Few people would go on a vacation without planning it in advance. Decisions about where to go, how to get there, how long to stay, how much money to take, and what clothing to pack are but a few of the important objectives to plan before going. Planning is especially important if you take someone with you. Before leaving they may want all the information or more. Taking that first step on a 1,000-mile journey is an objective; so is taking the last step. The better the planning, the more likely the goal will be achieved.

As a supervisor you may need to make changes to point A, the actual state. If the changes you make are likely to affect the work or routine of your employees you should involve them in the planning stage of the change, not just in the implementation stage. Often employees resist change because they were not involved in the planning. If you desire to move your employees to point B, to the desired state, you will need their motivation and cooperation to move, to change. An effective way to encourage this motivation is through involvement.

Setting goals can lead to the following benefits:

- *Achieving more:* You become more organized in your work. By prioritizing your activities, you can give more attention to getting the important things done first. You have more energy to devote to your work because your efforts are focused. Goal setting is synonymous with change. One sets a goal because the current state of affairs needs to change. If current productivity levels need to improve, specific productivity goals need to be set. The goal becomes the target for all activity.

- *Improving self-confidence:* Reaching goals builds self-confidence. Self-confidence promotes growth and personal development. As one achieves goals, one also becomes less fearful of risk taking. Resistance to change may be a by-product of fear. Setting goals and formulating a plan help to overcome fears. The confidence your employees have in you as their leader will improve also as your goals become reality, especially when they benefit directly from the goal.

- *Communicating more clearly:* An effective goal is precise, has set priorities, and is documented. It communicates to everyone where they are headed.

- *Meeting deadlines:* Deadlines or due dates cause things to happen; they are control measures. Procrastination may result from unspecified due dates rather than lack of motivation on the part of those the changes affect. Target dates for things help to move activity toward goal accomplishment.

THE ABC METHOD OF SORTING THINGS OUT

Some managers use a simple ABC system to help them prioritize tasks. Priority A includes "must-do" items that are critical. Priority B is "should do" items but without critical deadlines involved. Priority C constitutes "fun to do" or "when I have time" tasks that can usually be saved for slack periods.

A supervisor's priority list should be made up and constantly revised according to sound principles and sound thinking. Setting priorities is a decision-making process whereby you rank order the tasks that need to be done by you and the people who work for you—first, second, third, and so on down the line. Following such an order in taking care of tasks and problems will help you reach your goals. It is not as easy as it sounds, however. Listed here are eight questions to ask yourself when setting priorities.

- If I deal with this problem first, will it automatically solve others later?

- If I deal with this problem first, will it delay the solution of another that will eventually cause severe damage to productivity or my career?

- If I delay action on this problem, will it solve itself?

- What can I delegate on my list so that I can get to more serious problems sooner?

- Will taking care of this small problem first free my mind to take care of my number one problem later?

- What tasks must I complete quickly so that I will not hold up the schedule of other people or other departments?

- Can I group a few things together and save time by solving them all at once?

- Is the time psychologically right to take a problem up with my boss, or should I wait for a more appropriate time?

You can see that setting priorities is a complex, demanding process that you can never perfect. Yet the more effective you become at it, the more success you can anticipate. Many managers have learned that keeping a written list of priorities is best for them; others prefer to carry a list around in their minds, a list that constantly changes as changes occur in the work environment.

CRITERIA FOR SETTING PRIORITIES

Experts describe three basic yardsticks to follow in setting priorities. First is *judgment.* You are the best judge, so prioritizing is a do-it-yourself undertaking. Second is *relativity.* Relativity can best be determined by asking the question "What is the best use of my time right now?" Third is *timing.* Deadlines often dictate priorities, but starting times need to be made in advance, and these decisions involve the priority process.

ADVANTAGES OF A WRITTEN LIST

You may have the aptitude to keep a running priority list in your mind, but most beginning supervisors find it advantageous to write out a list on a desk pad for the following reasons:

1. Writing the list is a form of self-discipline. When you know what needs to be done next, you are better organized and less likely to waste time.

2. The list frequently eliminates forgetting, which can get one into trouble with superiors. Some supervisors simply prefer to trust visible lists instead of their memories.

3. Completing a list and checking off items is satisfying and motivating. A priority list is, in effect, a personal reward system.

Return to the Six-Month Model on page 184 and prioritize the activities. List them from highest priority (A) to lowest priority (C). By prioritizing you will readily recognize how it affects the completion of objectives.

KEEPING PRIORITY LISTS FLEXIBLE

The first thing you learn about setting priorities is that the order may not last long. All it takes is a call from your manager, an emergency situation, an unexpected human relations problem, or a mechanical breakdown to force you to make up a new list. A priority list is not a static thing and may need revision many times a day.

In fact, many supervisors automatically reevaluate their priorities every time they move from one completed task to another. Then, you may ask, why make a list in the first place? The primary reason is to keep all responsibilities, tasks, and problems in view. A priority list should include *all* tasks that need to be done to reach your goals as soon as possible. Obviously, a cardinal mistake would be to leave something off the list that should be on it. But even if your list is complete, you can still make mistakes by putting one task or problem ahead of another. For example, if you spend your time on what should be a lower-priority matter, you are neglecting something more crucial, resulting in more harm than benefit. To illustrate the importance of this concept, look at the following examples:

Sid was a department manager for a major retail chain. Last week it was announced that his store would have its annual inspection by a team of top officials. Sid wanted a good report so badly that he gave top priority to cleaning up and rearranging the department, and everything else was neglected. Predictably, Sid and the department received a 100 percent rating. But what happened to the other priorities? For one thing, Sid neglected to turn in a non-computerized merchandise reorder list on time and the department was out of stock for two weeks. Sid—and his company—paid a high price for a poor priority decision.

Gayle was so fed up with the poorly organized files in her department that she finally decided to reorganize them herself, making it her top priority. Once she got into the task, she discovered that things were worse and took much longer than she anticipated. As a result, she neglected other important matters, including annual reviews of the six people in her department. Her superior was upset about it. Later, as Gayle thought it over, she realized that if she had taken care of the reviews first, she could have used them to motivate her employees to clean up the files themselves. She permitted her frustration to overemphasize one problem at the expense of another that should have been first priority.

Duke was chief of a repair crew that had been working long hours due to heavy storm conditions. No sooner did they make one repair than they were sent to do another. Each day Duke was supposed to turn in written reports on finished projects, but last Tuesday he wasn't organized, failed to set any priorities, and forgot to turn in the report. As a result, another repair crew was sent 100 miles away to do a job that Duke's crew had already completed. It was an embarrassing situation.

EFFECTIVE PRIORITY SETTING

How can you set priorities that will make it easier for you to reach your goals and keep you out of trouble? Here are some suggestions.

Give priority to any problem that is rendering you ineffective as a supervisor. Sometimes an upsetting human relations problem might be bothering you, such as a conflict with one of your employees or a serious communications conflict with your superior. Such situations can disturb you emotionally and make you ineffective, or at least not up to standard in the rest of your work.

Do not focus only on your top-priority task. Frequently supervisors become so involved in reaching one goal that they neglect others, resulting in more harm in the long run. Keep all your priorities in mind and balance them to prevent shortsightedness.

Sometimes it is good to delay a problem or task, giving it a lower priority. Some problems become so complicated that an immediate solution is impossible. More time is needed to evaluate the facts and measure the total impact. In such instances, you might wish to drop the problem to the bottom of your list, where you can watch it but not forget it.

Sometimes you can group goals into a meaningful sequence. Many supervisors are good at putting their daily goals into a priority pattern that saves time and effort. Into this category fall such things as making one trip accomplish three goals or arranging tasks in sequence so that they are easier to accomplish.

If something has been on your list for a long time, either do it or forget it. An item that keeps showing up on a priority list soon becomes an irritant. Do not give it that power.

Do not push what should be a high-priority item to the bottom of your list because of fear. Some managers keep what should be top-priority items undercover because they are afraid to face them. This kind of denial is a serious mistake because time solves very few problems.

Oscillating back and forth from one priority to another is unwise. Once you put a task near the top of your list, try to complete it within a reasonable period of time. If you start something and then keep switching to another priority, you will lose all motivation to complete the project.

HOW TO GET STARTED

If setting up a priority list is a new experience for you, the following tips will help you get started. Later, after you have had additional experience, you can adapt the process to your own style. If you are not currently a supervisor, you may wish to set up a personal priority list.

1. Select the task or project that will, in your opinion, advance the productivity of your department the most, and put it at the top of your list. Leave it there until it is completed or a more important task surfaces.

2. List two additional tasks or projects that are less important but should still be numbers 2 and 3 on your pad. Frequently these tasks present less time pressure.

3. List, in succession, any tasks (reports, appointments, telephone calls, counseling) that either must or should be accomplished before you leave work.

4. Select and list a "fun" project—something you can look forward to doing as an end-of-day personal reward—near or at the bottom of your list.

5. Try to restrict the number of tasks on your list to about seven. Too many priority projects can lead to confusion and demotivation. Even though it may be your goal to accomplish as much as possible in a single day, some tasks will wait until tomorrow. Those who overschedule themselves take the risk of turning out poor-quality work with higher levels of frustration.

DAILY PRIORITIZED MODEL

1. Meet with computer software consultant at 10:30 A.M.

2. Handle late delivery complaint from key customer.

3. Get monthly quality-control report to boss on time.

4. Write complaint letter to supplier.

5. Clean and reorganize supply room.

6. Counsel Mary on absenteeism.

7. Compliment Gregg on his progress in reaching the personal productivity potential.

Check off the items on your priority list and prepare a new one at the end of the day. You will transfer some unfinished tasks to the new list, realign them, and add new ones. This process accomplishes two psychological goals. First, it helps you leave your responsibilities at work so you will be free to enjoy your leisure time. Second, arriving at work the following day with a list prepared saves time and can be self-motivating.

Setting priorities for personal tasks off the job can be as important as those at work. If you use what you have learned in this chapter in both environments, you will automatically do a better job of balancing home and career.

DISCUSSION QUESTIONS

1. Do you agree with the belief that those who do not keep a written priority list needlessly burden their minds?

2. What advantages might come from keeping a priority list on a computer instead of a personal notebook?

3. What is the relationship between setting long-term goals and setting daily priorities? How does priority setting fit into the formula presented in Chapter 17?

Mini-Game

Do not turn this page until told to do so.

Priorities

Objective

To provide simulated experience in setting priorities under pressure.

Problem

You (Supervisor Joe) left Monday morning for a one-day company-sponsored training program in supervisory leadership. Your department was turned over to Mrs. R, but she became ill and went home. You were called to return on an emergency basis and arrived five minutes ago. The time is 1:00 P.M. Monday. As you walk into your workstation, you face ten critical problems.

Procedure

These problems are listed on page 199. Read, evaluate, and assign a priority number to each problem. In other words, decide which problem you would handle first, second, third, and so forth. You have five minutes to prioritize the tasks.

Turn the page and read all ten problems. You are then ready to assign the priority numbers in the appropriate squares in the left-hand column. While participants are making their priority choices, the instructor or trainer should list the choices in abbreviated form on a blackboard so that the results can be compared. When the time is up, the instructor should invite one individual at a time to put her or his priority list on the board and explain it in front of the group.

Players

Everyone plays the role of Supervisor Joe.

PRIORITY LIST

❏ A formal grievance from Mrs. R is on your desk. To read and digest it would take fifteen minutes.

❏ Mr. Big has left word that he wants to see you in his office immediately upon your return. Anticipated time: sixty minutes.

❏ You have some very important-looking unopened mail (both company and personal) on your desk. Time: ten minutes.

❏ Your telephone is ringing.

❏ A piece of equipment has broken down, halting all production in your department. You are the only one who can fix it. Anticipated time: thirty minutes.

❏ Someone is seated outside your office waiting to see you. Time: ten minutes.

❏ You have an urgent electronic mail notice to call a Los Angeles operator. Both your mother and the company headquarters are located in Los Angeles. Time: ten minutes.

❏ Mr. X has sent word that he wants to see you and has asked that you return his call as soon as possible. Time: ten minutes.

❏ Mrs. Q is in the women's lounge and claims to be sick. She wants your permission to go home. It would take about five minutes to get the facts and make a decision.

❏ In order to get to your office by 1:00 you had to miss lunch. You are very hungry, but you figure it will take thirty minutes to get something substantial to eat.

Postgame Discussion

Discussion should center on the differences between the priority patterns put on the blackboard. Why might one be better than another? Should the broken equipment have received priority on all lists? Did anyone save time by grouping? Are some people intimidated by a telephone or their boss?

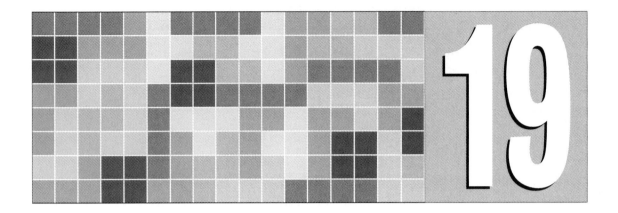

Managing Your Time

After you have finished reading this chapter, you should be able to complete the exercises and integrate the changes indicated into your behavior patterns to help you achieve a noticeable improvement in the management of your time.

If you establish sound goals for your department and yourself and learn to set priorities on a daily basis, will you automatically become more effective at managing your time? Not necessarily. You still need to deal with the basic problem of time allocation itself.

Why should you make a special effort to manage your time?

You will get employees off to a better start. Recent discussions with successful managers indicate that those who arrive at work twenty to thirty minutes ahead of their staff accomplish the following:

1. Improve productivity attitudes when they greet staff arrivals with an upbeat message or compliment to start the day.

2. Do a better job of organizing their day.

3. Set a better example for their own employees.

You will be less frustrated. A good manager senses and handles problems before they get out of hand. When you learn to manage your time well, you can prevent fires rather than spending more time putting them out. Because you are on top of your job—not always catching up—productivity is more even, fewer emergencies and unpleasant surprises emerge, and you have fewer problems to handle.

In short, you need to manage time well so that you can create the extra time you need to be a manager.

You will have the time you need to prepare for the future. Until you learn to organize and manage your time well enough to take on additional responsibilities, you are not promotable. You cannot prepare for the next position if you are bogged down in your present job. You cannot do a good job of personal career development if you habitually operate on a crisis basis. You must *make* more time now through better time management to prepare for a bigger role in the future.

The better you manage your work, the more family and leisure time you will have and the better you will manage your lifestyle.

Despite his young age and modest formal education, Frank is a successful, highly respected executive in a demanding field. He has time to play racketball each day, never neglects his family, devotes time to his church, takes care of personal business matters, and still has time left over for social and personal leisure activities. How does he do it? *Frank manages his time.* If you could meet with him and you asked the right question, he might supply the following answers.

Each day we are given 24 hours. Each week contains 168 hours. No more no less. We all have the same amount of time. We may know people who get a lot more done in those hours than we do. We may wish to better manage our time. Of course we really don't have the entire 168 hours to manage. We need to sleep for instance. If we sleep eight hours a day, that amounts to 56 hours per week. Subtracting out the 56 hours from the 168 hours in a week leaves us with only 102 hours to manage. This number is further reduced if we subtract out the time it takes to do things that can not be avoided or done while working. For instance, your personal hygiene takes time, as do eating and traveling to work. These types of activities require our undivided attention to complete. Sure, a person may use a cell phone while commuting to work to increase personal productivity but that person is four times more likely to have an accident than the driver who gives full attention to driving.

HOW TO MANAGE YOUR TIME

Change your attitude toward time. "Learn to value your on-the-job time more fully. For a long time I didn't worry how long it took me to do things, but then I suddenly realized I was spending more hours than necessary on certain assignments. As a matter of fact, I was spending more time than was necessary on the job itself because it was beginning to encroach on my leisure time and influence my lifestyle. I soon realized that time was one thing I couldn't stretch. I was expected to complete my work in eight hours. If I didn't, it was my fault, not the job's or the company's. The only alternative to better time management was to dip into my personal time. It was then that I decided that time *could* be managed. Know what I discovered? If you learn to manage your working hours, you seem to enjoy your nonworking hours more."

Delegate more. "The best way to save your own time is to let somebody else do the task. Many managers could save far more time than they think if they delegated more effectively. Nothing is more revealing than to see a manager who is overworked while his people are underworked. Yet it happens frequently."

Look for and take shortcuts. "There is usually more than one way to complete a task. Try to find the best way and the one that takes the least amount of time. Could you get people to come to see you instead of taking the extra time to go to see them? Would a written note to a superior in advance of a meeting help you accomplish more in less time when you arrive? Could you set up a luncheon meeting to accomplish a business goal and still enjoy it? Could you save time by discussing the problem with an expert instead of struggling with it too long yourself? You will manage your time better if you use a little more of it to figure out the fastest route to get where you are going."

Group tasks together. "If you watch a supervisor who has learned to manage time well, you will discover that little jobs and tasks are grouped together so that they can be accomplished at the same time. A trip or meeting might be delayed until it can accomplish more than one thing; a trip to the executive offices in the same building can be planned so that the mail can be picked up, a report dropped off, and an executive seen all in one trip instead of three; five or six people can be brought together to save time on communication; a list can be made in advance so that a counseling session will cover everything and make a follow-up unnecessary. Sometimes a manager has developed the skill to do more than one thing at the same time without offending others. When stalled on the telephone, the supervisor might read some official publications; a business matter might be introduced while walking to another meeting; when a dull staff meeting is tied up on a problem that does not involve the supervisor, he or she might plan a priority list for the next day."

Cut down on interruptions. To manage your time effectively, it is often necessary to keep others from using up time that is critical to your performance. The following list offers three ways to manage interruptions.

KEEP OTHERS FROM USING UP YOUR TIME

1. *Respect other people's time.* When you do, you send an unspoken message that you prefer not to interrupt others and would appreciate the same treatment in return.

2. *Indicate availability.* Let people know when interruptions are okay. Schedule blocks of time when you are free for visits.

3. *Decline to be interrupted.* When someone asks "Have you got a minute?" say "Not at this time because I'm in a deadline situation. I'll get back to you when time permits." If you do it in a pleasant voice, no one should be offended. Be sure to get back to them as you said you would.

MAKE MEETINGS MORE EFFICIENT

Most supervisors find that it is important to have short staff meetings on a regular basis. Such meetings provide an excellent opportunity to introduce changes, solicit input, explain, and ask questions. Staff meetings can dissipate tensions, improve relationships, communicate an important message quickly, and result in increased productivity. But if not conducted properly, staff meetings can waste time and thus do more harm than good. Here are some simple tips to organize your meeting to reduce wasted time and increase the chances for a productive meeting:

1. Do not call a staff meeting unless it is necessary.

2. Have a specific goal or purpose to accomplish, and announce it before you begin the meeting. Attendees need to know how to participate and arrive prepared.

3. Keep the meeting as short as possible.

4. Use care in selecting the location of the meeting to avoid distractions and interruptions.

5. If a group decision is involved, get as much participation as possible.

6. Seek alternatives to any decision proposed so that the final decision is the best one.

7. Keep the meeting upbeat and energetic.

8. Enjoy a little laughter.

9. Use the meeting to demonstrate your leadership.

10. Conduct a personal evaluation so that you can do even better the next time.

ELIMINATE TIME WASTERS

Eliminate the little time wasters. "Some manufacturing plants do microtime and motion studies on their production employees. Employees are filmed doing their work, and then they carefully view their motions in an attempt to eliminate unnecessary activities. Perhaps this technique would be good to use with supervisors. A film would probably show you many ways to save time through elimination of needless motions or activities."

Do not waste time looking for things that you use often. Put things back in their proper places. Organize your office so you can find what you need, whether a file or a piece of equipment. Searching for a misplaced item eats up time.

After sorting your mail, handle a piece of paper only once. It sounds easy, but it is often difficult. If a report, for example, comes across your desk, do it. Don't sort it and place it back on your pile to only resort later. If it is a lengthy report or assignment, see if all or part of it can be delegated. Much correspondence can be completed in a few minutes once you sort it. (More on this in the next chapter.)

If you wish to benefit from Frank's suggestions, take a close look at your present habits through the "Supervisor's Time-Waster Assessment Scale" that follows. As you complete it, keep in mind that in controlling your time more effectively, you do not want to squeeze all the joy out of your job. Your goal is to use your time wisely so that you will enjoy your job more, not less.

SUPERVISOR'S TIME-WASTER ASSESSMENT SCALE		
Circle the number that best indicates where you lie between the two extremes. Total your score at the end of the exercise.		
When I arrive at work in the morning, I get started immediately.	5 4 3 2 1	It takes me at least 30 minutes to get started in the morning.
I do not procrastinate; my priority list prevents delay.	5 4 3 2 1	I procrastinate because I never know what to do next.
I keep personal activities to an absolute minimum.	5 4 3 2 1	I let personal activities eat away my on-the-job time.
My schedule is rigid; I never overextend a coffee or lunch break.	5 4 3 2 1	Three-hour non-business lunches and 40-minute coffee breaks are common with me.

I'm an extremely fast reader and I waste no time on trash mail.	5	4	3	2	1	I need a reading-improvement course; I waste too much time reading.
My telephone conversations are to the point and deal only with business matters.	5	4	3	2	1	I socialize on the telephone—my number one time waster.
I delegate as many tasks as possible.	5	4	3	2	1	Failure to delegate is a serious problem with me.
I refuse to let others waste my time in pointless conversations.	5	4	3	2	1	When people use up my time just chatting, I can't seem to break away.
I don't waste a single minute oversupervising.	5	4	3	2	1	Oversupervising is killing my time-management plan.
I schedule my appointments so that I waste no time conversations.	5	4	3	2	1	I often keep either myself or others waiting.
I stay motivated until I go home.	5	4	3	2	1	"Afternoon drag" slows me down to a crawl.
My objectives are clear; I know where I am going.	5	4	3	2	1	My objectives are fuzzy; I often go in the wrong direction.
I socialize on the job only after the day's objectives have been reached.	5	4	3	2	1	I look for opportunities to socialize to escape from work.
I have no pet projects; I stick to my priority list.	5	4	3	2	1	I can't stay away from some time-wasting pet projects.
I counsel my employees but never become overinvolved.	5	4	3	2	1	Every time I counsel an employee, I become overinvolved.
I avoid mistakes by working steadily at an even tempo.	5	4	3	2	1	I make foolish mistakes by hurrying to catch up.
My priority list and general attitude eliminate crisis management.	5	4	3	2	1	I am always putting out fires and operating in a crisis.
I maintain a highly efficient personal filing system.	5	4	3	2	1	My personal filing system is a time-wasting mess.

| I ask for help with tough problems that consume time. | 5   4   3   2   1 | I would rather solve my own problem no matter how long it takes. |
| I make maximum use of time-saving equipment such as computers and copying conversations. | 5   4   3   2   1 | Doing things the old-fashioned way gives me more personal satisfaction. |

Total Points [   ]

If you scored more than 90, you are a highly organized supervisor and you waste almost no time. If you scored between 70 and 90, you need a slight improvement. If, however, you scored less than 70, you would probably enjoy work more and improve your future by eliminating some needless, perhaps frustrating, time wasters. If you scored a 3 or lower on any one area, you should look for ways to improve your time management skills in that area.

INVENTORY ANALYSIS CHART

Now that you have completed the "Supervisor's Time-Waster Assessment Scale," you may wish to log your time among various activities for a typical day. This approach (using the "Eight-Hour Day Inventory Analysis Chart" on the following this page) will help you compare the actual time you spend with the time you *should* spend.

Here are Frank's final comments: "Look, work is work. There is no way to make pure fun out of it. Certainly I want to enjoy my work as much as anyone, but I don't want it to drag on. I like to dispose of my work responsibilities with pride, vigor, and efficiency. My approach is to be professional, so when I get to work, I assume a 'let's get it done' attitude. I use my time in an orderly manner, and my employees pick up the tempo. Then sometimes we take a real break and relax. I learned a long time ago that the only way to enjoy a little fun time on the job is to control your time so well that there is some to spare. Then if feels good. There is no other answer. You have time working for you, not against you."

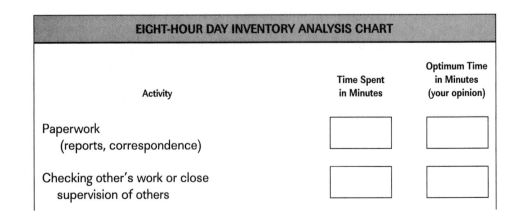

EIGHT-HOUR DAY INVENTORY ANALYSIS CHART		
Activity	**Time Spent in Minutes**	**Optimum Time in Minutes (your opinion)**
Paperwork (reports, correspondence)		
Checking other's work or close supervision of others		

Communication (counseling)

Telephone calls

Command meetings
    (imposed by management)

Problem solving (putting out fires)

Planning

Other_____

Other_____

Other_____

Total

1. Add both columns.
2. Subtract "Time Spent" from "Optimum Time."
The difference is time wasted.

DISCUSSION QUESTIONS

1. Do you agree or disagree with the concept that you have to invest a little time to save a lot of time? Explain.

2. What signals might a supervisor receive when his or her time is managed poorly? What signals might be received when activities are overorganized?

3. Do you support the idea of taking a daily time inventory to improve time management? Is logging time for only one day sufficient? Should time be logged during or at the end of the day?

Case Study

Analysis[1]

Supervisor Joe has been working extra hours to catch up on everything he needs to do in his department. No matter how he tries to save time, he never catches up. As a result, Joe has become increasingly irritable, haggard, and ineffective. Unable to solve the problem, Joe makes an appointment with Mr. Big and then makes a big pitch for an assistant to help release the pressure. But Mr. Big replies that better time management would solve Joe's problem. He asks Joe to log how he spent his time yesterday. Joe turns in the following table:

---

[1]Turn to page 266 to compare your thoughts with those of the author.

SAMPLE OF JOE'S TIME INVENTORY FOR ONE DAY			
Activity	**Time**	**Activity**	**Time**
Preparing written request to Mr. Big attempting to justify a 20 percent increase in budget next year.	60 min.	Typed up five extra copies of a productivity report so that all five employees would be informed.	30 min.
Discussing next month's production schedule with Mr. G; will do same with Mrs. R, Mr. K, and Mrs. Q later.	15 min.	Struggled again with a new layout plan that would free about forty square feet for a new piece of equipment on order. Got disgusted and tore up new and previous plans. Impossible.	50 min.
Handling thirteen telephone calls, only three of which were personal.	50 min.	Trip to union hall to talk to our agent about a grievance that had been continuing too long. Meeting took 30 minutes. Transportation time: 20 minutes each way.	70 min.
Worked in stockroom alone doing a reorganizing job. Left note so that Ricardo would understand	50 min.		
Interviewing woman sent by Personnel as a possible replacement for Mrs. Q, who is leaving in two weeks. Decided that individual is not suitable.	50 min.	Waited 20 minutes to see Mr. Big to discuss time-management problem. Conversation lasted 10 minutes.	30 min.
Repairing broken equipment that only I could fix. I asked Mr. K and Mr. G to take an early lunch while I repaired it so that they could continue working when they returned.	60 min.		

Based upon this time inventory, do you agree or disagree with Mr. Big? Support your answer. How might Joe improve his time management?

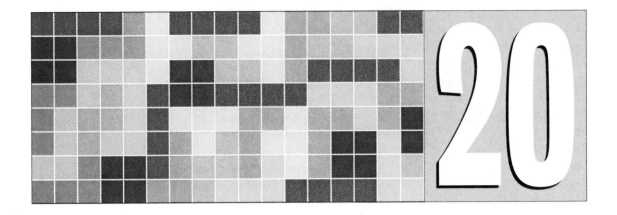

Make Decisive Decisions

After you have finished reading this chapter, you should be able to apply its ideas and improve your decision-making abilities to a noticeable degree.

FOR SALE

SUPERVISOR'S PROBLEM-SOLVING MACHINE

Guarantees Better Decisions with Less Worry

Easy to Use!   Write Scientific Systems for Further Details   No Tricks!

How would you react to the following advertisement if you found it in your favorite newspaper?

You would probably be highly skeptical and quickly pass it off as an unethical come-on or a joke. And you would be right because no such thing as a sure-fire decision-making device could replace the judgment of supervisors. The great majority of decisions you are paid to make as a supervisor must be made in your mind and not by gadgets, gimmicks, or even sophisticated computers. You can, however, do certain things to improve your decisions.

You can learn how to make decisions more systematically and train yourself to think through problems more logically. You can remember to take into consideration all factors that should influence the decision. In other words, you can become methodical. An example of how you can be methodical in dealing with paperwork is to choose quickly one of the following options:

- Act on it now.
- File for future reference.
- Refer it to someone else.
- Trash it.

Do not leave correspondence of any kind in your in-basket. Decide what to do with it the first time you touch it. If the task requires a large time commitment to accomplish, put it in a designated place marked for things to act on at your next opportunity. Making decisions (problem solving) is no job for a scatterbrained amateur, an impulsive individual who overreacts to every problem, or a person who sees only the surface of the problem. It takes emotional stability, a logical mind, and deep thinking to come up with sound answers to tough problems. This point is illustrated by some sample management comments.

"I'd make Helen a supervisor tomorrow if she could only learn to make clear-cut decisions instead of being so wishy-washy about every little problem."

"We finally had to transfer Drew back to his old job. He had great potential as a supervisor, but when it came to making even simple decisions, he fell apart. Fear and frustration took over, and everyone lost confidence in him."

"Gregg keeps getting into hot water because he makes impulsive decisions instead of using his head. His career is grounded until he puts more thought into his decision making."

THREE APPROACHES TO PROBLEM SOLVING

As a supervisor, you will find that each day a constant variety of large and small problems will come to you from all directions. You can use one of the following three approaches in dealing with them:

1. You can stall or delay action through any number of often-used ploys. For example, you can bury the problem in red tape, shuffle it in a circle until it disappears, overconsult with your boss until he tells you to forget it, or simply procrastinate until (you hope) a decision is no longer necessary. Using this wishy-washy approach will doom you to failure. Not only will you lose the respect of your superiors, but you will kill the productivity of your employees. The very nature of your job forces you to become a decision maker, and there is no escape from the responsibility. You will be expected to make good decisions, but good or bad, they must be made. Except in unusual cases, stalling or delaying will only compound the original problem.

2. You can temporarily dispose of your problems by making quick, superficial decisions with little or no thinking and even less logic. If you adopt this approach, you will do the following:
   a. Use your hunches instead of your rational powers.
   b. Refuse to consider side effects.
   c. Give each problem (large or small) the same off-the-cuff treatment.
   d. Violate the concentration techniques you learned in Chapter 16.
      If you take this road, you will create more problems than you solve. You will survive for a while, but in the end you will drown in your own confusion.

3. You can be professional in your approach and learn to solve your many problems through sound decision-making practices. It means following a system, using logical steps, and thinking. It is not easy, but it is the only way you can make decisions that will contribute to greater departmental productivity, that will be enthusiastically accepted by the people who work for you, and that will build a good reputation for you with management.

THREE KINDS OF DECISIONS

Supervisors make three kinds of decisions. The *autocratic decision* is one that you make by yourself. You do not consult anyone, and you accept full responsibility for the consequences of your decision. Your second choice is talking over the problem with another person, perhaps a more experienced superior. The result is called a *consultive decision.* Two heads are frequently better than one when a serious decision must be made. It is foolish to make a poor decision on your own if an expert is available to help you make a better one. The *group decision* is a third possibility. When a problem involves the entire staff, they should participate in the decision, especially if their own decision will satisfy them better and motivate them more. This approach would be the only acceptable process in a true team operation.

For autocratic and consultive decisions you may find that the following "Seven-Step Decision-Making Model" will fit into your personal comfort zone. If so, embrace it and use it whenever appropriate. Its use can measurably improve your decision-making track record.

SEVEN-STEP DECISION-MAKING MODEL

Assume that you have accepted a new position with an organization located several miles away in an unfamiliar urban area. While studying a map at your kitchen table, you decide to experiment with the seven-step method. Here's what might happen.

Steps	Example
1. Define the desired outcome.	You see at least three different routes you might take. You want the best one.
2. Establish decision criteria.	You want the shortest, fastest, safest route, the one that will cause the least wear and tear on your car and use the least gas.
3. Define alternatives.	Mark off what appear to be the three best routes on your map.
4. Get all the facts.	You will measure the time, number of stops, gas usage, traffic density, and other factors on each route. You will drive a different route each day for three successive days.
5. Weigh and compare.	Compare all facts and opinions to decide which route is best under all conditions.
6. Opt for the best alternative.	Once you have *thought it through,* you can make the decision with confidence.
7. Follow-up.	After implementing decision, evaluate its effectiveness against desired outcome.

Often it is best to take a few seconds to decide what is involved in a decision before you start applying any logical procedure. As in taking a trip, you need to stop and figure out how to proceed. (Consider this step the "decision before making the decision.") For example, for many supervisors it is helpful to divide problems into those that are job oriented and those that are people oriented. Once they make this preliminary decision, they can apply the seven-step procedure.

For decisions that directly affect your employees' work or routine it is wise to involve them in decision making, especially when decisions bring change. Any time you need the motivation of your employees to carry out a decision, it is a good idea to involve them; participation is a motivator for many employees.

DECISION-MAKING MODEL

The following Group Decision Making Through Needs Clarification Model is an effective model for group decision making. The supervisor, acting as facilitator, with an appointed recorder from the group, follows the model. The model is ideal for fostering group consensus.

1. *Communicate the situation to the group:* Openly discuss the need for a decision. Decisions are often needed when changes are being considered. It is a good time to differentiate the "Actual State of Affairs" from the "Desired State of Affairs." Maintain an open atmosphere where questions, concerns, and perceptions about the situation can be explored. In this step it is important that everyone understand why a decisioni is being considered.

2. *Brainstorm all possible decisions:* As a group, with the recorder writing on a flip-chart or white board, generate as many ideas as possible. Be creative. Do not evaluate or choose any one decision at this time. Let the ideas flow. The selection process comes next.

3. *Evaluate the list of possible decisions:* Examine the idea list generated and begin to evaluate the pros and cons of each item. Evaluate the alternatives by asking at least three questions. The answers to these questions are the criteria for the selection and become the justification for your choice.

   Question 1: Will the choice improve the situation; will it solve the problem; what is the probability that we will achieve our desired state or goal?

   Question 2: Will the choice meet the needs of those involved in carrying out the decision; will those involved in implementing the decision be motivated to carry it through to completion?

   Question 3: Do we, as a group, have the resources, such as time, money, and expertise, to carry out the decision; how much help will we require from others not in our group?

   Asking these questions for each alternative will eliminate some ideas immediately. Others look good and are put on a short list of possibilities to be evaluated again.

4. *Choose the best alternative:* Do not rush to a decision. It is best to postpone a decision when more discussion is needed. Be sure everyone buys into the decision. It is useful to ask everyone whether they are motivated to carry out the decision. If the answer is no, start over.

5. *Develop an implementation strategy:* The decision of the group must be put into action. Clarify and organize the timed, sequenced series of steps (objectives) needed for implementing the decision. This step is best left for another meet-

ing. Allowing your group time to think about how they will implement the decision will help in the long run, but schedule an implementation meeting soon. Group decision making should be used during the implementation meeting.

6. *Follow up:* Evaluate the effects of the decision. Has the situation changed in the desired way? If so, celebrate. The supervisor must personally thank everyone involved.

Some may think that this level of participation in decision making takes too much time. It does take time, but consider it an investment. People are more motivated to carry out a decision if they have had a part in making it. Overcoming resistance to unilateral decisions takes a great deal more time in the long run. This Group Decision Making Through Needs Clarification Model works in family situations as well as it does at work.

JOB-ORIENTED PROBLEMS

The two basic kinds of job-oriented problems are minor problems that require quick answers but have little permanent influence on department operations, and major problems that have deep and lasting influence. Most of your decision making will deal with minor job problems that you should be able to handle on the spot. Where should this new item be stored? Which report should be completed first? Should I delegate this task or do it myself? Which color would be best? Should I write or telephone my answer?

LOW-CONSEQUENCE WORK-ORIENTED DECISIONS

Most job-oriented decisions the front-line supervisor makes are low on the consequence scale. Even a bad decision will have little impact on productivity or the image of the supervisor. Faulty low-consequence decisions are usually easy to correct. Generally speaking, minor problems can be solved immediately and then forgotten. They should be disposed of in an orderly and efficient manner without consuming too much time. The major threat with these problems is that they may become psychological hangups for the supervisor when a clear-cut decision is not obvious and, through indecision, the supervisor permits the problem to become a major source of frustration. This kind of distortion is a luxury the supervisor cannot afford. The following half-minute procedure will help you make quick, frustration-free, low-consequence decisions.

1. Take time to restate the problem and review the facts in your mind (about ten seconds).

2. Compare the first answer you think of with at least one other possibility. Weigh one against the other and try to come up with the best choice. If a decision is not obvious, make one anyway (about fifteen seconds).

3. With confidence that you have made the right decision, announce it to those involved and move on to something else (about five seconds).

It is a serious mistake to make a big thing out of a low-consequence decision. You will lose the respect of your supervisors and the confidence of your employees. Recognize a small problem for what it is, give it the treatment recommended here, trust your judgment, and then move on to something more important.

HIGH-CONSEQUENCE WORK-ORIENTED DECISIONS

Major job-oriented problems that will have a permanent influence on the operation of your department, on the other hand, must be given more serious treatment and more time. These problems probably challenge existing policies or procedures or involve changes in technology, layout, design, reporting methods, procedural patterns, control systems, safety rules, or basic production methods. They are major because they touch on something basic in the department and because they probably have complicating side effects. Job-connected problems of this nature and scope deserve careful attention and your best logical thinking. When they occur, lean heavily on the seven-step procedure and these additional suggestions:

- *Avoid the temptation to make a quick decision.* Gather all the available facts even if it means making a major project out of it. Ask yourself these questions: What has been done in the past? Why isn't it working today? Will a new system or approach work better? What is the real source of the problem? What are the other factors? Write down all these facts so that you clearly see the detailed overall picture.

- *If you decide to make an autocratic decision, write down and study each possible solution.* Slowly eliminate those that do not conform to company policy or have side effects that might do more damage than good. Reduce the list to the two or three possibilities that offer the best permanent solution.

- *If a clear choice is not evident, use the consultive-decision approach.* Ask your superior or a key employee to talk over the remaining solutions. Sometimes possibilities need to be talked over so that the person making the decision can compare one solution with another.

- *After some careful weighing, choose the solution you feel is best and take it to your immediate superior for his or her reaction and approval.* Tell why you made the decision and what results you expect. If approved, take the time to communicate the decision to all the people involved.

- *Follow up.* To make sure the decision is properly implemented and that misunderstandings are eliminated you need to check back with those involved.

Major job-connected problems should not be solved in haste or under pressure. When they occur, slow down and follow the logical steps outlined here.

LOW-CONSEQUENCE PEOPLE PROBLEMS

The most important thing you can learn about decision making is that people problems are quite different from job problems and demand special treatment. Job-connected problems deal with tangibles or procedures that influence people;

people-connected problems deal with the people themselves—their disappointments, frustrations, hostilities, and personality conflicts. People problems may stem from job problems but they exist primarily inside the employee. Approaching people problems requires your most sensitive handling. Success with these problems depends both on making a fair decision and on the way you work with the people involved.

People problems fall into two categories: simple employee requests that require only limited decision making, and deep-seated, complicated problems that require considerable time and all the skill you can muster.

Supervisors often receive special requests from employees concerning work schedules, procedures, breaks, and personal matters that are important to the individual but relatively insignificant in the total operation of the department. In most cases, you can listen carefully and give an on-the-spot, yes or no answer within a few seconds without spending a great deal of time and effort. To play it safe, however, ask yourself these three questions before answering such requests:

1. Is there a written policy that governs such requests? If so, it should apply (except in unusual cases) and should be carefully explained to the employee.

2. Will granting the request damage relationships with other employees in your department? If so (except in unusual cases), it should be refused and the reasons made clear to the person making the request.

3. Will granting the request seriously endanger the health and safety of others? If so, it should be refused and the reasons given.

When a special request does not violate any company policy, will not damage the supervisor's relationship with others, and will not endanger the safety of others, it should be granted graciously and quickly.

HIGH-CONSEQUENCE PEOPLE PROBLEMS

Any people problems other than simple requests should be considered potentially high-consequence problems. They fall into two classifications: (1) those pertaining to one individual only—these problems are usually highly personal and psychological and should concern the supervisor only because they influence productivity; (2) those that involve two or more employees—these often involve friction in the relation between two or more departmental employees and usually affect productivity. Supplement your seven-step procedure with the following suggestions:

■ *Listen carefully to all problems or complaints.* If something is important to one of your employees, it is also important to you. Do not ignore or belittle any problem, no matter how trivial it may seem at the beginning.

■ *People problems usually involve two or more people, so always make an effort to gather information from all sides.* Do not take sides while you are gathering the facts.

■ *Weigh all the facts carefully before you make a decision.* Ask yourself these questions: Will the decision be fair to all concerned? Will it violate any company personnel policies? Do any potential serious side effects need consideration? Will the decision violate any human relations principles? Write down two or three possible decisions for careful evaluation before you choose one.

- *Using good counseling techniques, openly communicate to all parties involved your decision and why you made it.* Take time. Encourage a two-way conversation. Listen to any negative reactions, but stand firm on your decision.

- *Follow up by working to restore or rebuild any relationships that may have been temporarily injured because of your decision.*

THE GROUP DECISION

The group-decision approach can accomplish a great deal if the supervisor uses it skillfully. When should it be used? (1) When the decision will have an influence on employees; (2) when the decision requires no urgency; (3) when departmental priorities permit; (4) when you are willing to abide by the decisions the group makes; and (5) when you have created and maintained a team approach. Here is how one successful supervisor puts it:

> "When I left college three years ago, I thought I would be a Theory Y person at least 90 percent of the time. I really believed in it because I was convinced that it would improve morale and achieve great individual productivity. My goal has not been achieved. In fact, I feel good if I am 60 percent Y and 40 percent X. Why? Too often I have deadlines to meet.
> "When I can't spare the time, I make autocratic decisions or consult with a single person. Perhaps when I get into middle management, I will be more successful in meeting this goal."

Leadership and decision making are inseparable. As you start out, do not expect to bat a thousand, but be satisfied with the best average you can achieve, learning as you go. If you make a mistake, do not hesitate to make a second decision to correct it. Nothing will effect more forcefully your upward mobility than your willingness to improve your decision-making style.

Once the decision is ready to be announced, do it in a *decisive* manner. The more confidently you communicate that you have made the *right* decision, the more acceptance it will receive—and the more leadership you will have demonstrated.[1]

DISCUSSION QUESTIONS

1. Why do some beginning supervisors find it so difficult to make even minor low-consequence decisions?

2. Challenge or defend the practice of dividing decisions into two categories: job oriented and people oriented.

3. Do most supervisors involve their employees in the decision-making process as much as they should? If not, why don't they?

---

[1]See Chapter 24 to learn more about the importance of decision making.

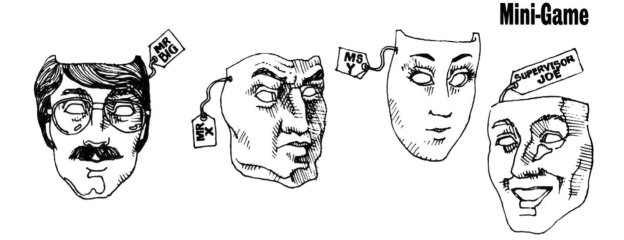

Termination

Objective

To provide a simulated experience in evaluating the causes for and potential dangers in termination.

Problem

Supervisor Joe has made up his mind that he wants to give Mrs. Q the required two-week termination notice. He bases his case on the following: (1) Her productivity dropped about six weeks ago and has never come back up to previous levels. (2) She has been absent twice during this six-week period and late several times. (3) She has, despite suggestions from Supervisor Joe, consistently overextended her coffee breaks. (4) Mrs. R has threatened to quit if Mrs. Q is not transferred out of the department. (5) At 3:30 yesterday afternoon, Mrs. Q walked off the job crying. (6) Under a staff reduction policy, should Mrs. Q be terminated her position might be eliminated.

Mr. Big claims that Supervisor Joe does not have sufficient cause for termination. (1) He has not formally "written up" Mrs. Q twice previously about violations, as required by company policy. (2) Supervisor Joe has not had a heart-to-heart talk with Mrs. Q for two weeks. (3) Although walking off the job is technically a cause for dismissal, Mr. Big feels the case has not been fully investigated. (4) He fears that Mrs. Q might appeal her case to the Civil Rights Commission. (5) If the case is not investigated, Mrs. Q could draw unemployment insurance by contesting the termination procedure, which would cost the company money and deplete the reserve fund at the state headquarters.

Players

All four management roles.

Procedure

Mr. Big and Supervisor Joe argue the case before Mr. X and Ms. Y, who comprise a two-person jury. After each has presented his case, Mr. X and Ms. Y retire from the room to make their decision. While they are out, those left in the class discuss the situation and vote independently for Mr. Big or Supervisor Joe. You win the game if you agree with the jury.

Postgame Discussion

Discussion should center on causes for termination and why business organizations must protect themselves against unfair practices in this area.

Where Do I Go from Here?

"There go my people. I must find out where they are going so I can lead them."

ALEXANDRE LEDRU-ROLLING
1807—1874

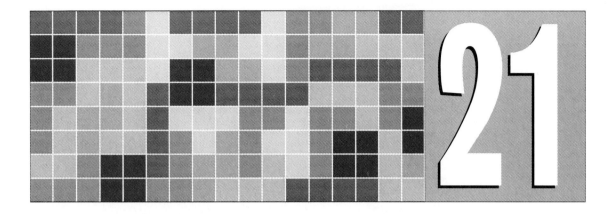

Common Mistakes You Don't Want to Make

After you have finished reading this chapter, you should be able to improve your upward mobility through the elimination of some common mistakes.

"I've been in upper management for twelve years and, in my opinion, the greatest mistake most supervisors make is to back away from and be too soft with the employees in their departments. Sometimes you'd think the supervisor is working for the employee and not the other way around."

"I can't help but think that for many supervisors their biggest mistake is old-fashioned stubbornness. They appear to listen to their employees and superiors, but they go right ahead and do it their own way. They lock themselves in with their closed minds."

"I've been supervising supervisors for more than twenty years with the same company and, in my opinion, their biggest mistake is underestimating the true potential of the people they supervise. They write off people before giving them a chance. This one failure has cost my company millions."

"Most managers multiply their problems because they *think* they communicate with their people when, in fact, they do not. It's their biggest mistake."

If you were to do a survey asking fifty different management people to name the biggest mistake made by first-line supervisors, you could easily receive twenty or

so different answers. But if you examined the essentials of all those responses, they would probably all fit into one of the following categories.

FAILURE TO COMMUNICATE

All work is a process that is accomplished by communicating. Whether they will admit it or not, many supervisors fail to establish and maintain a good communications system within their department and their company. If the people around you are to become sufficiently informed, you must set up a system to ensure that it happens. You will have to weave it into your departmental plan and put it on your priority list. You must *make* time to communicate. If you don't, you'll be faced with a constant flow of human relations problems from your employees because they will feel left out, neglected, unappreciated, and frustrated. Serious misinterpretations will occur between you and others both inside and outside your department. Morale will eventually drop, and so will productivity.

How can you set up a communications system to prevent this deterioration from happening? Here are some suggestions.

Create daily two-way conversations. Consider taking ten, twenty, or thirty minutes each day to talk things over with your employees. If you supervise many people, you might rotate among them so that you will have some personal communication at least every week or so. Keep in mind that it is sometimes more important to listen than to talk.

Set up a bulletin board as a communications headquarters. When the proper physical facilities are available, a bulletin board can be a valuable tool. Let's look at how it is used by one supervisor.

> Linda has trained her nine employees to check the bulletin board the first thing in the morning and two or three times during the day. Sometimes she leaves messages for the whole group and sometimes for individuals. Employees are, of course, encouraged to leave messages for others, including Linda. Here is how she puts it: "My little bulletin board is an integral part of my system. I just don't have time to contact everyone personally all the time, so I write a lot of bulletins and notes. It really works."

An "electronic bulletin board" can be accomplished on a network of computers to replace or supplement the traditional kind.

Hold group meetings. Try to hold short group meetings from time to time for communication purposes. Nothing can substitute for the interplay of group communications if such meetings do not take too long, are not overstructured, and are held when necessary. Group meetings are extremely useful when major changes in procedure are necessary.

Send interoffice communications. Many organizations have a voice mail or electronic mail system to keep upper management, supervisors, and other staff people informed. This written form of communication should be used to (1) keep others informed, (2) initiate requests, and (3) reply to inquiries, whether written or by telephone.

Use other communication techniques. In addition to the frequent use of the telephone, the supervisor can arrange formal two-way meetings in the office, arrange for luncheon communication sessions, and sometimes take advantage of coffee breaks and trips outside the plant or office for communication purposes. Conversations between supervisors of different work units promote teamwork. Look for ways to help peers. Regular informal communication helps you learn about the business and how you can make a greater contribution.

You will, of course, have to develop your own system based upon your particular situation and needs. The most important factor, however, is to maintain the system on a daily basis. It is a difficult responsibility and no one has created a perfect system, but everyone seems to agree that unless you keep people informed, they can and will misinterpret you, resulting in problems for everyone involved. Constant and effective communication with your employees sends the message that you value them as people.

FAILURE TO EXERCISE STRONG LEADERSHIP

A shocking number of both new and old supervisors seem reluctant to exercise the forceful leadership management wants, employees respect, and the job requires.[1] Too many supervisors back away from an aggressive employee or avoid any confrontation with those who work for them.

---

[1]Chapter 24 is devoted to the subject of leadership.

Why? Several reasons seem to explain such behavior. Some supervisors would rather be popular than effective. In other words, they are simply too sensitive to the possibility of receiving a negative reaction from an employee if a firm stand is taken. In other cases, the manager is intimidated by those he or she is supposed to lead. Both responses may stem from a fear of people that needs to be dissipated. Leo is a good example.

> Most of the employees in Leo's department loved him. Some said he was the finest supervisor they had ever known. He was kind, sensitive, and calm in all situations. There was a very harmonious climate inside the department most of the time. It naturally came as a shock to the employees when Leo was given a nonsupervisory job and replaced by another man. Why did management take this step? They removed Leo because he was permitting a few employees to take advantage of him. Rules were being broken, and production was down. Leo had been counseled on the problem, but he couldn't face taking the necessary disciplinary action to correct the situation. As a result, management had no choice but to transfer Leo to a nonsupervisory job.

Some supervisors mistakenly believe that time solves all problems. The people who perpetuate this myth fail to see that one unsolved problem often sets up a chain reaction that creates others. They also fail to recognize that a problem left unsolved can fester and damage a relationship beyond repair. Marge was naive in this respect.

> Marge grew up in a home where problems were never dealt with openly. Communication was restricted to pleasant subjects. As a result, she formed the habit of keeping most of her personal problems inside. The habit had become so much a part of her that when she became a supervisor she followed the same pattern. What happened? She soon had so many unsolved problems that her boss had to come to her rescue.

Solving problems too quickly (without getting the facts) can be a serious mistake, but expecting time to solve them for you is simply going to the opposite extreme.

These reasons, among others, are why many supervisors fail to provide the strong leadership needed. Some people are much too introverted to communicate their feelings to others. Others have more faith in the behavior of their employees than is justified. A few simply refuse to recognize that the supervisor *must* be a leader to survive. The precautionary measures suggested here will help you avoid such traps.

Talk about it when it first affects you. Learn to say what is on your mind when you first have a reaction. At least two good reasons make this step an important one: (1) If you don't discuss something that is troubling you as soon as it begins to affect you, it will bother you until it emerges too harshly. The pressure caused by holding it back may make you hostile, leading to misinterpretation. (2) When your employees are permitted some small infraction a few times, they begin to build a defense against the time when you reprimand them for it. The defense makes them less communicative and sometimes adds an explosive element that would not exist if you had corrected the infraction at the beginning.

Say what is on your mind and say it often. Don't bury your thoughts until they become distorted. Open and frequent communication is an effective way to demonstrate strong leadership.

Tell it the way it is. It is a mistake to cushion your verbal communication in soft words and tones so that what you say is taken too lightly or disregarded. Be firm, be clear, and let people know you mean it. Employees can take more frank talk and constructive criticism than you think. Be specific and focus on the behavior or situation that bothers you. Never insult an employee by calling him a name such as lazy or incompetent.

Let your employees feel that you are leading them. Most employees like the security of strong leadership from their supervisor. Be considerate, sensitive, and fair—but above all, be decisive. If you are, you will dissipate a great deal of apprehension and confusion among your employees.

Seek respect rather than popularity. You are ill advised to run a popularity contest in competition with other supervisors. Be content to build honest working relationships based upon the integrity of doing a good job and not upon personal favors that bring immediate gratification but destroy respect. Recognize the difference and you will be a more successful leader.

As a supervisor, you may need to take a firm position with a problem employee, with a fellow supervisor, or during a management meeting. But *how* firm? How assertive need you become to be effective as a supervisor? What kind of balance between passiveness and counterproductive aggressiveness should you strike? Here are some tips:

- Keep in mind that strong leadership is as important with teams as under the traditional approach.

- Becoming more assertive may be uncomfortable for you at the beginning. If so, it may take time to establish the balance you seek. Be patient with yourself, but don't err on the side of weakness.

- In general, you want to show strength without aggressive behavior that will injure relationships. It means being firm but understanding, taking a position but also being open to compromise, and maintaining respect for others and the position they take.

- To protect the productivity of your department (and the firm's profit), you have the right to speak up and take a stand. Your challenge is to do so and, at the same time, build good human relationships in all directions.

- As you make your moves, assume a "win-win" attitude. Be assertive to the point where you, your colleagues, and your company come out ahead. But no further! Keep in mind that you can show strength in your eyes, posture, and demeanor, as well as your voice. Choose your words carefully.

You know you are showing the right degree of assertiveness when others are equally open, direct, and forceful with you.

MAKING AND BREAKING PROMISES

A promise can be exciting and ego building to make but sometimes a distressing impossibility to keep. A promise kept may bring a great deal of inner satisfaction, but a promise broken can be embarrassing and humiliating beyond expectation. Unnecessary promises are too easy to make. The supervisor with a great desire to build good relationships and to increase productivity is prone to make unnecessary promises.

> John, a successful supervisor, was so impressed with one of his new employees during the first-month review that he promised the new employee all his support when the time came to appoint a new assistant. Two weeks later (much sooner than John expected), he was forced to appoint someone else as his assistant because the new employee had not served the ninety-day probation period necessary for eligibility. Having to go back on his promise put John in an awkward position. He paid a high price for breaking a promise he didn't need to make in the first place.

A promise is emotionally accepted. Promises made in a climate of excitement may appear different to you in the cold light of reality, but the changed perspective may not have reached your employees. They fail to understand that busy supervisors with many responsibilities can easily forget a promise even though it was sincerely made. In other words, the receiver sees and feels a promise differently from the giver. The supervisor who ignores this difference is asking for trouble.

Promises easy to keep are also easily forgotten. It is easy to convert a request into a promise and then promptly forget it. For example, an employee might ask you for a special favor such as requisitioning a new, inexpensive tool. If you don't do it immediately or write it down to remind yourself to do it later, you may forget it. The world won't end because of your neglect, but sooner or later your poor memory will cause you embarrassment and make it necessary to rebuild a relationship. Even small promises must be kept, and only the organized person who can follow through should make them. A broken promise may be labeled a lie.

How can you guard against making foolish promises you may not be able to keep? Tell the employee making the request that you can't promise, but you'll do everything in your power to make it come about. Such an approach helps you avoid making a promise, but it still enables you to support the employee. Don't permit yourself to be carried away by your own enthusiasm so that you make promises to create or maintain good relationships with employees.

Of course, you are not expected to avoid completely making promises. Sometimes you must and should make them. Try the following suggestions to help you keep them.

Write them down. You will have a much better chance of keeping promises if you write them in your notebook or on your desk calendar.

Admit you might forget. Tell the employee you intend to keep the promise but you would appreciate a reminder at the appropriate time. It puts some of the responsibility on the employee and helps ensure that you will keep the promise.

If possible, keep it now. If you can fulfill a promise before the day is over, do it. It is a mistake to postpone a promise that can be kept immediately.

If, in your role as a supervisor, you can learn to make few promises but keep those important ones you do make, you will avoid a common and costly mistake.

STRAITJACKETING EMPLOYEES

Call it *prejudging, underestimating, downgrading,* or *prejudice.* Whatever the name, many supervisors put their employees in a psychological straitjacket, preventing them from growing into the kind of workers they could become. This problem usually arises because supervisors are unaware of the restrictive climate or barriers they build. They may think they are communicating with the employees, but they aren't. At least three kinds of supervisors restrict their employees in this way.

The typecaster. This supervisor wants to classify and pigeonhole all employees. Rather than accepting and treating everyone as a separate, unique individual, this manager insists upon putting people into groups. For example, a male manager may think that all women who work are first and foremost housewives, so he overlooks the professional career woman; a mature manager may think that all young people prefer not to have early responsibility and ignores those who do; the manager may think that all employees work primarily for money and thus pays little attention to psychological needs that are often more important than money; a manager who has had a bad experience with one employee from a different culture may assume that all future employees from the same background will behave in the same manner. Such managers refuse to be convinced that typing people automatically sets the stage for getting exactly what they expect, no matter how things could have been.

The snuff-out artist. This supervisor squelches the ambition and creativity of employees without knowing it by having an overpowering demeanor, which may include speaking in a gruff voice, using a bulldozer approach, or adhering to a stiff, militaristic style. This supervisor's personality is so powerful that he or she snuffs out the sparks of creativity in employees.

The poor perceiver. This supervisor is not sensitive enough to see the potential abilities of employees. He or she doesn't see hidden talent and therefore fails to recognize a special contribution that deserves a compliment, or doesn't recognize improvement in a new employee and thereby fails to reinforce it. The poor perceiver does not recognize and treat employees as separate individuals because he or she does not see their differences. Employees recognize this behavior and may give up.

How can you guard against putting your employees in straitjackets? How can you train yourself to bring out the potential of your employees instead of restrict it? Here are three suggestions that may help.

Take time to know your employees. Occasionally relax for a few moments with each employee during coffee breaks or other informal sessions so that you can better perceive and understand their special needs and individual personalities. What are their interests and ambitions? Are they going to school part time? Gaining insight into individuals as people instead of as employees will help you avoid putting anyone in a psychological straitjacket.

Look for potential first and performance second. Although all employees must be judged on their performance, it is a mistake to evaluate performance without first looking at the individual's potential. Most employees have an undiscovered skill, talent, or aptitude that could be used in their work if they were encouraged to use it. Discover and encourage the use of hidden abilities in those who work for you.

Give employees the reassurance they need to take advantage of the opportunities you provided. To realize their potential, some employees need large doses of encouragement that you can provide. Sometimes it means giving people something to do on the spur of the moment so that they won't have time to worry about it or helping them forget a mistake and letting them try again. It is amazing how many people will grow and bloom under the supervision of a person who provides both reassurance and opportunity—these build confidence.

FAILURE TO ENJOY YOUR ROLE AS A MANAGER

Many psychological rewards and perks come with a supervisory position. If you don't isolate and enjoy them, you will render yourself less effective. For example, one of your rewards is more freedom. Enjoy this freedom by giving yourself workdays filled with variety and special challenges to eliminate boredom. Remind yourself that your employees can afford to be negative or have occasional down days, but you can't. If you appear overburdened, washed out, haggard, and down, those who work for you will pick it up and the entire department will reflect your negative attitude. No matter how effective you are in other ways, if you don't stay positive and upbeat, the productivity of your department can drop and your own career will be damaged.

The very nature of the supervisor's job involves making minor mistakes. You will be no exception. With so many responsibilities, you can't avoid it. It is important, then, to avoid making the serious mistakes, the costly ones that damage both the department and your future as a supervisor. Reflect on your mistakes and learn from them—doing so is the cornerstone of personal growth and development.

DISCUSSION QUESTIONS

1. Why do many managers fail to receive the obvious signals (low productivity, complaints, and so forth) that they are not communicating with their employees?

2. Which supervisor would you prefer to work with? Supervisor A is a strong leader who knows when to get tough, but at least you always know where you stand. Supervisor B is a more quiet and soft leader who is consistent and easy to work with but at times gets pushed around a little. Explain your point of view.

3. What can be done to help a manager who consistently stereotypes employees and thereby fails to encourage the development of their potential abilities to contribute?

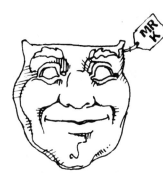

Intimidation[2]

Since he took over the department, Supervisor Joe has been under subtle pressure to grant Mr. K a series of special favors. Most of the pressure has come from Mr. K himself, who let Joe know from the beginning that he would support him in turn for certain freedoms to which he was entitled anyway because of his seniority and special knowledge. Some of the pressure, however, has come from outside sources in the form of warnings. For example, one supervisor told Joe: "Treat Mr. K with kid gloves because he has powerful connections upstairs." So far Joe has gone along with the requests, with growing resentment. It all came to a climax yesterday, however, when Mr. K asked if he could leave early Friday for personal reasons that he did not explain. Joe came back with a fast and emphatic no and walked away. Since then the following has happened: (1) Mr. K has been silent and sulky; (2) Mr. R came to Joe and complimented him on his stand in behalf of the other departmental employees; (3) Mr. X has reminded Joe that a previous supervisor resigned because Mr. K initiated a campaign to get rid of him.

Joe discusses the following options with you in confidence:

1. Stand pat and do nothing.

2. Protect your flanks by going to Mr. Big and explaining the history of the problem and why you feel you must stand pat or lose the respect of the other employees. Tell him you want his complete support or he can have your resignation.

3. Back down by calling Mr. K into your office and telling him he is free to leave early Friday but must keep his special favor requests to an absolute minimum in the future.

4. Call Mr. K into your office and tell him firmly that you resent his going over your head to Mr. Big and talking outside the department, and that you intend to stand by your decision and defend it all the way to the top.

Which option would you support? Why? What changes would you suggest to Joe in using it? What other option (not on this list) might you propose?

---

[2]Turn to page 266 to compare your thoughts with those of the author.

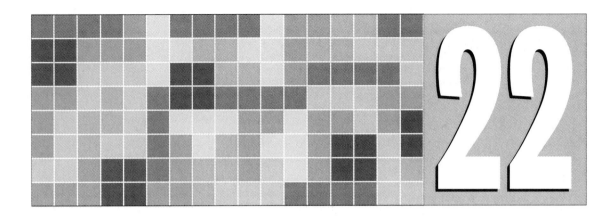

Converting Change into Opportunity

After you have finished reading this chapter, you should be able to convert most changes into career opportunities for you and your staff.

When you hear the words *downsizing, layoffs, lean and mean, restructuring, relocating, decentralizing, new information technology,* and *retraining,* you know that change is around the corner. Change is anything that happens in our environment that requires a human adjustment. The dramatic tempo of change continues to accelerate, and the impact falls more on the supervisor than on staff employees. As a beginning manager, the *way* you accept and interpret changes to your staff and how you cope personally will have a measurable effect upon departmental productivity and your future success.

Many times an individual hears about a pending change and promptly converts it into a dragon instead of an opportunity. You hear comments like these:

"There is no security in a big company anymore."

"This constant changing may force me into a nervous breakdown."

"Early retirement may be my solution."

How you cope with change as a supervisor will depend upon your attitude. Some people have the capacity to view change as opportunity; others reject even

good changes with hostility. What is your attitude toward change? The "Attitude-Toward-Change Scale" has been prepared to provide a few clues. Please rate yourself on all factors and compute your total score.

Not all changes are good or necessary. Resisting an ill-advised change can be a worthy mission that will protect and benefit your firm and your employees. But most changes are inevitable, and the sooner they are accepted by you as a supervisor, the better it will be for your employees. In spite of short-term adjustment disadvantages, many changes have long-term advantages that make the adjustment worthwhile. It will be your responsibility to communicate this situation to your employees when it occurs.

TECHNOLOGICAL CHANGES NOW IN THEIR INFANCY

Alvin Toffler, in his book *The Third Wave*, develops the concept of the *electronic cottage*. At some distant time, he predicts, most employees will work in their own homes, where electronic equipment will permit instant communication with and directions from a central management source. Teachers will teach from their homes. Production workers will use sophisticated equipment to produce parts for a company miles away. Commuting to factories, skyscrapers, and other workplaces will be a thing of the past for many. People who live together will work together.

ATTITUDE-TOWARD-CHANGE SCALE

I view any change as an opportunity, not a threat.	4	3	2	1	0	I reject all change as a personal threat.
If my organization should introduce new equipment for me to use, I would be delighted.	4	3	2	1	0	If forced to learn how to use new equipment, I would be openly hostile.
A reorganization of my firm would be welcome; my flexibility would give me an advantage.	4	3	2	1	0	I would hate any form of reorganization; I like things stable and totally predictable.
I have an excellent superior, but a change would not bother me.	4	3	2	1	0	I have an excellent superior; a change would devastate me.
New work assignments and responsibilities motivate me.	4	3	2	1	0	New work assignments and responsibilities demotivate me.
All the social and political changes taking place today are exciting to me.	4	3	2	1	0	I wish I had lived 100 years ago.
Predictability is dull.	4	3	2	1	0	Predictability is beautiful.
The possibility of a career change intrigues me.	4	3	2	1	0	The possibility of a career change deflates me.
I have confidence that I can quickly change my behavioral patterns to fit any contingency.	4	3	2	1	0	In all honesty, it is almost impossible for me to change my behavioral patterns.
I can change my career and lifestyle goals quickly.	4	3	2	1	0	My career goals and values are bedded in cement.

TOTAL [   ]

If you scored greater than 25, you appear to have a positive, flexible attitude toward change. You should be able to handle future changes effectively. If you scored less than 25, you have less flexibility than you may need to cope well with future changes.

The electronic cottage may or may not become a reality, but many other changes will occur. Transportation, manufacturing, banking, medical, retailing, education, and government facilities are feeling the impact of change. As a management person, you will be caught in the middle. When sweeping changes come from above, it will be your responsibility to see that they are accepted by those who work below you. Even more critical, you will need to teach employees new techniques and procedures so that change can take place. Wherever you work as a supervisor, technological change will make your role more difficult. You can view these changes as opportunities to prepare yourself for a higher position, or you can take a negative view and eliminate yourself from the race.

When May heard that her firm would adopt a more sophisticated computer system, her first reaction was negative. As an operations officer, she knew the change would involve substantial new responsibility for her. She would have to undergo additional training that would be difficult. Besides learning new skills, she would have to spend many hours of additional time helping her nine employees adjust. At first she even considered changing her career. But after talking things over with a close friend, she decided to turn the announcement into an opportunity. She said to herself, "If computers are going to dominate this industry, then I am going to dominate the computers so that I can use my skills to increase my upward mobility." She promptly enrolled in an Institute of Financial Education course that would improve her skills with computers. She also enrolled in a general course in data processing at a local college, and she welcomed the information provided by the computer firm. May was determined to take advantage of change to improve her own future. Her superiors were quick to recognize her positive attitude toward changes over which they, too, had little control.

ORGANIZATIONS CHANGE TO SURVIVE

At one time in the United States, a supervisor felt lucky to work for a stable, predictable corporation. The supervisor could anticipate security and upward mobility within the framework of a single large organization. The corporate womb was a safe, comfortable place to be. A first-line supervisor could blueprint a career path to the top with confidence. The supervisor knew, at least to some extent, what was ahead.

Today, the supervisor should feel lucky if he or she works for an organization that is sufficiently flexible to adjust to changes and survive. Organizations that are too slow to adjust will be left behind. Supervisors and employees who belong to such organizations will find themselves unemployed.

Changes are hitting firms of all sizes with increasing magnitude. Mergers, takeovers, and staff reductions are in the headlines. You should not infer that the organization you are currently working for is so vulnerable to change that it may turn belly-up. But if your organization is not adaptable enough to survive, your job may disappear. Your attitude should be, "I'm lucky that the management of my organization is flexible enough to keep the organization alive and changing." It should *not* be, "I hope my organization can resist change and stay the way it is."

As a supervisor, you are in a key role to help your organization survive and prosper. You will need to be flexible enough to reorganize your department, accept new technology and assignments, and, most of all, assist your employees in making their adjustment.

Doug couldn't understand why his firm needed to make changes. As a result, he resisted what few changes were made and refused to learn new techniques that were revolutionizing his particular career area. Because of inflexible, shortsighted management, his firm went into bankruptcy, and Doug was left out on a limb. His failure to learn new techniques left him unprepared for a similar job with another firm. He had contributed to the demise of his organization and permitted himself to become obsolete in his career specialty.

THE WORKFORCE CHANGES

The U.S. workforce has been changing rapidly during the last ten years. It is becoming multicultural and multilingual. Women are moving into all occupations and making faster progress up executive ladders. African Americans, Hispanics, Orientals, and a growing number of people from other cultures are improving their skills and earning greater upward mobility. First-generation workers from foreign cultures are arriving and making adjustments to the workforce. The new workforce is a challenge to the front-line supervisor because it is he or she who must work with all individuals on a personal, one-to-one basis.

> Ten years ago Herbert had twenty employees in his department: seventeen white males, two white females, and one African American male. Today, thanks to his human relations skills, productivity is higher with only sixteen employees. The composition is as follows: five white females, four white males, two African American males, two Oriental females, one African American female, one Hispanic male, and one Hispanic female. Herbert takes pride in the cultural mix of his department. From the start, he accepted the change as a personal challenge and enjoyed helping the few remaining senior employees in his department to adjust.

MANAGEMENT BURNOUT

Supervisor's Survival Kit is designed to prevent burnout. The chapters on managing yourself have been written to help you do the best possible job and still protect your emotional health. Supervisors who establish realistic goals, maintain comfortable priorities, and manage their time are in a position to balance their careers with their personal lives. This balance helps prevent burnout when things are stable. When major changes occur, they always introduce stress; the perceptive supervisor is prepared for temporary adjustments until career and home are again properly balanced. A balanced, happy, activity-centered, relaxing home life is one of the best insurances against stress generated in the workplace.

CHANGE AS A SOURCE OF STRESS

Employee stress comes from many sources: work overload, role conflicts, over-supervision, ambiguity, insecurity, and change. Although you want to protect your employees from such pressures, you cannot provide a 100 percent stress-free work environment. In fact, mild positive stress (eustress) stimulates greater productivity. Some work environments such as the media, advertising, and political activity have built-in eustress. The way you handle change in your department, however, can eliminate a great deal of harmful stress (distress) that might injure employees and eat away at productivity standards.

To convert dragons into caterpillars, you should portray changes as opportunities for growth instead of problems to overcome. You should communicate such changes in a nonthreatening way as far in advance as possible so that employees have time to adjust. You should also explain why such changes are necessary. Employees who participate in the planning of change experience a reduction in the stress that change can bring.

SUMMARY

As you accomplish these goals, consider the following suggestions:

Turn change into opportunity for yourself. When it comes to change, it doesn't hurt to think of yourself first because if you don't succeed, those working for you will be left unprepared. It is bad enough to work for a supervisor who is negative about change; it is even worse to work for one who neglects to prepare you for the future.

Communicate the advantages of change. Tell your staff that changing now may save their jobs later. State that the way to protect their retirement pensions in the future is to change to greater profitability now. Communicate this message individually, in staff meetings, and during formal appraisal periods. Prepare your people to anticipate change and learn to roll with the punches. You will be doing them an immense favor.

Follow up with advanced, hands-on training. Frequently, highly capable persons take their skills with them to a new company or community, only to discover that their competencies are obsolete. Do not let obsolescence happen to your staff. Provide them with the kind of training they need to stay up to date with career demands where they are or where they move in the future. Allowing your staff to rest on their career laurels is doing them a disservice.

When one accepts the premise that change is inevitable, it is possible to take pride in being able to cope with change effectively. Anything you can do to help your employees experience this pride will make you a superior supervisor.

DISCUSSION QUESTIONS

1. Can all changes be converted into opportunities? Defend your answer through examples.

2. What can supervisors do to minimize stress within themselves? For the employees? Evaluate such possibilities as physical exercise and meditation.

3. Would you agree that change is the primary source of stress in our society?

4. Think of your own situation. How much change is in your life? How do you react to change and how might your reaction be modified to reduce stress?

Mini-Game

Change

Objective

To provide the supervisor with insights and techniques to help a negative mature worker accept change.

Problem

Ms. Y is concerned about Mrs. B. During more than twenty years with the organization, Mrs. B was highly productive. For the last year, however, she has been negative to both co-workers and customers. Every time a change is mandated by top management, Mrs. B becomes more vocal and more negative. Now co-workers are complaining and customers are turning to competitors. In addition, Mrs. B's inflexible attitude toward change is hurting the productivity of everyone who works with her. Ms. Y agrees that something must be done. The organization has a nontermination policy for employees in Mrs. B's category.

Procedure

The seminar, workshop, or classroom is divided into small groups of four or five. Each group selects its own chairperson. The group then develops a counseling strategy that will help Mrs. B to cope with change and restore her previous positive attitude and high productivity.

The strategy should include (1) counseling techniques, either directive or nondirective; (2) a decision on whether Mutual Reward Theory (p. 47) (MRT) would be effective; (3) the number of sessions recommended; and (4) the choice of superiors who will be involved.

Give each group at least twenty minutes to develop a strategy, followed by an opportunity to present its conclusions to the class or seminar.

Postgame Discussion

Compare the strategies presented and evaluate their probable effectiveness in improving Mrs. B's attitude.

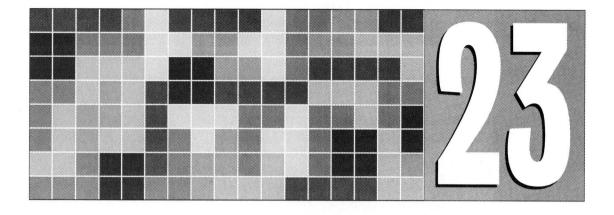

Having a Personal Plan B

After you have finished reading this chapter, you should be convinced that it would be smart for you and your staff to develop a personal plan B.

If you are happy and effective as a front-line supervisor, chances are excellent that you will eventually aspire to further upward mobility. Success at one level has a way of pushing an individual toward a higher level for many reasons, including the prospect of additional financial rewards, greater ego satisfaction, and the opportunity to test one's leadership ability in more demanding situations.

What about you? Would you like to use your first supervisory position as a springboard? Do you have ambitions to climb the management ladder? If so, this chapter will have special meaning for you because it is designed to take you above and beyond the realm of operating a successful department. You, too, can reach the upper levels of management by building strong working relationships with other supervisors and executives as well; you can play the management game with experienced professionals in a way that will help you contribute to the growth of both the organization and yourself. Sound interesting? Here is the way Bob Spencer sizes up the situation:

> Even with a four-year degree in business administration, it took me more than two years to become the kind of front-line supervisor I wanted to be. I had more to learn than I suspected when I started out. Once I had everything under control,

however, I became intrigued with taking the next step. I then discovered a whole new dimension of communications, human relations, decision making, and management know-how. The first-line supervisor is a babe in the woods compared to the experienced middle manager. I suddenly realized I had just started to learn what I would eventually need to know to move up to more competitive middle management positions. It appeared far more demanding than I had expected, but I decided to start preparing myself. I had taken the first step successfully, so why stop? Besides, I had a feeling that if I didn't keep preparing for something bigger, I might lose interest in what I already had. I work for a rather high-powered organization and if you stand still too long, others often pass you by.

Do you agree with Bob? Do you feel it might be wise to prepare for a more demanding role in management? If so, most executives would agree that you must start playing the management game from your present position as a front-line supervisor. Consider making the following moves now.

MAKING YOURSELF VISIBLE

Make yourself visible. To make yourself visible, you must be seen and talked about by management people above you. You must be noticed, which you can accomplish in a number of ways.

- Speaking up (sometimes critically) in staff meetings

- Turning in written suggestions through channels

- Making appointments with upper management people to ask questions but always going through channels

- Being seen around the facility

- Leading a cross-functional team

- Participating in organizational events or recreational activities

- Taking advantage of lunch to meet other people

Of course, the best way to be visible is to do a quality job and get recognition from doing it. In fact, it may be more important to be visible silently rather than physically or verbally. You need to avoid being visible in a negative way. Some supervisors become too aggressive and play the management game too forcefully, hurting instead of helping their personal progress.

Show strength from your present position. If you are to move up toward executive management, you must occasionally stand pat and refuse to be pushed around. It may mean quietly standing up to your own superior and other management people when you know you are right and have all the facts to document your case or holding your own in a controversy over the role of your department; it may mean fighting back in an acceptable way when someone tries to invade your area of responsibility. You cannot build a reputation as a strong leader if you always back down under pressure. When you know you are right, stand up for your ideas. It is the best way to win the respect of some top managers.

Always defend and protect your employees to outsiders. You cannot move up the executive ladder without the enthusiastic support and loyalty of the employees in your department. You earn some of this loyalty when you go to bat for them with outsiders. This way you keep departmental problems inside the department, where they belong. The easiest way to destroy a good departmental image is to air dirty laundry with outsiders, which your employees are free to do any time they wish. However, if you defend and protect them, they will probably do the same for you.

Do your homework. If you keep your department in top shape at all times, you will not be vulnerable to those who may wish to stop your personal progress. Some extremely ambitious supervisors spend so much time playing management politics that they neglect their department and defeat themselves. You can afford to work on outside communications only when your department is completely under control. You can make outside moves only when you yourself are safe from attack.

Stand firm with other supervisors. You will need the support of other supervisors if you hope to join middle management because in many cases you will be supervising them following your promotion.

Sound, healthy relationships with other supervisors can be developed, but it is naive to expect them all to be open and supportive. You are their competitor, so some may use devious tactics to undermine you, try to outmaneuver you to gain something you both want, or even try to trick you into making a poor move that will give them an advantage. Of course, most will be aboveboard and easy to work with. Even when other competitors use unfair tactics, your best move is to win their respect without resorting to the same methods. Protect yourself and your department while maintaining your personal standards and your belief in human relations principles. Be tough in defending what you feel is right, but avoid revenge or vindictiveness. Such conduct will only destroy the reputation you are attempting to build.

Be a team player in staff meetings. The staff meeting is the perfect setting to make either good or bad impressions, so it will be a challenge to get the right kinds of reactions from other management people in this environment. Here are some suggestions that might help: (1) Don't hesitate to speak up when you have something to say, but don't overdo it.Overtalking and underlistening are serious problems. (2) Make a critical contribution now and then, even if it is something your own manager doesn't want to hear. In short, say what you really believe; don't just accommodate the group. (3) When you do say something, be brief and stick to the topic at hand. (4) Support others enthusiastically if you agree with them. It is a sound way to build relationships with other supervisors. (5) If you lose interest in a staff meeting that is dragging, try not to show it. Sometimes you can tolerate it by arranging your priorities, thinking about a problem, or engaging in some other mental activity so long as you don't miss anything vital. (6) Never show personal hostility in a staff meeting.

Read and study. The supervisor who stops reading is locking the doors to opportunity and throwing the key away. Required reading includes company brochures, bulletins, reports, and research papers, as well as outside articles and books on management techniques. The ambitious supervisor must keep informed on company matters and prevailing management practices or, sooner or later, he or she will be passed by.

Look as though you are ready. It should go without saying that a junior manager on the way up must look ready. You should project an image of confidence, demonstrate leadership, stay constantly organized, and handle problems with finesse. In short, you should communicate upward—through your leadership style—a readiness factor that shows you are stronger than your competition.

Two different routes can take you to the top: on the straight-line route, you climb the ladder of your present organization; on the zigzag route, you change employers. The choice you make is critical and should involve a careful study of your own personality, values, and lifestyles.

THE STRAIGHT LINE TO THE TOP

If you are currently a supervisor for a sizable organization you respect, you may prefer to work your way to the top within this firm. You might say to yourself, "This strong organization has a bright future, and I prefer to settle in and build my career without looking outside for better opportunities." The straight line is a comfortable pattern to take. It permits you to enjoy your work, build long-term working relationships, and feel secure without constantly working to build outside contacts. It also permits you to stay in one geographical location without making frequent moves. You can enjoy staying in the same home, permitting your children to mature in the same school system, and generally establishing your roots in the community of your choice. In the past, most top executives followed this pattern to the top.

You should, however, take the following three precautions. First, you must make certain that the organization you select has growth potential and can survive under changing conditions. Second, you must stay motivated. When ambitious supervisors who accept this strategy become complacent, management is forced to go outside to fill top leadership roles. Third, you must assertively communicate to management that you are capable, loyal, creative, and dependable, and because of these characteristics, you deserve the next promotion available. You cannot assume that management will recognize your accomplishments.

THE ZIGZAG PATTERN

The alternative to the straight-line approach is zigzagging your way to the top by moving from one organization to another, always making a major contribution as you go. The zigzag pattern takes more energy, involves more risk, and requires greater flexibility. Those who make this pattern work (scramblers) usually stay with one firm for a minimum of two years. They are highly motivated and constantly learn new ideas to take with them as they travel on. They spend a great deal of time making contacts. These individuals talk about their "Plan Bs." A *Plan B is a well-devised strategy that permits the individual to move quickly to a new firm if promotional opportunities begin to fade.* While most supervisors spend all their energy on their jobs, scramblers work hard to contribute where they are but exert extra energy to locate better opportunities elsewhere; they put their personal careers ahead of the organization. Being more assertive in promoting themselves, they do not always play by traditional rules.

Are you a scrambler? To gain some indication as to whether you could be a successful scrambler, complete the following scale.

SCRAMBLER-STABILIZER SCALE

Please circle one number to rate yourself honestly on a scale from 0 to 4.

I will always welcome any-geographic move that enhances my career.	4	3	2	1	0	I would turn down any job opportunity that involves moving.
Zigzagging from one firm to another would be intriguing to me.	4	3	2	1	0	I hate the process of adjusting to new work environments.
My career is first; my personal life is second.	4	3	2	1	0	My personal life is first; my career is second.
Getting to the top through zig-zagging is more of a challenge.	4	3	2	1	0	Getting to the top in one organization is more of a challenge.

I am willing to take risks even though I might lose my job.	4	3	2	1	0	I will not take any risks that put my job in jeopardy.
My ultimate loyalty is only to myself and my career.	4	3	2	1	0	I am 100 percent loyal to my organization.
I do not intend to follow traditional rules in order to get to the top.	4	3	2	1	0	I intend to follow traditional rules to the fullest extent.
I enjoy the job-seeking process, especially interviews.	4	3	2	1	0	I hate the job-seeking process, especially interviews.
I am willing to spend the extra energy to have a Plan B ready and waiting.	4	3	2	1	0	I do not bother with a Plan B. I devote my energy to my firm and my job.
It would not bother me in the least if I lost my job tomorrow.	4	3	2	1	0	I would be devastated if I lost my job tomorrow.

TOTAL [   ]

If you scored 25 or higher, you should give the zigzagging pattern (scrambling) careful consideration. If you scored lower than 25, the straight-line pattern appears to be a better choice for you.

DEVELOPING A PLAN B

Seven steps are involved in the preparation of a Plan B.

Step 1: Revise and keep up-to-date a superior résumé.

Step 2: Streamline and become more effective in your Plan A so that you will have more free time to design an excellent Plan B.

Step 3: As difficult as it may seem, start learning more from your Plan A or present job. (This step sometimes requires an attitude turnaround.)

Step 4: Verify your competencies to make sure you are up-to-date in your professional arena.

Step 5: If necessary, return to college for additional training or engage in a do-it-yourself upgrading project.

Step 6: Do some creative networking from your present position. Make it a major effort!

Step 7: Use your Plan B to gain a promotion where you are (Plan A), or use it to win a better position outside. Include it in your résumé and refer to it during interviews.[1]

As you can see, an effective Plan B is much more than something you devise in the back of your mind. Rather, it is a sophisticated strategy that usually takes a minimum of six months to complete. A Plan B is equally effective for both stabilizers and scramblers.

IT'S OKAY TO PLAY BOTH ENDS AGAINST THE MIDDLE

Nothing unethical is involved in preparing a Plan B while you continue to operate effectively in the job you were hired to perform. You have the right to improve your competencies whether you eventually wind up using them where you are or in a new role. In most cases, people engaged in preparing a Plan B start doing a better job with their Plan A and everyone winds up ahead.

Most observers agree that the zigzag route will take a person to the top faster, but it has its disadvantages. First, the individual must occasionally uproot his or her family to make a geographical move. Second, the person needs more talent and energy to make it work. Third, if not careful, the individual may create resentment among fellow workers—which can, in turn, force the person to make a move more quickly.

Although the zigzag route is attractive in many respects, not everyone can make it work. The scrambler is a person with high intelligence, great energy, and a willingness to take risks. Although moving from one work environment to another is demanding, some evidence indicates that it builds better leadership. The individual has to make more adjustments and decisions. The very act of moving seems to enhance the individual's personal growth.

If you want upward mobility, your master plan should take into consideration the advantages and disadvantages of both patterns. The "Scrambler-Stabilizer Scale" (pp. 243) will assist you in this undertaking. Assume that you are highly ambitious and capable of excelling in higher leadership roles. Which pattern fits your personality and values?

THE IMPORTANCE OF A PLAN B

Although scramblers *must* design and implement a Plan B if they intend to zigzag their way to the top, stabilizers can also benefit from a Plan B for the following reasons:

1. As discussed in Chapter 22, mergers, takeovers, and highly volatile market conditions may render your position (or even your employer) obsolete. Without a Plan B you can, through no fault of your own, be unemployed.

---

[1]See *Be True to Your Future*, by Elwood N. Chapman, published by Crisp Publications, Inc., 95 First Street, Los Altos, CA 94022.

2. Having a Plan B will help keep you informed about what is going on in the marketplace and thus contribute to your professional growth where you are now employed. For example, in forming a Plan B, you may discover that you need to return to school to upgrade your competencies. The new skills will help your present firm.

3. A Plan B can help keep you motivated. Knowing you are capable of building a career elsewhere can make you feel better where you are currently employed. You will feel more secure. You will be more inclined to speak up and contribute more without fear. If you are doing an excellent job and your superior discovers you have a Plan B, she or he may appreciate you more.

Stabilizers can benefit from a Plan B without ever exercising it.

NETWORKING

All scramblers and most stabilizers believe in some form of networking. Networking is the practice of actively seeking out and building relationships with colleagues inside and outside your firm—significant people who can keep you informed and, if necessary, come to your aid at a later date. If sound, mutually rewarding relationships are built, such networks can provide you with a *career support system*, an inner circle of colleagues who can help you professionally.

Network inner circles can include co-workers and superiors in the same company, counterparts in competitive organizations, trade association friends you may see only at conventions, college professors you have maintained relationships with, and many others. Three professionals who endorse the networking system comment:

"The idea of building relationships with other professionals so that you can experience greater personal growth is an excellent idea."

"I have made two beneficial career changes in the last five years; in each instance, I found my new job through a network contact."

"My career has been enhanced through membership in the local chapter of my trade association. Should I seek another career opportunity, I would contact association members first."

Taking a leadership role in a trade association is an excellent way to enhance career growth."

PROTECTING THE CAREERS OF YOUR STAFF FROM THE WINDS OF CHANGE

Just as you will want to protect your career from the winds of change, you will want to be concerned with the future of your staff. You will want to help them keep their skills upgraded by providing as much on-the-job training as possible. The more you enhance their careers (whether they stay with your firm or eventually move on), the more productive they will be now and the more they will respect you as a supervisor.

DISCUSSION QUESTIONS

1. How, in your opinion, can ambitious stabilizers compete more successfully with talented scramblers within the same organization?

2. Do you agree that moving from one organization (environment) to another is a good way to improve one's leadership ability?

3. Should stabilizers develop a Plan B even if they have no intention of leaving their firms?

4. What are some benefits of joining a trade or professional organization associated with your profession?

Case Study

Decision[2]

Eric is thirty years old and an engineer for a giant utility. Commuting daily from the suburbs to a central city headquarters, he arrives early but refuses to work beyond 4:30 P.M. except in emergencies. Eric puts his personal life first and clearly separates work from his private life. He is highly family and church oriented.

Management believes that Eric is talented, ethical, and patient enough to play the corporate game. Eric's co-workers know he is extremely ambitious and is growing increasingly impatient. Eric is usually motivated, but now his ambition is beginning to flag. He has the impression management is keeping him in an unnecessary holding pattern, possibly because of a prior image resulting from some unfortunate experiences early in his career. The solution is aggravated now because management is heaping responsibility on Eric without giving him additional recognition. He senses that they view him as "good old dependable Eric."

Eric prefers the straight-line pattern to the top because it gives his family stability and permits him to maintain his present church connections. He is, however, considering the zigzag pattern. Other firms would recognize his skills and experience, and a new job in a new environment would provide greater personal growth. Eric freely admits that he is in conflict between the two upward mobility patterns.

What advice would you give Eric? Upon what values should he base his decision? Can Eric take the zigzag path without sacrificing family values? What impact could adverse economic conditions have on such a decision?

---

[2]Turn to page 267 to compare your thoughts with those of the author.

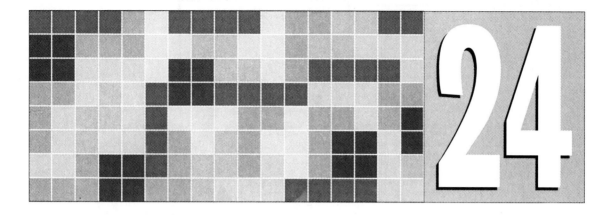

Leadership: What Every Manager Should Know

After you have finished reading this chapter, you should be able to become a stronger, more effective leader.

Leadership is not a gift awarded to some and denied to others. No magic is involved, and no special personality or unusual charisma is required. Most individuals who truly wish to become leaders can develop leadership ability.

Leadership is stepping out in front of others with confidence, taking charge, and earning the support of followers.

A perceptive observer can sense the presence of strong leadership. The group under observation is pulling together in an organized, efficient manner. Members show enthusiasm and a sense of direction. Tension is absent because everybody expects to benefit from the group's activity. Everybody supports the leader because of respect that the leader has earned. A strong leader is as important in a traditional department as in a team arrangement, although the leadership styles are different.

YOUR OPPORTUNITY TO BECOME A MANAGER/LEADER

For most workers the leadership-building process starts when they become supervisors. Some may get a head start through experience as club officers, team captains, chairpersons, and officers in trade or volunteer organizations, but supervisory jobs are the primary leadership builders.

It is possible to be a good supervisor without being a good leader, but it is impossible to be a good leader without being a good supervisor or manager. Those who become leaders without first becoming supervisors must ultimately learn management skills such as setting priorities, learning to delegate, and other principles and techniques covered in this book. They must do these things to free themselves to lead. Many supervisors become so bogged down with administrative details that they do not have time to put more leadership into their styles, denying themselves the opportunity to move up the ladder to higher management/leadership positions.

The better you are as a supervisor, the more freedom you will have to lead. Although most people are in middle or upper management positions before they have had the opportunity to stretch their leadership "wings," it can all start at the supervisory level. It is the combination of management and leadership that usually creates upward mobility.

Leadership is often the missing ingredient to greater productivity. Leaders who meet the needs of their followers inspire greater productivity than managers who do not.

Your leadership style should reflect your personality. Although you can learn about leadership from others by using them as models, you must nevertheless create your own style, a style that reflects your personality, supervisory approach, and the kind of leader you want to be. You can learn a lot about leadership by observing your superiors, but you should feel free to adapt or reject their methods in forging your own individual style.

In building your own leadership style, it is important that you identify your strong personal characteristics and strengthen them. Your style is an extension of these characteristics. When you emphasize a unique trait, such as a strong, powerful voice, you are building a style that causes you to stand out from others. It is vital, however, that you channel your special characteristics into certain areas that reflect strong leadership.

A LEADERSHIP FORMULA FOR PERSONAL GROWTH

This chapter introduces you to a prescription, or formula, for increasing your own leadership potential by teaching you how to acquire the successful skills, techniques, and principles practiced by men and women who occupy leadership

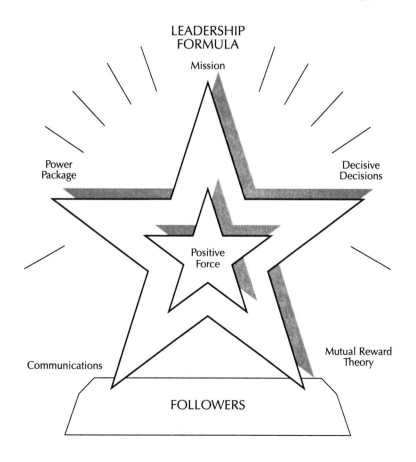

roles in a variety of settings. The formula was not developed merely from reading and observation but was synthesized from the results of interviews with more than sixty successful leaders in business, education, sports, religion, youth organizations, politics, and community groups. It has since been revised and strengthened based on the advice of professional users both on and off campus and converted into the publication: *Leadership: What Every Manager Should Know.*

The leadership formula[1] (strategic model) is presented here in graphic form. All five points in the STAR represent a foundation upon which successful leadership can be built. The smaller inside STAR (Positive Force) is the luminous spark that extends energy to the outer points. The two legs are firmly embedded in the foundation that holds up the STAR. They remind us that the power to lead comes from followers, not from superiors or organizations.

All foundations are interrelated and interdependent. For example, without effective Communications from the leader, it would be impossible to create and maintain a motivating Mission, make Decisive Decisions, have Mutually Rewarding relationships with followers, and effectively utilize a Power Package.

BE A STAR COMMUNICATOR

Starting at the bottom-left point of the star, your first step in putting more leadership into your style is to become a more dynamic communicator. Followers like their leaders to speak with authority. They want them to *sound* like leaders.

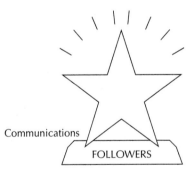

Communications
FOLLOWERS

Dixie was an outstanding supervisor, but she was so soft-spoken in her approach to group meetings and counseling that those in her department became impatient. Some even went so far as to say she was "too nice." Dixie's superior and mentor, a woman with a strong, commanding voice, suggested that Dixie take a course in public speaking. Dixie rejected the idea but took the suggestion to mean that she should demonstrate more leadership through her voice. She started to exercise more control through her voice in both private counseling and group sessions. Within three months her superior complimented her on the change and asked what grade she had received in her public speaking course. "I didn't take one," Dixie replied. "I used you as a model and made the changes myself."

---

[1]The leadership formula, briefly presented here, is fully developed in the book *Leadership: What Every Manager Should Know.* For further information, write to Prentice-Hall, Inc., Upper Saddle River, NJ 07458.

Of course, speaking with confidence is only one part of your communications system. A good communications system is a planned program of daily two-way communications to keep those who work for you informed. An effective communication system can include all or part of the following: daily personal contact with workers on the site, a bulletin board where both supervisor and employee can leave messages that will be picked up daily, regular group staff meetings, informal communications during break periods, and use of in-house communications media (newsletters), telephone calls, distribution of personal notes, and voluntary or designed counseling sessions. Each leader must design a two-way system that works on a daily basis. A breakdown in the communications system is as serious as a breakdown of production equipment.

Why is such a system so important?

It is essential to keep everyone informed and prevent misunderstandings. Silence—not knowing what is going on—destroys morale. When workers are involved in decisions, or at least informed, they can cope with changes. Being left out in the cold develops hostility that can even lead to mutiny in extreme cases.

Employees need to know how they are doing as individuals and how their contribution relates to departmental goals. Knowing their status provides job security and reassurance, which many desperately need almost daily. When employees know where they stand, they relax and produce more. Within the security of the group, they feel they belong. A good communications system keeps workers from feeling neglected, misinterpreting, or becoming suspicious. It keeps them involved.

Leaders need the ideas that can come only from their followers. They must listen to suggestions and then give credit to those who make them. A good leader discovers problems and solves them before they become disruptive. The only way to make such discoveries is through a sound two-way communications system that brings problems to the attention of the leader. Weak and ineffective leaders usually discover problems too late. A leader with a strong, commanding voice who does not have a two-way communications system eventually loses the respect of followers. A leader with an authoritative voice and a well-maintained communications system has the winning combination.

As managers move into leadership roles, they go through a transition similar to a baseball player's experience in shifting from the minor to the major leagues. In no area is this change more dramatic than in communications.

Interviews with recognized leaders revealed a surprising number who gave high praise to Dale Carnegie courses and public speaking teachers for preparing them to lead. In recognition of the need for special training in this area, some professors are now suggesting that business administration majors consider a minor in communication arts.

THE MUTUAL REWARD THEORY

The best way to convert employees into enthusiastic followers is to put the Mutual Reward Theory (MRT) to work with more intensity. The supervisor (leader) and employee (follower) can easily reward each other with more conviction. For example, the supervisor can provide an enjoyable, consistent work environment, opportunity to learn, and freedom to operate without being stifled. The employee

can provide productivity, dependability, and freedom from unnecessary problems. A natural *reward exchange* takes place between a supervisor and an employee, and rewards can be considered trade-offs.

It stands to reason that a leader cannot be a leader without having followers. But what is a follower? Is a follower really different from an employee? If so, how can a manager convert employees to followers and become a leader?

The line that separates an employee from a follower is a fine one. Three basic factors are involved in the transition:

1. Employees cannot be forced or cajoled into becoming followers. It is a purely voluntary action on their part. If they want to move in the direction the leader has chosen, they join up. Naturally, they reason that it is to their advantage to do so.

2. The vision projected by the leader is a primary converter. The goal or mission presented must offer the promise of transforming the nature of the work and raising expectations to a high level, so that following is a natural and enjoyable thing to do.

3. The personality of the leader plays a significant role in the conversion. Sometimes charisma is present; sometimes it is not. There must, however, be a high degree of confidence, trust, and a strong belief that life will become better as a follower than as an employee.

All leaders go about converting employees to followers in their own way. The supervisor who provides unusual opportunities for self-improvement, for example, may gain an increase in productivity in return. Mutual rewards strengthen the relationship and enhance the image of the leader. Both parties come out ahead, and they know it.

Leadership, in a sense, is an impression in the mind of the follower. If the needs of the worker are satisfied, the supervisor appears to be a good leader; if the needs are not satisfied, then the worker feels thwarted and neglected and has a poor image of the supervisor. And when workers produce at high levels because their needs are amply satisfied, they convert their supervisors into leaders in the view of upper management. The workers turn their supervisors into management/leaders.

When Ralph was first introduced to MRT, he dismissed it as nothing more than the old truism "You scratch my back and I'll scratch yours." But later, after a discussion with a superior he respected, he decided to try it. As a supervisor, he discovered that he could furnish many rewards he had previously neglected. When he sat down with an employee and openly discussed the reward exchange that was possible between them, a better relationship and higher productivity resulted. In six months Ralph had progressed from a good supervisor and average leader to a better supervisor and a good leader. Through the application of MRT he had put more leadership into his style.

DEVELOP YOUR POWER PACKAGE

As discussed earlier, you have three basic sources of power to draw upon to establish your reputation as a leader:

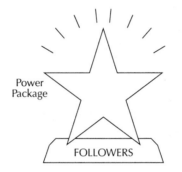

1. You have power that comes from your *role* as a supervisor. Anyone in your job as a manager has the same power. It gives you authority to require certain behavior from your workers. You must be careful, however, not to overuse this source.

2. You have power because of your *knowledge.* Your followers respect you because they recognize you have skills and know-how. This source of power is seldom overworked.

3. *Personality* power is important because, as a supervisor and leader, you need to show confidence in yourself as you take various actions and make decisions. You can and should influence your followers through the strength of your own personality.

You should draw carefully from the power bank composed of your role position, knowledge, and personality, but you should not hesitate to draw from it when necessary. Without a firm and consistent discipline line, a department cannot reach productivity goals. When such goals are not reached, everyone suffers. Utilizing your power sources in a sensitive, balanced manner may be the best way to put more leadership into your style.

Janice knew she had replaced an authoritarian manager. After careful consideration, she decided she could gain greater productivity from the nine workers in her department if she relied primarily on her knowledge power and soft-peddled her role and personality power. Janice said to herself: "If I can teach them more about the automated equipment and increase their competencies, they will sense my knowledge power and little else will be necessary." Things progressed in a satisfactory manner for some time, but gradually her employees began to slow down and take advantage of her. Janice had made the classic mistake of depending upon one source of power. She quickly fell back on her role power by demonstrating her strength as a firm, no-nonsense supervisor. In addition, Janice became a stronger personality—using her special characteristics (warm voice, persuasive manner, etc.) to project more leadership. It took only a few weeks to return to higher productivity and a more cohesive department.

MAKE BETTER DECISIONS MORE DECISIVELY

In all leader-follower situations, good decision making eventually surfaces as a characteristic followers value highly. Leaders say the same thing in many ways:

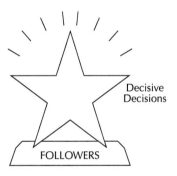

"Poor decision making is the downfall of most leaders."
"Decision making is a symbol of leadership."
"It's not just making good decisions, it's making them with authority and decisiveness."

Although you will eventually be judged by the quality of your decisions and your long-term record, the way you announce your decision is important. A good decision forcefully announced communicates the presence of leadership. In fact, a poor decision forcefully announced communicates the presence of leadership. A poor decision timidly announced communicates the absence of leadership. Even an excellent decision that is announced in a wishy-washy manner turns out to be weak if it is not accepted and put into operation by followers.

From the viewpoint of followers, leadership is decisiveness. A strong leader carefully analyzes the problem and then chooses one direction or another with confidence. Supervisors who straddle the fence and sweep problems under the carpet do not communicate strong leadership.

Kenneth had spent all afternoon evaluating the new advertising campaign. He had seen all the layouts and considered their probable impact on sales and on the corporate image. He was not satisfied with the program, but he had no time to develop a better proposal. He decided to support the advertising staff, accept their plan, and do everything in his power to make it work. He called in the staff and complimented them on their proposal. Then he wrote a short, enthusiastic article about the campaign for the in-house bulletin. In every possible way, he communicated the idea that the right decision had been made. As it turned out, the advertising program was moderately successful, primarily because of the enthusiasm behind it. Equally important to Kenneth, he had protected his leadership image. In fact, he was never criticized because the program's success was only moderate. His staff and other followers continued to support his leadership.

Leaders who expect to bat a thousand in making sound decisions will, of course, fall short of their expectations. But those who are afraid to make any decisions are doomed to failure. As one supervisor stated, "You can't expect to win 'em all, but you can win often enough to keep your workers' respect. And a decision made with confidence has a better chance of success because your employees will try to make it work. When you're indecisive, you only get into trouble."

Workers often interpret your decisions from a personal point of view. "Does the decision give me more or less job security? Will it enhance my career progress or slow it down?" Employees like decisions that are good for themselves as well as for the organization. The skillful leader makes sure that employees see how they benefit from whatever is best for the organization. Involving your followers in decision making increases their motivation.

Decisions that involve too many compromises do little for the supervisor's leadership image. Those decisions that are based upon facts and made with gusto are usually well received. A good decision maker inspires respect. Employees feel they are in good hands, and the department is making progress and headed in the right direction.

LEADERS CREATE AND ARTICULATE A MISSION TO THEIR FOLLOWERS

Being a star communicator! Providing followers with the right rewards! Developing a balanced power package! Making decisive decisions! All are part of the leadership star model. But on top of everything else, leaders must furnish direction. They must lead to something of meaning and significance. A possible victory must be provided somewhere down the road.

On a flight to Washington, D.C., I sat next to a young Native American who was flying to the capital to accept a Small Business Administration award for starting a successful business to recycle steel slag. We touched on many subjects, but I was most impressed with how he interpreted the mission of his small company. "Our purpose is to live in harmony with the land—to use what we take, to return what we do not need. It is the Indian way." The goal of his company was to make money and survive; its mission was conservation of natural resources, and he knew exactly how to articulate it.

Peter Drucker, in his book *Managing for Results*, discusses the importance of a single organizational goal for both managers and employees.[2] If such a goal exists (and is articulated), it can and should be converted into a mission. A mission has two purposes: It gives the whole organization (managers and employees alike) a sense of unity and purpose, and it keeps everyone moving with enthusiasm in the direction to accomplish it.

Most people underestimate their own need and that of others to have a higher vision or dream. The majority of managers fall into this category. So do some leaders. That is the reason many organizations falter. It is also the reason work is nothing but work for most people.

As sad as it is to acknowledge, individual productivity in America (taking into consideration technological advances at the time) was never greater than during World War II. Why? Because almost everybody had a bigger mission. They wanted to be part of a victory that was over the horizon. Of course, peacetime missions may be more difficult to form and articulate, but the possibility exists in all situations where people operate as a group.

True leaders acknowledge with enthusiasm that people do not live or work for bread alone. They know that employees really want something beyond dollars, benefits, security, promotions, recognition, and the promise of retirement. They want to be a part of something bigger. And the key word is *part*. Workers become followers when they become part of an effort that has significance. They feel differently when they are a part of a movement, wave, or team. It is not just little personal victories that most employees seek; rather, they want to participate in and share in a possible group victory.

CREATE A POSITIVE FORCE

Drawing upon all power sources, especially personality power, a leader creates and maintains a positive force that pulls followers in one direction with enthusiasm and dedication. Nothing is ever dull or routine in the presence of a leader with spirit and a sense of urgency. Things are always jumping! This physical, psychological, and spiritual "force" constitutes the heart of our strategic model (STAR).

In creating this intense sense of power, the leader must also make maximum use of her or his communication system, see that followers receive proper rewards, make decisive decisions, and keep the mission in focus. Not an easy combination! Although all points in the STAR are equally important and interrelated, the energy that keeps them functioning at the maximum level emanates from the center. It is this leadership power that energizes and illuminates the STAR. Like any

---

[2]Harper & Row, New York, 1964.

POSITIVE FORCE

power system (generator, battery storing an electrical charge, etc.), the central force keeps the communication network alive; provides the vehicles to deliver rewards; creates good decisions; and, drawing heavily from role, personality, and knowledge power sources, leads the organization to high productivity and success. And all in the direction of a preestablished mission!

> When Bernie took over as supervisor, apathy prevailed. The staff was lethargic and difficult to motivate. Within six weeks the opposite was true. Employees were full of energy and anxious to contribute. How did Bernie turn things around? He put the five foundations of the leadership STAR into operation and topped them off by setting loose a moving force from his own energy source and personality. Bernie stirred things up through his own activity; he seemed to be everywhere at the same time. Through a new wave of delegating, he made sure that every staff member had more to do and received more satisfaction from doing it. He stayed in constant communication with staff members, creating and releasing their talents. Using his personality power, he created laughter where previously there was silence. Like a centrifugal force, Bernie expressed his leadership by being in the center of things but at the same time encouraging others to demonstrate their own talents in new directions.

By carrying out the responsibilities of a supervisor as outlined in this book, you will automatically develop a certain amount of leadership. But don't stop here. Once you survive and feel comfortable as a successful supervisor, you may want to accept the challenge of becoming a manager/leader. Later, after receiving more responsibility and promotions, you may have the opportunity of becoming a leader/manager. Keep in mind that your future as a manager or leader is based upon the success you achieve as a beginning supervisor.[3] To measure your future as a manager/leader, you are invited to complete the scale on page 260–261.

---

[3]A thirty-minute film, *Put More Leadership into Your Style,* is now available from Barr Films, 12801 Schabarum Ave., Irwindale, CA 91706-7878. Telephone: (818) 338-7878.

DISCUSSION QUESTIONS

1. Do you agree with the statement that it is possible to be a good manager without being a leader? Explain fully.

2. Do you feel that most supervisors would be more successful if they put additional leadership into their style?

3. Do you feel that the leadership formula is complete? What, if anything, should be added?

MANAGEMENT/LEADERSHIP POTENTIAL SCALE

If you have not had the opportunity to demonstrate your leadership talents, you may have more potential than you think. This scale is designed to help you evaluate just how much potential you possess.

Circle the number that best indicates where you fall in the scale. A "10" indicates super-high potential. A "1" indicates no potential. After you have finished, total your scores in the space provided.

	High									**Low**
I can develop effective two-way communication.	10 9 8 7 6 5 4 3 2 1									I could never develop two-way communication with my employees.
I can set a strong authority line and make it stick.	10 9 8 7 6 5 4 3 2 1									I cannot become an authority figure in any situation.
It would not bother me to discipline those under my leadership.	10 9 8 7 6 5 4 3 2 1									I would find it impossible to discipline someone under my leadership.
I can determine what rewards others seek.	10 9 8 7 6 5 4 3 2 1									I could never become effective at determining the needs of others.
I am confident that I would make an excellent decision maker.	10 9 8 7 6 5 4 3 2 1									I do not see myself making decisions that affect others.
I can make hard decisions that may cause others to be upset with me.	10 9 8 7 6 5 4 3 2 1									I don't want anything to do with hard decisions.

I can inspire fol-lowers to accom-plish our "mission."	10	9	8	7	6	5	4	3	2	1	I'd rather let upper management in-spire employees.
I am highly moti-vated and seek responsibility.	10	9	8	7	6	5	4	3	2	1	I am not motivated; I do not seek responsibility.
I have great com-passion for others.	10	9	8	7	6	5	4	3	2	1	I have little or no compassion for others.
I can remain com-pletely positive in a negative environment.	10	9	8	7	6	5	4	3	2	1	I have a difficult time remaining positive in a nega-tive environment.

TOTAL [＿＿＿]

If you scored 80 or more, it would appear that you have very high leadership poten-tial. You have the confidence to be a top-flight leader. If you scored between 60 and 80, you have above-average leadership potential. You will probably do well in many leadership roles. If you scored less than 60, you may have underrated yourself or you may simply not be ready for a leadership role at this stage of your life. It is suggested that you complete the scale again after you have finished the book.

Keep in mind that the scale is not a scientific instrument; it is nothing more than a self-assessment aid designed to help you measure your own potential for leadership.

Mini-Game

Reward Trade-Offs

Objective

To give participants practice in applying Mutual Reward Theory (MRT).

Problem

Mr. Big wants Supervisor Joe to put more leadership into his style. He feels that Joe must first learn how to make MRT work.

Procedure

All nonmanagement players (five roles) select from the following employee list what they believe are the five most important employee needs that Joe should provide to gain greater productivity. In a separate group, all management players (four roles) choose from the management list the five rewards they feel would do the most to increase productivity. Those in the class or seminar not assigned roles should make their own selections, either individually or as a group.

After twenty minutes, a member of the employee group and a member of the management group will write their selections on the board. Each group (in turn) will answer questions regarding their five choices out of these long lists.

Postgame Discussion

Consider how Supervisor Joe might maintain an even exchange and what MRT might do to improve his role as a leader.

EMPLOYEE NEEDS

- Opportunity for self-improvement on the job

- Freedom from close supervision

- Ample time for socializing

- Freedom to take breaks without following a schedule

- Opportunity to express oneself in group situations

- Chance to have some enjoyment on the job

- Opportunity to rotate among different tasks

- Credit for accomplishments

- Involvement in the decision-making process

- Knowing what is going on

- Opportunity to use limited work time for personal business

- Chance to learn the supervisor's job

- Opportunity to talk about personal problems

- Chance to extend coffee and lunch breaks without asking permission

- Opportunity to use the telephone for (local) personal calls

- Assurance that the job is secure

- Having a supervisor who is accessible

- Knowing about changes in advance

- Selecting one's own vacation schedule

- Learning new things from one's supervisor

- Other: _____

    _____

    _____

MANAGEMENT NEEDS

- Quality work

- High productivity

- Acceptable attendance record

- Creativity

- Cooperative attitude toward co-workers

- Cooperative attitude toward management

- Desire to learn

- Self-motivation

- Willingness to accept new assignments

- Willingness to pitch in during emergencies and, if necessary, work overtime

- Willingness to teach co-workers

- Tolerance of problem co-workers

- Minimum of socializing on the job

- Control over misuse of the telephone for personal reasons

- Awareness of safety regulations

- A consistently positive attitude

- Other: _____

    _____

    _____

Suggested Answers to Case Problems

The typical supervisory problems presented in this book were designed as springboards for individual thinking and discussion. None of the problems have exact answers because only the essential facts of each problem are outlined. It is therefore impossible to give definite or complete answers to any problem. The following so-called answers, then, are nothing more than an account of how the authors would approach the problem with the available facts. Each suggested answer should serve only as a guide to the independent thinking of the reader and the discussion leader.

CASE: CHOICE

Both Mrs. R and Mr. G should make good supervisors. The author favors Mr. G because his greater sensitivity to the needs of the employees could lead to greater productivity. Mrs. R has a more Theory X oriented style (authoritative rather than permissive), and because she has neglected to build strong relationships with co-workers, they may resent her being promoted over them. Resentment plus a heavy-handed attitude could make productivity increases difficult. Mr. G's sensitivity (and the fact that he has built better relationships with co-workers) makes him more acceptable to the employees, which could be converted into higher productivity.

CASE: APPROACH

Mr. G's approach could fail because of the following pitfalls: (1) Overemphasis on being a good model could be so time-consuming that Mr. G might neglect other important duties. (2) Those inexperienced at professional customer relations often need to learn skills and techniques that are best communicated through training. Being a good model is important as long as Mr. G does not devote too much time to it, but it does not replace individual or group training. (3) "Good guys" do not always make the best supervisors. Some discipline is usually necessary. Mr. G needs to come up with the right combination of being a good model, providing the right kind and amount of training, and maintaining discipline.

CASE: REQUEST

The following three steps are recommended for Mr. X:

Step 1: Mr. Big needs to show and discuss the letter openly with Mr. X so that he can verify the contents of the letter and Jane's productivity contribution. In doing this, Mr. Big needs to be extremely careful to protect the ego of Mr. X.

Step 2: The termination procedure of the firm needs to be reviewed carefully so that Mr. X does not make a decision too soon. Also, such a discussion should (hopefully) lead to a solution whereby Jane can be retained.

Step 3: The possibility of working out a flexible schedule should be explored. Mrs. Pitts appears to be a most valuable employee. If this fact is substantiated, adjusting to her needs might be in the best interest of the company and of all individuals concerned; however, no company rules or procedures should be violated.

CASE: TECHNIQUE

In this situation the author recommends technique 2 (nondirective) because the facts have not been verified. Joe needs to know Ricardo's side of the story. It is possible that Ricardo has a good explanation for both irregularities reported. If a violation has occurred, Joe should check with Mr. B to determine whether a written warning should be issued first to Ricardo. The nondirective technique could save Joe from an embarrassing mistake if he were to come down hard on Ricardo only to find out that the night watchman reported unverifiable facts.

CASE: STAFFING

Complete a job analysis to determine the required skills needed to do the job. Construct a questionnaire to be used during the interviews that explores the applicants' abilities and experiences. Contact your local EEOC office for pamphlets on conducting interviews. Ask for information and guidance about interviewing from your Human Resource office.

CASE: TRAINING

The author believes that orientation training for new employees should be tied to personnel turnover and productivity, both of which are already measured by most firms. To superimpose Mr. Big's complex system on these instruments could be interpreted as a duplication and somewhat heavy-handed. The proposal also violates sound principles of delegation, in that the supervisors should be given authority to orient employees in their own style. If turnover and productivity results do not come up to standard, then supervisors should be held accountable. In addition, the plan appears to be overambitious. It is doubtful whether Mr. Big will be able to follow through with so many evaluation meetings.

CASE: THINKING

The author agrees with both Lisa and Lester. Lisa has a point when she says that concentration comes first and thinking comes next. Until supervisors focus their attention on a problem or project, it is impossible for them to get their thinking "gears" in motion. Lester makes a good point, however, when he states that learning to concentrate for study purposes prepares people to concentrate in the workplace.

CASE: PLANNING

It would appear that Mr. Big may be guilty of overdoing a good thing and stifling the creativity of his staff. Few people enjoy doing things "by the numbers." Ms. Y, on the other hand, may be going too far in the other direction. The majority of high-level managers feel it is helpful and motivating to have written goals submitted by those in lower positions. Perhaps a blend of both planning patterns would be best, giving some autonomy to supervisors so that they express their management/leadership styles.

CASE: ANALYSIS

A close look at the time inventory submitted shows that Joe is not delegating enough. He could save additional time by having staff meetings instead of individual communication sessions on matters such as productivity schedules. A more serious problem for Joe is that he appears to be guilty of what might be termed fragmented management—going from one activity to another without an overall plan for the day. Joe needs more guidance and support from Mr. Big on how to manage himself.

CASE: INTIMIDATION

The author favors parts of option 2, with some important variations. First, Joe should counsel with Mr. K, at which time he should take a pleasant but firm position. Second, Joe should communicate the results to Mr. Big, and during this meeting he should also take a strong stand. He should not, however, threaten to resign because he would be using the same intimidation technique on Mr. Big that Mr. K is using on him. Such emotionally charged actions often backfire.

Supervisors who permit an employee to intimidate them lose some of their role power and effectiveness in dealing with others, thus undermining their own chances of success.

CASE: DECISION

Eric is in a perfect position to prepare a Plan B. In fact, he should have started one some months ago. Apparently he does not sense that it is ethical in this situation to play both ends against the middle. A true Plan B would prepare him for upward mobility in his present firm, but if things don't work out, he will be ready to accept excellent outside opportunities. Chances are good that by the time Eric has a Plan B ready, he will have solved the problem. One reason a resolution is likely is that in doing his Plan B, Eric will have restored his positive attitude.

Role Profiles for Cases and Mini-Games

Identifying with the nine profiles that follow will help make the cases and mini-games in *Supervisor's Survival Kit* more realistic and enjoyable. If you have the opportunity to play a role in a mini-game (group situation), you will be expected to make decisions from the viewpoint of the character you portray. For example, if you are given the role of Mr. Big, you will attempt to act in a way you feel a top-management person with his personality would act.

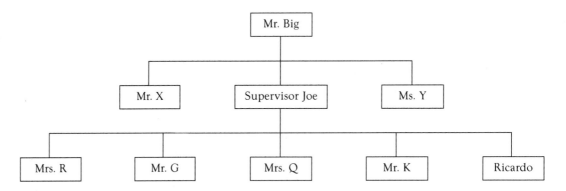

The chart gives you the power positions of each individual in our hypothetical organization. The more you study and identify with these roles, the more intriguing will be the case studies and mini-games.

MR. BIG

As Mr. Big, you occupy the number one power role. You consider yourself a professional manager and a strong leader. Your superiors recognize you as ambitious, efficient, and a good listener. You are a stabilizer (as opposed to a

scrambler[1]) in that you intend to stay with your present organization and take a straight line to the top. You measure your people on the basis of productivity, not personality; because you are good at setting priorities and managing your own time, you expect the same efficiency from others; you maintain a clear and firm discipline line. You sense you are an excellent model for the supervisors who report to you.

You feel fortunate to be in your present position at the age of thirty-five. You credit your rise in the company to your four-year college degree in business management, your leadership qualities, and your willingness to work harder than others. You are married and have three children. You are a runner and have participated in three marathons. You spend a great deal of time at home reading management books and periodicals because you want to be known as a supervisor's supervisor.

You like Supervisor Joe as a person, but you feel he was promoted to his job without proper training. As a result, you have a tendency to be impatient with

---

[1]Scramblers are highly motivated, unorthodox people who zigzag from one organization to another to get to the top; stabilizers are loyal, hard-working people who prefer to stay with a single organization and take a straight line to the top.

some of his decisions. For example, you supervise Joe's department much more closely than you do Mr. X's or Ms. Y's.

SUPERVISOR JOE

As Supervisor Joe, you are the key personality in most case studies and mini-games. You consider yourself a hard-working, conscientious supervisor, but sometimes you feel insecure in your job. For about two years, you were an employee in the department you now supervise. You know all the skills and techniques to teach others, but so far you have not been able to raise productivity as high as Mr. Big expects—and consequently, you feel uneasy around Mr. Big. You are learning to delegate, manage your time, and build good relationships with your people, but you realize you are still in a transition stage.

You are twenty-four years old, and your wife works as a secretary. You have no children. You earned a degree from a two-year community college, where you concentrated on business courses. You are a car buff who likes to restore antique automobiles.

People seem to react quickly and favorably to your warm personality and friendly attitude. As far as you can tell, all five of your employees like and respect you. You feel they come to you without fear to discuss problems of all kinds. You strive for a department that is happy and free of conflict. Mr. Big has recently told you to exercise stronger leadership and to distance yourself from your employees so that they will learn to respect you more. Mr. X seems to resent your personal progress and frequently interferes in the operation of your department. Ms. Y also seems highly critical of you at times.

You look upon your job as a stepping stone to middle management. In fact, you have already started to study Mr. Big and his job because you feel his position is the next one up the ladder for which you must qualify. You recognize that you would be in a better position if you had graduated from a four-year college instead of a two-year institution, but you feel you can make up the difference with extra performance. You are thinking about taking some night courses that will lead to a four-year degree. You consider yourself to be a scrambler and would not hesitate to move to another firm if the salary and benefit package were right.

MS. Y

(*Note:* Ms. Y is a typical Theory Y supervisor—that is, one who operates on a low-key and somewhat permissive basis but nevertheless often achieves high productivity.)

As Ms. Y, you are a recent college graduate who believes in participative management. You involve your employees in departmental decisions when possible and pride yourself on your sensitivity to individual needs. You have developed your own informal communications system. You are assertive in manner and consider yourself a scrambler rather than a stabilizer. Although you do not intend to stay with your present firm more than two years, you will not move until another employer offers you a substantial increase in salary. You like the idea of becoming a top executive. So far your personnel turnover has been lower than in Mr. X's department, and your productivity is as high as his.

You are single, like to ski, and enjoy the challenges of work. You are moderately assertive and self-motivated. You persistently study the leadership styles of others. You like Supervisor Joe but feel he is uninformed and clumsy. You feel Mr. X is much too demanding and a poor listener. You sense a deep conflict between your style and his. You intend to learn as much as possible from Mr. Big even though you have no intention of staying under his supervision for long.

MR. X

(*Note:* Mr. X represents the Theory X style of leadership. Mr. X is therefore painted as authoritarian and demanding but fair. His controls are strict and definite.)

As Mr. X, you have been with the organization longer than many others, including Mr. Big. It is your opinion that employees feel more secure and produce more under a firm and predictable discipline line.

Certainly you expect some conformity and high productivity from your employees, but they always know where they stand and they respect you for it. Although you believe in control more than participative management, you respect the people who work for you and treat them as individuals.

You supervise one of the departments located next to Supervisor Joe's. The two of you must work together closely to achieve the productivity goals set by management. You feel superior to Joe for three reasons: (1) you have twenty years' more experience; (2) you helped the company through some tough times, thereby demonstrating your loyalty; and (3) you have trained many people who are now in upper management positions.

You feel that you are the supervisor best qualified to succeed Mr. Big, and you take advantage of every opportunity to demonstrate that you are ready for the job. You are rather proud that others feel you are a demanding supervisor. This reputation works for you, and management knows it. All this attention to modern psychology in order to motivate people is not your style. You have let everybody know that you think Ms. Y and Joe are too people oriented, too permissive, and too friendly with their employees. You didn't go to college but you are an avid reader, have enjoyed many management seminars, and take pride in teaching skills to those in your department.

MR. K

As Mr. K, you have seniority over all the other employees in Joe's department. In fact, you have served under five different supervisors. You are married and have five children. Two are outstanding students in the local high school.

You feel you are a loyal, friendly, helpful employee, but you see no reason to extend yourself. You manage to keep your productivity at a safe average, and that is about as far as you intend to go. Joe is an acceptable supervisor (no better or worse than some of the other young ones you've adjusted to), but he probably won't last too long, so why worry? After all, you taught him most of what he knows about the job, and he still comes to you for advice.

You could have become department supervisor some years ago, but you turned it down because you didn't want the people problems involved. You feel the pay is fairly good and the benefits are great, so you coast along. Your main interest is fishing, and the more time you spend in your camper, the better life is for you.

MRS. R

As Mrs. R, you classify yourself as a reentry scrambler; you will not be content to mark time and wait for advancement. You are thirty-six years of age but entered the labor market only two years ago, after your divorce. You have a sizable mortgage and two children to raise. Everyone can see that you are active socially, but you never talk about your private life. You are well groomed and able to communicate in a persuasive manner. People in management respect your assertiveness.

Although you had only two semesters of college, you know you are above average in intelligence. You learn quickly and are currently taking a course at the local community college in the elements of supervision. You become impatient with Joe as a supervisor (as well as with other employees), but as yet you have said little. You figure that if Joe stubs his toe or is moved up, you will be next in line. Meanwhile, if you sense a little hostility from your co-workers, you pass it off as unimportant. Your goal is to impress Supervisor Joe, Mr. Big, and their superiors.

Supervisor Joe and Mr. Big know that your personal productivity is substantially higher than that of others in the department, but you are not going to sit around and wait for further management recognition. You intend to promote yourself. Although you have been with the organization for less than a year, you hope to be the next supervisor, either in your own department or in another one. If nothing happens soon, you will exercise your Plan B and move to a competitive organization at a higher salary.

MR. G

As Mr. G, you are forty years of age. You were raised in an inner-city neighborhood, but you seldom think about it anymore because you have worked hard and now have a nice home and most things you need to achieve the lifestyle you desire. Your wife works in a government job, and you have two children.

You were a high-school dropout some ten years ago, but you worked hard during your four-year hitch in the Marines and took an examination to receive your high school diploma. You are still weak in English and mathematics, but you have been going to adult evening classes to improve your proficiency in these two areas. Because of your advancement in the Marine Corps (you became a noncommissioned officer), you feel you have leadership ability.

You have earned the respect of Supervisor Joe, Mr. Big, and (you feel) all of your fellow employees except Mrs. R. You hope to become a supervisor in a few months and perhaps qualify for Mr. Big's job a few years from now. You are next in line in terms of seniority after Mr. K, and you know he's not interested. You feel you are better qualified than Mrs. R for promotion because you are more sensitive to people and therefore have a stabilizing influence upon the department. Although you recognize that your personal productivity is not as high as Mrs. R's, you feel you contribute more than she does to the productivity of others.

MRS. Q

As Mrs. Q, you are twenty-three years old and have two years of college behind you. Everyone agrees that you are good at your job. You like your position, but it would not upset you should you be terminated tomorrow. You somehow feel you could get a better job if you really tried. You are seldom absent from work and never late. You know your productivity is above average, but you also know it could be higher if you felt there was someplace to go in the organization. If a promotion came along now, either Mr. G or Mrs. R would get it, so why push? You recognize that you are not highly motivated and believe nothing management can do will change you.

Joe isn't the kind of guy you'd go all out for anyway. You think he is doing his best, but as far as you're concerned, he doesn't understand people well enough to get them to work together as a team. It's not the worst place in the world to work, though. The physical facilities are excellent, and the pay is okay. At this point, you are making slightly more money than your husband.

RICARDO

As Ricardo, you are the only part-time employee in the department. You work twenty hours a week while taking a full program at a local college. You are nineteen and come from a large family. You are very handsome, a sharp dresser, and the first member of your family to go to college. You like the company and Supervisor Joe, but after you get your degree, you are going to look elsewhere.

You like your job because of the good pay, but it seems that most of the dirty work is left for you. The company's attitude appears to be that as long as you are a student, you don't really count and should be happy to do anything available. You resent this attitude, so whenever you get a chance to speak up in a staff or group meeting, you do not hesitate to do so. After all, even though you work only part-time, you still have a right to be heard.

Supervisor Joe has been good about changing your work schedule so that you can attend classes. You feel, however, that the full-time employees take advantage of you, and you welcome any opportunity to voice your feelings.

Now that you are familiar with the nine roles, the mini-games and case problems should provide more intrigue, meaning, and value, whether or not you receive the opportunity to discuss them in a classroom or seminar. If you are using this book for individualized study, treat the mini-games as cases and devise your own solutions. In the classroom or workshop, the teacher or trainer will provide further instructions on how to play the mini-games.

Index

ABC method of sorting, 193–194
Advance training of supervisors, 25
Appraisal. *See* Formal appraisal
Art of Communicating, The, 106
Attitude, 62
  multicultural teams and, 92
Attitude-toward-change scale, 234
Authority line, 63(1)
Autocratic climate, 65
Autocratic decisions, 212, 213
Autonomy of supervisors, 25

Barker, Joel Arthur, 77
Behaviors (in teams), 94
Buffer between superiors and subordinates, 16

Career planning and appraisals, 156
Case studies
  analysis, 208–209
  approach, 44
  choice, 11
  decision, 248
  intimidation, 231
  planning, 190
  request, 61
  staffing, 136
  technique, 109
  thinking, 179
  training, 153
Change
  communicating, 67
  gradual, 16
  source of stress, 236–237
  See also Converting change into
      opportunity
Chemical dependency, 118
Climate. *See* Productive working climate
Communicating privately, 99
  art of communicating, 106
  case study—technique, 109
  individual goals and, 108
  MRT discussions and nondirective technique,
      107–108
  principles for (five Rs), 101–106
  what is involved, 100–101

Communication
  of changes, 67
  daily, 70
  failure of, 224–225
  star communicators, 252–253
  two-way, 47
  See also Communicating privately
Compassion vs. control, 65
Computers, supervisors and, 187
Concentration
  barriers to, 175–176
  case study—thinking, 179
  defined, 173
  effect of personality on, 176
  eliminating distractions, 174–175
  to learn vs. to manage, 175
  steps to success, 178
  tips for, 176–177
  wearing two hats, 177
Conflict or disagreement, 115–116
Consistency, 68
Consultative decisions, 213
Continuous learning, 72–73
Control and discipline in teams, 91–92
Converting change into opportunity, 232
  attitude-toward-change scale, 234
  changes as a source of stress, 236–237
  management burnout, 236
  mini-game—change, 238
  in organizations, 235–236
  technological changes, 233–235
  in workforce, 236
Core-ring approach to hiring employees, 132
Corrective interviews, 114–115
Cultural communications quiz, 91
Customer focus, in TQM, 79

Decision making, 210–211
  group decision, 218
  Group Decision Making Through Needs
      Clarification Model, 214–215
  high-consequence people problems, 217–218
  high-consequence work-oriented decisions, 216
  job-oriented problems, 215
  kinds of decisions, 212–214

low-consequence people problems, 216–217
low-consequence work-oriented decisions, 215–216
mini-game—termination, 219–220
problem-solving approaches, 212
seven-step model, 213
Decker, Bert, 106
Delegation, 137, 202
    failure to delegate, 139–140
    mini-game, 144–145
    part of larger plan, 142
    when and how to delegate, 140–142
Democratic climate, 65
Departmental plans, 183–184
Departmental productivity, 36–38
Deterioration of productive departments, 68
Directive communication, 105
Disagreement or conflict, 115
Discipline line, 63–65, 113
    fine-tuning, 69
    ideal, 68
    low, firm, 68
    monitoring, 67–71
    poor, 68
Drucker, Peter, 31

Electronic cottage, 233–235
Emergencies, handling, 66
Employee accountability, in TQM, 79
Employee turnover, 123–124
Employees
    assistance from, 17
    challenging, 69–70
    empowerment of, 88
    sensitivity and, 15
    See also Problem employees
Empowerment of employees, 79
Empowerment of line supervisor, 24–25
Equal Employment Opportunity (EEO) guidelines
        for managers and supervisors, 133–135
Exploratory interviews, 114

Feedback
    from employees, 68–69
    to employees, 73
    form for teams, 95
Forbes, B. C., 1
Formal appraisal
    benefits to employees, 162
    benefits to management, 156, 162
    career planning and, 156–161
    conducting the appraisal, 166–167
    formal appraisal exercise, 165–166
    instruments, 154–155
    long-form appraisal, 158
    MBO (management by objectives) and, 155–156
    mini-game—option, 169–170
    positive approach, 162–163
    short-form appraisal, 157
    using appraisal as a positive tool, 167–168
    using the appraisal form, 164, 166
Foundations of motivation, 40, 54
    case study—request, 61
    communicate, 56
    give clear and complete instructions, 55–56
    give credit when due, 56
    involve people in decisions, 57
    maintain an open door, 57–58
    mastering, 59–60
    reasons seldom used, 58
Front-line supervisor
    major changes from middle management, 24–25

managing oneself, 26
middle-management views, 23
mini-game—downsizing, 28–29
minor changes from middle management, 24
pacing oneself, 25–26
responsibility and support, 22–23
*Future Edge: Discovering The Paradigms of
        Success*, 77

Gantt bar chart, 182
Gantt, Henry L., 182
General Motors, experience with TQM, 80, 81
Goals, 191–193
    benefits of, 193
    departmental productivity and, 36–38
    individual, communication and, 108
    initial, of supervisors, 17–18
    See also Planning; Priorities
Group Decision Making Through Needs Clarifi-
        cation Model, 214–215
Group decisions, 213

Hawthorne experiments, 41
High-consequence people problems, 217–218
High-consequence work-oriented decisions, 216
High (permissive) discipline line, 64
Home and career, balancing, 19
Human resource department, supervisor's rela-
        tionship with, 133, 135

IBM, experience with TQM, 80
Increase in staff, justifying, 131
Individual productivity, 35–36
Integrity, 16
Internal motivation, characteristics of, 71
Interviews
    corrective, 114–115
    ending, 128
    exploratory, 114
    interviewer's self-assessment exercise, 126
    job qualifications checklist, 128
    noncorrective, 116–117
    preparing for, 125
    questions, 127–128
    techniques, 127
Inventory analysis chart (for time), 206–207
    sample, 209

Jensen, M. C., 96
Job-oriented problems, 215
Job qualifications checklist, 128

Knowledge power
    case study—training, 153
    four-step process of teaching, 148–151
    group instruction, 151–152
    teaching by not teaching, 147–149
    training responsibilities, 151
    your attitude toward teaching, 148

Leader's role in teams, 93
Leadership
    create a positive force, 258–259
    create and articulate a mission, 257–258
    develop your power package, 255–256
    formula for personal growth, 251–252
    make better decisions more decisively, 256–257
    management/leadership potential scale, 260–261
    mini-game—reward trade-offs, 262–263
    Mutual Reward Theory (MRT), 253–255

opportunity to become a manager/leader, 250–251
   star communicators, 252–253
Leadership: What Every Manager Should Know, 249
Learning attitude, 17
Ledru-Rolling, Alexandre, 221
Long-form appraisal, 158–161
Low-consequence people problems, 216–217
Low-consequence work-oriented decisions, 215–216
Low (tight) discipline line, 64

Managing oneself, 26
Management
   advantages, 7–8
   burnout, 236
   case study—choice, 11
   definition and checklist, 7
   disadvantages, 8–9
   pressures, 9–10
   prior-image problem, 10
Maslow, A. H., 41
Maslow's hierarchy of needs, 41
Master calendar, 182–183
MBO (management by objectives), 183
   appraisals and, 155–156
Middle (intermediate) discipline line, 64
Mini-Game
   change, 238
   climate, 74–76
   confrontation, 121–122
   delegation, 144–145
   downsizing, 28–29
   intervention, 52–53
   option, 169–170
   philosophy, 83–84
   priorities, 198–199
   pyramid to circle, 98
   reward trade-offs, 262–263
   strategy, 20–21
   termination, 219–220
Mistakes to avoid, 223
   case study—intimidation, 231
   failure to communicate, 224–225
   failure to enjoy your role as a manager, 230
   failure to exercise strong leadership, 225–227
   making and breaking promises, 227–228
   straitjacketing employees, 228–230
Motivation
   defined, 71
   techniques, 39–40
   theories, 40–41
Multicultural team, 89–91
Mutual respect, 89
Mutual Reward Theory (MRT), 47, 51, 106–108, 253–255

Network analysis plan, 182
Networking, 246
Noncorrective interviews, 116–117
Nondirective approach to problem employees, 112
Nondirective communication, 105, 106–108
Normative conditions for effective teams, 96

Observer's role in teams, 95–96
Opportunity. *See* Converting change into opportunity
Orientation, 128–129

Pacing oneself, 25–26
Paradigm, 77
Part-time employees, 131–132

Patience with self, 15
Permissive climate, 65
Personal performance contract (PPC), 188
Personal plan B, 239–240
   case study—decision, 248
   developing, 244–245
   importance of, 245–246
   making yourself visible, 240–242
   networking, 246
   playing both ends against the middle, 245
   protecting your staff from change, 246
   scrambler-stabilizer scale, 243–244
   straight line to the top, 242–243
   zigzag pattern, 243
Personality, effect of, on concentration, 176
Planning, 180
   case study—planning, 190
   department success, 186–187
   formula for success, 183
   importance of, 181–182
   management by objectives (MBO), 183
   master calendar, 182–183
   personal performance contracts (PPCs), 188
   software packages to help supervisors, 187–188
   supervisors and computers, 187
Planning time, 16
Power, sensitivity and, 15
Pressures, absorbing, 66–67
Prior-Image Predominance Theory, 10
Priorities
   ABC method of sorting, 193–194
   criteria for setting, 194
   effective setting of, 195–196
   goals, objectives, and plans, 191–193
   how to start setting, 196–197
   mini-game—priorities, 198–199
   need for flexibility, 194–195
   written lists, 194
Problem employees, 110
   chemical dependency, 118
   corrective interviews, 114–115
   disagreement or conflict, 115–116
   employees unable to reach standards, 117
   exploratory interviews, 114
   mini-game—confrontation, 121–122
   noncorrective interviews, 116–117
   objectivity required, 113–114
   professional perspective of supervisor, 111–113
   reduction in staff, 119
   sexual harassment, 118–119
   testing of supervisor's image by employee, 117
Problem solving. *See* Decision making
Problems. *See* Decision making
Productive working climate
   absorbing pressures, 66–67
   challenge employees, 69
   communicate daily, 70
   communicating changes, 67
   compassion vs. control, 65
   consistency, 68
   continuous learning, 72
   discipline line, 63–65
   encouraging self-motivation, 71
   feedback from employees, 68
   feedback to employees, 73
   fine-tuning discipline line, 69
   handling emergencies, 66
   low, firm line, advantages of, 69
   maintaining lively climate, 69
   mini-game—climate, 74–76
   purposeful and meaningful work, 72
   Web surfing on the job, 70–71

Productivity, achieving through people, 33
    case study—approach, 44
    departmental productivity, 36–38
    deterioration of, 69
    individual productivity, 35–36
    motivation techniques, 39–40
    motivation theories, 40–41
    supervisor-employee relationship, 41–43
    turning work over to employees, 34–35
Program Evaluation Review Technique (PERT), 182
Pyramid to circle, 86, 87
    mini-game, 98

Quality comfort zone scale, 80–81
Quality first, in TQM, 78–79

Recorder's role in teams, 93, 95
Relationship channel of supervisors and em-
       ployees, 46–48
Relationships, sound, 48–50
Rotation of staff. *See* Staff shifting and rotation

Sales productivity, 36
Scheduling, art of, 132–133
Scrambler-stabilizer scale, 243–244
Self-motivation
    continuous learning, 72–73
    feedback on performance, 73
    ideal climate and, 71
    purposeful and meaningful work, 72
Self-protection with problem employees, 112–113
Sense of humor, 89
Sensitivity, 15, 89
Service productivity, 36
Sexual harassment, 118–119
Shakespeare, William, 171
Shared vision, 88
Short-form appraisal, 157
Small plans, 184–185
Software, for supervisors, 187–188
Staff shifting and rotation, 129
    justifying a larger staff, 131
    supervisor's orientation checklist, 130
    transfers, 130–131
Staffing
    case study—staffing, 136
    core-ring approach, 132
    employee turnover, 123–124
    orientation and training, 128–129
    part-timers, 131–132
    scheduling, 123
    staff shifting and rotation, 129
    supervisor's relationship with human re-
       sources department, 123, 135
    See also Staffing process
Staffing process, 124–125
    ending the interview, 128
    interview questions, 127–128
    interviewing techniques, 127
    preparation for the interview, 125
Stress, change as source of, 236–237
Superiors, demanding, 50–51
Supervisor-employee relationships, 45
    building sound relationships, 48–50
    demanding superiors, 50–51
    mini-game—intervention, 52–53
    productivity and, 41–42
    relationship channel, 46–48
Supervisors
    computers and, 187
    software packages to help, 187–188

testing of image by employees, 117
    See also Front-line supervisor; Management;
       Transition to supervisor
Supervisor's orientation checklist, 130
Supervisor's time-waster assessment scale, 204–205

Tangible productivity, 36
Teaching. *See* Knowledge power
Team boundary, 87
Team leaders
    effective, 89
    personal characteristics, 89
Teamwork
    leader's role, 93, 96
    normative conditions for effective teams, 98
    observer's role, 95–96
    recorder's role, 93, 95
    team behaviors, 94
    team feedback form, 95
Third Wave, The, 233
Time management
    case study—analysis, 208–209
    efficient meetings, 203–204
    eliminate time wasters, 204
    how to manage time, 202–203
    importance of, 200–201
    inventory analysis chart, 206–207
    protecting one's time from others, 203
    supervisor's time-waster assessment scale,
       204–205
Toffler, Alvin, 233
Total Quality Management (TQM), 42, 77
    basic elements, 78–79
    IBM and GM experiences, 80–82
    mini-game—philosophy, 83–84
    quality comfort zone scale, 80–81
Training, 128–129
    See also Knowledge power
Transfers, 130–131
Transition to supervisor, 14
    balancing home and career, 18
    difficulty of, 14
    first step after, 14
    initial goals, 17–18
    integrity, 16–17
    mini-game—strategy, 20–21
    surviving first weeks, 15
    whether to make, 3–4
Tuckman, B. W., 96
Two-way communication, 47

Upper Level Leadership Dearth Theory, The, 7

Web surfing on the job, 70–71
Western Electric Company, 41
Work, purposeful and meaningful, 72
Work teams, 85
    control and discipline, 91–92
    employee empowerment, 88
    idea of team not new, 87–88
    multicultural, 88–91
    pyramid to circle, 86, 87
    transition dangers, 86–87
    when to try the concept, 96–97
    See also Team leaders; Teamwork
Working climate. *See* Productive working climate
Workplace friendships, 16
Written lists, advantages of, 194